Creative Blogging

Your First Steps to a Successful Blog

Heather Wright-Porto

Apress®

Creative Blogging: Your First Steps to a Successful Blog

ISBN-13 (pbk): 978-1-4302-3428-9

ISBN-13 (electronic): 978-1-4302-3429-6

Printed and bound in the United States of America 9 8 7 6 5 4 3 2 1

President and Publisher: Paul Manning
Lead Editor: Ben Renow-Clarke
Technical Reviewer: Thomas Rushton
Editorial Board: Steve Anglin, Mark Beckner, Ewan Buckingham, Gary Cornell, Jonathan Gennick, Jonathan Hassell, Michelle Lowman, Matthew Moodie, Jeff Olson, Jeffrey Pepper, Frank Pohlmann, Douglas Pundick, Ben Renow-Clarke, Dominic Shakeshaft, Matt Wade, Tom Welsh
Coordinating Editor: Jessica Belanger
Copy Editor: Sharon Terdeman
Compositor: MacPS, LLC
Indexer: BIM Indexing & Proofreading Services
Artist: April Milne
Cover Designer: Anna Ishchenko

Distributed to the book trade worldwide by Springer Science+Business Media, LLC., 233 Spring Street, 6th Floor, New York, NY 10013. Phone 1-800-SPRINGER, fax (201) 348-4505, e-mail orders-ny@springer-sbm.com, or visit www.springeronline.com.

For information on translations, please e-mail rights@apress.com, or visit www.apress.com.

Apress and friends of ED books may be purchased in bulk for academic, corporate, or promotional use. eBook versions and licenses are also available for most titles. For more information, reference our Special Bulk Sales–eBook Licensing web page at www.apress.com/info/bulksales.

The source code for this book is available to readers at www.apress.com.

To Gerry, my dear husband, my love,
Thank you for your continued support, love, and encouragement,
but most of all, for being you.

To my beloved children, my heart, Michaela and Luke,
I love you more than words can say.

To Mom, Dad, Kim, and Laura, my family,
I love you.

Contents at a Glance

Contents

About the Author

 **Heather Wright-Porto** has a master's degree in computer information systems and has had her own computer consulting company since 1995 (Premier Computer Solutions LLC). She has trained clients on Microsoft Office, as well as on Photoshop, Illustrator, Quark, and other graphic design applications, in addition to developing databases (using Microsoft Access, Microsoft SQL Server, and Oracle), programming in Visual Basic, and creating web sites (using ColdFusion, HTML, and JavaScript). Heather also worked at NYU School of Medicine as a senior database developer for more than nine years. In November 2009, her focus shifted to expanding and building her Blogs by Heather business, www.BlogsByHeather.com.

In July 2010, she published her first book, *Beginning Google Blogger*, and that fall began writing her second, this book, *Creative Blogging*. Heather enjoys writing and sharing her blogging knowledge and experience with her readers. She hopes to continue writing technical books and maybe will even write a children's book some day. Besides her business and her writing, Heather's days are also filled with raising her young children, Luke and Michaela.

As a creative outlet and for her love of art, she became a Stampin' Up! Demonstrator in October 2006. She is what is considered a "hobby" demonstrator, but enjoys making and selling cards at local shops, and holding child and adult craft programs at local libraries, as well as workshops at her home for customers, friends, and family.

Heather is easy going, but very ambitious and detailed-oriented—how does that combination work? She gets great enjoyment in helping others, and even more in making people smile. She is blessed and fortunate to have the life she has, and to be surrounded by a loving family and wonderful people.

About the Technical Reviewer

■ **Thomas Rushton** has been slaving over hot keyboards since the early 1980s when he started with a Sinclair ZX80, and was on the Internet before the World Wide Web was unleashed and the place got crowded. He is a long-standing denizen of a precursor to the social web, Monochrome (see www.mono.org for more information), which has provided many of the core features now seen on blogs and other sites, such as Facebook and MySpace.

In the Real World (TM), Thomas spends his time working as a SQL Server Database Administrator (currently on contract at MessageLabs, part of Symantec), and as an occasional technical reviewer for Apress. He has, in the past, worked for a variety of financial and legal institutions, some of which have survived the ravages of the latest recession. He has only recently started working as a contractor, rather than as a permanent employee, so is interested in this idea of managing one's personal brand through blogging.

Thomas lives in England and has one wife, one child, one dog, and one chinchilla. When they let him, he likes to play double bass with various local opera groups and orchestras.

Acknowledgments

I still remember the day that Steve Anglin, Assistant Editorial Director, approached me about writing my first book, *Beginning Google Blogger*. I was so thrilled to become part of the Apress family, and I still am! I'm so happy to have worked with so many wonderful people. I would like to extend a warm "thank you" to Ben Renow-Clarke, Acquisitions Editor, for assisting me through the entire process in writing *Creative Blogging* and for always being there to help; and to extend a special thanks to Jessica Belanger, Coordinating Editor, who continuously followed up and kept me on track, in addition to offering encouragement and support.

I greatly appreciate all the comments, advice, and hard work of the technical reviewer, Thomas Rushton, as well as the assistance of copy editor, Sharon Terdeman, the formatters, the art team, and all of those who have a part in the production of this book. I am very grateful. Thank you all.

About This Book

Hi and welcome to *Creative Blogging*! In this book we'll create a new blog. We'll start at the very beginning with a discussion of how to decide on a name for your blog and what you're going to blog about, and we'll finish by looking at how to use HTML and CSS code to customize the blog's layout or to better format blog pages. And, oh yes, there is a lot in the middle as well! In this book, we'll cover not only all of the basics, we'll also delve into many aspects of blogging and what's involved in creating and managing a personal or business blog.

Inside This Book

This book has eleven chapters, all filled with exercises, pictures, and content to get you started blogging; Some of the chapters are quite large, such as when we examine working with images and video (Chapter 4); others are fairly short, such as our walk through purchasing and setting up a custom domain for your blog (Chapter 6). All are written with passion and heart, and I can't wait for you to get started.

Chapter 1

In this chapter we'll discuss how to decide on a name for your blog. Although you can change the name after you've created your blog, it's not recommended as there may be a lot of work you have to do to complete such a name change. So we brainstorm about what factors to consider when choosing a name; what you envision your blog will look like; and what story you want to tell.

Chapter 2

We follow that vision and begin bringing it to life by discussing the elements you can use to make your blog look just as you want: color and font, size and placement of images, and the overall design and organization of your blog; To help you here, we'll also see how to keep your blog clean and neat and where you can find design templates online for free!

Chapter 3

Now you're ready to create your first blog! In this chapter, we'll review the pros and cons of three popular platforms to give you an idea of which is best for your personal or business blogging needs. Blogger, TypePad, and WordPress are the three we examine, and we'll use them throughout the rest of this book. In this chapter, we go through the setup process, pick a blog design template, and create a first post.

Chapter 4

If you've wondered about getting images and videos up to your blog, this chapter is for you! We look at how to get them from your camera and video recorder to your computer and then to your blog. We also see how to resize an image, how to apply a watermark, and how to do some minimal video editing. And yes, you will learn how to load your videos to YouTube and then how to embed them into a blog post.

Chapter 5

We start with a discussion of images and image management, then focus on how to modify your blog's design. We add a custom banner and modify the colors of the blog to coordinate with your new banner—and we do this in Blogger, TypePad, and WordPress.

Chapter 6

After setting up a blog and modifying its design, and after posting and uploading images and videos, you are ready to share it with the world. At this point, many bloggers decide they need a custom domain that says exactly what they want—and doesn't include the "blogspot," "typepad," or "wordpress" in the address. And that's what we cover in this chapter— how to purchase a domain and map it to your blog.

Chapter 7

Once you've created and announced your blog, you want to drive traffic to it and keep track of visitor activity. There are many wonderful tools to help you do just that, and we look at them here.

Chapter 8

It's time to socialize! Learn how to integrate your blog with Facebook and Twitter! In this chapter you will see how to configure the social networking giants so that your blog posts will post to them automatically, saving you lots of time and effort.

Chapter 9

Do you have items you'd like to sell right from your blog? Well, now you can. You'll learn how to set up pages to display whatever you want to sell, and then how to add PayPal buttons so you can accept payments online.

Chapter 10

We continue setting up the store page, using an HTML table to organize your sale items in rows and columns, which makes it easy to fix many items on one page. This table starts our discussion of HTML, and we continue with a look at other HTML tags and creating links, and then work with CSS code to further customize the layout and formatting of your blog.

Chapter 11

This book is full of information to help you get started, but there's a lot more to do and learn about blogging, and about the technology, tools, and gadgets that continually change. So we take a look at many help-related sites and review common errors and how to resolve them.

The Lingo

Without further ado, it's time to get started! You may be asking, what is a blog? What is HTML or CSS? What is a gadget, page or post? No worries, we'll review them now before you begin! The terms appear throughout the book and discussed in much greater detail.

Table 1. Blog Lingo

Element	Description
Blog	A blog is a type of web site that is updated regularly and frequently, with content about almost anything. Blogs are typically easier to maintain than a traditional web site and they actually get more traffic as well. Blogger, TypePad and WordPress are three popular blogging platforms (sort of like blog operating systems) where you can build and host your blog—for free!
Post	A post is an article or journal entry you'll write and publish to your blog. It can contain text, images, videos, hyperlinks, and other media. If you can use a word processor or write an e-mail, you can create a post! As in most word processing programs, you can even do some text formatting (bold, italic, changing the font, font size, and alignment) using a toolbar.
Page	A page is basically a post but with one major difference (and not one for you to be concerned about right now as we're just talking terminology). The difference is that when you post something new to your blog, people who subscribe (or follow) your blog will receive updates, but that's not the case when you create or modify a page. We'll discuss pages in more detail in Chapter 9.
Gadget	A gadget or widget is just another name for an item or element you add to your blog, most commonly in the sidebar. Popular gadgets are subscription links (which allow people to subscribe to your blog), links to favorite sites, your picture, or contact information.
HTML	HTML (HyperText Markup Language) is the language that's used to build web sites, and you can use it to format your blog. HTML is a special language that enables your blog to be read by all the different web browsers (such as Internet Explorer, Mozilla Firefox, Google Chrome, or Safari for the Mac).
CSS	Like HTML, CSS (Cascading Style Sheets) is a language that can be read by web browsers, but it is specifically designed for formatting posts, pages, and the overall blog layout.

Let's Go!

Are you ready? I hope so! Thank you for taking this journey with me. I would love to see your blogs when you've completed the book! Don't worry that blogging is too technical or that you are not computer savvy enough—you don't have to be! Just take it step by step and you'll quickly see this is something you can do and enjoy, and maybe even use to make some money! Let's get started!

CHAPTER 1

■ ■ ■

Where to Begin

In the introduction to this book we reviewed common blog lingo, such as blogging, posting, pages, and gadgets and widgets. We also discussed popular blog practices and concepts and the tools we'll be using and experimenting with throughout this book.

Now you'll actually begin the process of creating a blog! No, we are not signing up for TypePad, Blogger, WordPress, or any other blog platform just yet. There is a lot to consider before registering or setting up an account:

- What is the name of your blog?

- What are you interests?

- What do you want to blog about?

- Will you be the only one writing on your blog or are you part of group who will be posting content?

- What have you seen in other blogs that you like?

- Do you know what you want your blog to look like?

- What colors do you like?

After determining what you want to write about and what your blog should look like, you're going to need exciting, well-written content— free of grammatical errors—that gives your followers information they want to read, such as a funny story, a challenge or contest, details of a current promotion, professional advice, personal experience, or the benefits of using your services. With that in mind, in this chapter, we also supply some writing tips!

By the end of this chapter, you'll be armed with ideas and enthusiasm, and on your way to be a blogger!

Name Your Blog

Now you get to experience what parents go through in trying to find the perfect name! Or maybe you'll be one of the lucky ones who think of a great name on the first try. Either way, whether it takes you a minute or a month, you need to come up with a name for your blog. Although you can change your blog name later, it can be a big deal on some platforms (you may lose all your images, for example, and have to reinsert them, which is very time-consuming and not fun). So, take the time now to think about a name, before getting started.

The name of your blog should be related to its purpose, whether it's a personal journal, a fundraiser, a school project, or a professional blog about a service or product you provide. For example, if you'll be blogging about yourself, you may want to use your name. If you're using your blog for business, perhaps the blog name should be your company name or slogan, or it might describe the type of service you provide. Here are some examples:

- My blog development business is called "Blogs By Heather," (www.BlogsByHeather.com), which uses part of my name in the title, and indicates what my blog and business is about (see Figure 1–1).

Figure 1–1. The Blogs By Heather home page

- Many celebrities, athletes, professionals, and everyday bloggers like you and me use their own names for their blog. Figure 1–2 shows The Cooley Zone (http://chriscooley47.blogspot.com/; Chris is a professional athlete, #47, of the Washington Redskins). Others are blog.drphil.com (official blog of Dr. Phil) and www.sandimaciver.com (a fellow stamper blogging about her passion).

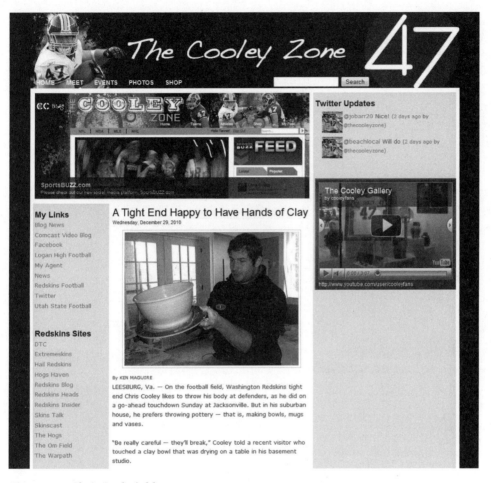

Figure 1–2. Chris Cooley's blog

- Some blog names include a cause or foundation name, such as www.donationsfordiabetes.com (a fundraiser site for a child with diabetes), www.fromourhearts.info (a site that gathers handmade cards to give to troops overseas so they can send them to their families), and the New York Times' blog on Breast Cancer (http://well.blogs.nytimes.com/tag/breast-cancer/), shown in Figure 1–3.

Figure 1–3. The New York Times's breast cancer blog

To find more inspiration, lists of many, many different types of blogs, and what others are blogging about, visit `www.blogs.com/topten`. First, however, I want you to come up with a name for your blog.

EXERCISE — COMING UP WITH A BLOG NAME

By the end of this exercise, I hope you'll figure out a name for your blog. This will take some time—as it should. If you are a business owner, you probably took some time to think of your business name. If you're a parent, you probably went around in circles searching for the perfect name for your new baby. Choosing the right name is important.

1. Consider if having your name as your blog name suits your blog's purpose. Is this blog about you and your life? Are you a business professional known by or for your name?

2. Get out a piece of paper or open your favorite word processor on your computer. Jot down all the names that come to mind, all of them, even if they don't quite make sense! Sometimes the best names are created by mistake. Note the ones that

   a. Involve your name, your business, your company name, what you love to do.

   b. Include a specific cause or upcoming event you are promoting.

   c. Refer to a group you belong to.

3. When you have a list of names, go to the Web and start searching for them to make sure they don't already exist.

   a. First use www.google.com or another favorite search engine.

   b. Then go to www.GoDaddy.com to see if they're used in a domain name (see Chapter 6, Setting up a Custom Domain; you may wish to use a domain with your blog, such as www.HeatherPorto.com instead of heatherporto.blogspot.com, for example). In Chapter 6, we actually purchase and setup a domain through GoDaddy. I mention this now as many bloggers do decide to purchase a domain later on, so you want to be sure at the outset that your name isn't already taken.

What to Blog About

Brainstorming about a name for your blog may have helped discover new ideas to write about. Or maybe you still haven't come up with the perfect name. This section may help you figure out what to write about as well as what to name your blog. The following ideas and creative writing tips should help you get started.

- Write about what you know. For example, I have a strong computer background and currently set up blogs for people daily, generally using Blogger or Typepad. So it was second nature for me to write my first book on Google Blogger. I simply wrote what I knew.

- Recount an event or experience. In remembering a specific event or experience, you may wish to write the entire story, but it can be even more compelling to simply share what you gained from that experience, what you learned.

- Share your memories of someone. Maybe you want to dedicate a blog to your grandfather or brother or aunt who has served or is serving in the army or fought in a war. In telling this type of story, you'll most likely interview people who also knew them and use the interviews and knowledge in writing your blog.

- Detail your personal research. If there's a subject that fascinates you and you want to learn more about it, start investigating it and then share that information on your blog.

- Start an argument. If you feel strongly about something going on in the world, from healthcare reform to the slow food movement to the overbreeding of dogs, let others know what you think, and why. Do be sure, however, to do your research to support your point of view.

- Tell your story. Use your blog as a diary to share your life—daily, weekly, or whatever suits your fancy. Many people use Facebook for this type of scenario, but it's just as easy to use a blog. And a blog allows you to write more content.

While thinking about what to write, know that not all blogs are meant to last forever. You may develop your blog for a particular purpose, say to promote an annual event or fundraiser, and then afterward no longer need it. Some are designed for business and will remain active as long as the company lasts and as long as you wish to continue. You may choose to blog as a diary, a journal of your life or someone else's, and keep it going as long as you have the interest in sharing. You can use your blog for any purpose and for any length of time. In any case, you should post often to keep people coming back—and to increase visibility and appear higher in search engine results. You don't have to post every day, though, and there are no specific rules to follow. This book is all about blogging practices and concepts, and the tools you can use to enhance your blogging experience and reach your blogging goals. The rest is totally up to you! My goal is to get you blogging and enjoying it!

Some people actually have more than one blog, such as one for family and another for a fundraiser they're running for a child's school. Or they may later start a business and create yet another blog for that. There's no limit and the topics to discuss are endless. I want to help you get started and unleash your creativity.

Family

Family is a very popular topic of conversation. I love to talk about my children, my husband, our dogs, and even the lizards! (Yes, we brought lizards home from a street fair—what were we thinking?) You can use a blog to jot down all your fun family times or to journalize your child's first year. You can share all those special moments—when did your baby first sleep through the night, what was her first word, when did he first smile—with the world or with just those family members and friends you allow to view your blog (yes, your blog can be protected).

For this, you can think of your blog as a digital scrapbook. You can include pictures, videos, and the "who, what, when, how, why, and where" details! This eliminates the need for printing or mailing copies of updates and photos, and lets your entire family experience these special moments day by day, month by month.

Of course you can use this concept for any type of family function, event, or history, such as birthday parties, school functions, vacations, and more! The possibilities are endless.

Personal Experience or Journey

Since all of us have a story to tell—a personal experience we've gone through or a personal journey we may still be on—let's brainstorm about one you might like to share with others in your blog. We'll discuss a series of personal topics and I'm sure there will be one you can relate to or one that will spark interest or an idea for a blog.

Take me, for example. I've been married for almost 10 years (June 2011), have two beautiful children, two wonderful dogs, and two "why did we take these home from the fair" lizards. So, with raising two young children, taking care of household chores, operating my blog services business, consulting, writing books, and holding paper crafting classes occasionally (for fun), you can surely understand how I get so preoccupied with everyday life and too busy being a mom, that I end up with no time to be a wife. So now I'm in the process of creating a blog called "100 Days of Kindness," which is totally dedicated to my husband and my personal journey of showering him with 100 days of kind gestures (and then hoping it continues after the 100 days!). Yes, it's personal, but it's in good taste and my whole family, friends and blog followers may have a good laugh or cry or just come along for the ride. I'm excited about it.

Now let's take you. Your personal journey may involve sharing your love of dogs or cats, or a life-altering experience you think others may benefit from, or writing about your hobbies or books you've read. You may be part of a book club or a design team where a group of you will author your blog and share the week's accomplishments.

Many like to share a weight-loss journey—where you started, all the steps in between, your ups and downs, your exercise routines, a special diet, a personal trainer, etc.

Teens may want to focus on school events, track the development of a school project, recount volunteer or job experiences, or detail the plusses and minuses of various colleges before applying.

Have any ideas yet?

Specific Cause or Event

There are many, many sites dedicated to cancer, or that serve as a fundraiser for a particular person, church group, or cause, or to promote and detail an upcoming annual event, such as a Breast Cancer Walk.

You may have visited blogs dedicated to autism, attention deficit disorder, or depression, or someone's personal battle with another type of illness or disorder. Many people share such experiences in order to help others.

Do you have a specific cause or yearly event you could write about or promote?

Business

Do you own your own business? Regardless of its size, it may benefit from having a regularly updated blog. People can subscribe to your blog to read about tips you may be sharing, promotions you are running, new products you are releasing, or whatever is coming soon.

For a business, a blog can serve as a powerful marketing and analysis tool. Later in this book (Chapter 8), we'll learn how to track visitor activity and, based on what areas of your blog people are visiting more or less frequently, you can learn more about your audience and possibly modify your marketing and business strategies.

As a business owner, you'll want to keep your blog's content focused on your areas of expertise or your particular business field. So, if you have a landscaping company, for example, you won't be writing about hair dye. I have a blog services business, so I regularly post about how to install new gadgets on a blog, or tips I've learned about blogging, or how to use blogging tools. Everything about blogging, in other words, but not about other topics. Not in my business blog.

Keep your posts centered on your business and share what you can without giving away trade secrets!

Hopefully, you've been thinking about what you'd like to write about — your life, your experiences, your profession, your family, your hobby, your cause. In this exercise, we'll continue to brainstorm.

1. Get out a piece of paper or open your word processor.

    a. Write down any topics that have captured your interest.

    b. Note any upcoming events, such as vacations, you may want to share.

    c. Are there any specific personal experiences that have changed you as a person?

    d. Are any family members suffering from an illness, such as cancer, where you'd like to share their triumphs and battles?

2. When you're done, review your list and choose the topic you'd like to start with!

Multiple Authors

Still have trouble finding something to write about? Or maybe you're afraid you're so busy you won't have the time to post as often as you should, but you still want a blog that remains active, is updated regularly, and keeps your customers and blog followers coming back. Don't worry, you are not alone!

Many blog owners have ghost writers—people hired to write material on their behalf, as themselves. For example, I am a Stampin' Up! Demonstrator (yes, I like to make homemade, hand-stamped cards) and have a personal blog where I post new cards and projects I've created, describe the products and techniques I use, or share what inspired me to create the project. However, I have also been hired as a personal designer for another demonstrator. As a result, I was a "ghost writer" and created unique, one-of-a-kind projects just for her, as her, on her blog. It was fun for me ad, at the same time, helps her focus on other aspects of promoting and growing her business. So, you may want to hire someone to help you (whether for a personal or business blog).

Moreover, you may have a business with many partners or a design team or club with many members, where all parties need to be able to post on the blog. The blogging platforms discussed throughout this book (Blogger, Typepad, and WordPress) all allow multiple people to access and post to the same blog.

1. Under the Permissions tab in Blogger, you can add Blog Authors by entering their names and e-mail addresses. Added authors then receive an invite in their inboxes and, after accepting, can post to your blog.

2. In Typepad, under Settings, click Authors. There, in the middle of the screen, you can add additional authors by entering the name, e-mail address, and level (junior or guest). Junior authors may create new posts and save them as drafts, but can't publish (the owner of the blog reviews and publishes these posts). Guest authors may create and publish posts or schedule them to post at a later time.

3. Under Users in WordPress, you can add a new user and designate her role to be Author, Administrator, Contributor, or Editor. An administrator has complete ownership and control of the blog and can do anything and everything. An author can edit, publish, and delete his own posts. An editor can edit, publish, and delete any posts or pages in the blog. A contributor can edit only his own posts but can't publish them; an administrator reviews and publishes them. Once these posts are published, the contributor can't revise them.

By using additional authors, you can reduce the amount of work you personally have to do on your blog while providing your customers with frequent updates, keeping your blog active, and therefore maintaining your online presence.

Writing Good Content

Let's review some good writing practices. One of the reasons you create a blog is to have lots of people follow its content. Posts make up the majority of your blog, so there are some basic tasks you should perform regularly.

Check Spelling and Grammar

Many bloggers use Microsoft Word to write up their posts, and then copy and paste the information into the post editor. If this is how you like to compose your posts, don't forget to use Word's great spelling and grammar feature (in Word 2007, it's under the Review menu). However, if you compose your post from within your blog, use the post editor's spell check option in Blogger, Typepad, and WordPress, which you'll also find on the post editor toolbar. It only takes a few minutes to perform and it is well worth that time to post a flawless article that reads well. However, we all know the spell checker itself is not flawless (as I often write "form" instead of "from" and the spell checker finds nothing wrong with that). So, even after running a spelling and grammar check, you should definitely reread your work before publishing.

Stay Focused

Keep each post focused on one particular topic, date, or event. You may lose readers if your posts are too busy or contain too much information, or try to cover too many topics at once. Besides appearing disorganized, it's too time-consuming to read all the content, so you may lose readers—and business if your sales pitch is at the very bottom of a lengthy post. You want to keep your readers' attention!

Use Keywords

It's also a good idea to include keywords in your posts, in both the content and the title if possible. This helps potential customers find you on the Internet when they search for those keywords. For example, a landscaping company's blog posts may include the keywords or phrases landscaping, landscape, lawn service, waterfalls, masonry, and the like, as well as, of course, the business name and the town or county it's in. The ultimate goal in using keywords is to have a search engine (like Google) rank your site on the first page or two of search results.

Although it's important to use keywords, it is equally important not to overuse them. If you do, your site will be flagged as spam and will not show up at all on result pages. Years ago, I downloaded free software from Apex, Dynamic Submission (http://apexpacific.com/submission.html), and at the time it stated that keywords should only be between 2 and 3 percent of your content. Therefore, out of 100 words of content, you should use a keyword no more than three times. This software is still available. However, today, 3-6 percent as a keyword ratio is average.

English and Writing

You're in luck! My husband is an English teacher and has a few tips to share with us regarding writing blog posts. Note that the rules that apply to writing blog posts are different and much less strict than those that apply to writing academic or formal papers, resumes, or business correspondence. In general, your tone is informal, relaxed, and conversational, and you speak to your blog readers as to a friend. This is not intended to be an English 101 class, but to review a few practices to help you write better posts:

- Use a conversational tone. As previously stated, your writing should be relaxed and informal. You don't have to worry about an editor reviewing your work or that your sentences are structured perfectly. This book is written in a conversational tone as I speak to you about blogging in a friendly manner (not as your professor or English teacher).

- Keep track of your tenses (past/present/future). If you're writing about the past, keep it in the past, and the same goes for the present and future. Nothing makes writing more difficult to follow than a jumble of tenses.

- Me or I. If you are writing or speaking about yourself, use "I" as in "Billy, Mary, and I are going to the mall." Use "me" when you're receiving an action, such as "Charlie gave me the game ball." or "My mother is angry with me for staying out late."

- Numbers. You can use either digits or words to write a number (10 or ten, for example) in the body of a sentence, so which you use is up to you. However, the first word or letter of a sentence should be capitalized so you shouldn't use a number there unless you write it out (Ten).

- Using commas. Unfortunately, some writers use commas to combine too many thoughts into one sentence. It's better to use shorter, simpler sentences than to create run-on sentences.

- Its and it's. In general, "it's" is a substitute for "it is," as in "It's cold outside." "Its," on the other hand, is a form of ownership—"An elephant uses its trunk to pick up food."

- Apostrophes. In following the rules of ownership, in most cases you would use an apostrophe "s" such as "Heather's jacket is red with black trim." However, if the noun is plural, use just an apostrophe, as in "The princesses' crowns sparkled with diamonds."

- Quotations and ending punctuation. In general, keep the period, question mark, exclamation point or other punctuation inside the quotation marks. While blogging, chances are you won't use many direct quotes that require quotation marks, but if you are specifically quoting someone else's work, you should certainly credit them in some way (remember the saying "give credit where credit is due").

- Proofreading. In addition to using a spelling and grammar checker, be sure to proof read your work. If you inadvertently use the wrong word, but it's a real word, chances are good that neither the spell checker nor the grammar checker will pick it up. So don't forget to reread your work before posting. It's even better to have someone else read your work!

Blog Design

What do you want your blog to look like? Have you seen other blogs that you absolutely love? Or totally dislike? In the next chapter we'll cover Blog Layout and Design, and later in Chapter 5 we'll focus on Advanced Blog Design. So take some time now to start thinking about what you want your blog to look like.

- What colors do you like?

- Have you seen sites you like? What do you like about them?

    - Color

    - Font

    - Layout

    - Organization

- Do you want a blog that looks and acts like a traditional web site?

- Do you like tabs across the top?

All of this is important to note. You want your blog, whether for personal or business use, to reflect you, your personality, and your likes. For example, on my blog, I use shades of blue, as blue is easy on the eyes and is used by many corporate sites. However, I keep it fun with the waves down the sides. At some point I may switch the samples you see in the banner area, but other than that, I'm really happy with the way it turned out!

EXERCISE – BLOG DESIGN

In this exercise, I want you to explore the Web, looking for sites you like and dislike, noting the attributes you find compelling or that put you off.

1. Do you know what you want your blog to look like? If so, then open up Photoshop, Illustrator, InDesign, Acrobat, Publisher, Word, or any program you like to start creating a sketch. Or, use a pencil and paper instead!

2. If you really don't have any idea, go to `www.blogs.com/topten` and start looking through the lists of blogs on all different topics. You'll find tons of interesting blogs, and that will give you exposure to lots of different designs and layouts.

With Figures 1–4 through 1–9, I'd like to share a few different types of designs that my design partners Michelle Laycock (`www.LaycockDesigns.com`) and Amy Celona (`www.WebsByAmy.com`) have worked on, each displaying something unique. Just a little imagery to spark your imagination!

Figure 1–4. A blog layout with a design to the left and a navigation bar at the top

Figure 1–5. A fun and cheery layout with a unique design

Figure 1–6. A traditional look with a more masculine color scheme

Figure 1–7. A full blog layout, including a floral design with decorative banner and footer

Figure 1–8. A blog for a cause, and another more masculine sample

Figure 1–9. A seashore design with navigational tabs that move up and down

Summary

I hope you enjoyed your first chapter on blogging! Have you come up with a name for your blog? And a subject? We covered some writing tips and discussed potential topics, such as family, a personal journey or experience, your life in general, your business, a child's school project, or a specific cause like cancer or diabetes; I hope through the exercises you've found material to begin writing your blog!

Furthermore, you learned that you do not have to blog alone! Lots of people are members of a group, team, or association, where many people may contribute to your blog's content. You may even want to hire someone to post for you—someone who knows the subject(s) you want to blog about.

We also saw that it's important to use a spelling and grammar checker, and to reread your work before publishing it.

We finished up by starting to explore our next topic—your blog's design. In the next chapter, we will continue our discussion of blog design and the overall layout and organization of your blog.

CHAPTER 2

■ ■ ■

Blog Layout and Design

You've decided what to blog about and you've come up with a name that reflects your goals. Now it's time to consider how you want your blog to look, what you want to accomplish, what sort of mood you want to evoke. Hopefully, the exercises in Chapter 1 gave you some good ideas and you've turned your vision into a basic sketch.

To help you realize the vision you have for your blog, in this chapter we'll discuss the building blocks of design. We'll start with color—what colors are primarily used for a variety of businesses, when to use certain eye-catching colors like red or yellow, and what kind of feeling the different colors evoke. We will also cover the dos and don'ts of fonts and the use and misuse of images, as well as the size of different elements (the banner, sidebar images, images in posts, and so forth).

No matter how pretty your blog looks, if visitors can't find what they need or find the navigation clumsy and confusing, they won't come back. So, in this chapter we'll also consider the overall layout and organization of your blog and its elements—where to place items in your blog and how to assist visitors in finding posts and topics of interest.

Finally, we'll examine how different screen resolutions or web browsers can affect how others view your blog, and we'll see how you can use free blog templates to enhance your blog's appearance.

Using Color

When you're starting out, it's a good idea to take advantage of other people's knowledge of what works. Although you may love the color red, for example, it's hard on the eyes and not recommended as the major color in your blog's design. Blue and green, on the other hand, are most easy on the eyes, and therefore among the most popular colors used online.

Color is a personal choice, of course, and there's nothing written in stone about what colors you can or can't use. There are no official rules, just recommendations and, of course, exceptions. For example, sites directed at children often use red—it's eye-catching, exciting, and cheerful (see Figures 2–1 and 2–2). (The black and white images don't do justice to these sites, so visit www.FAO.com and www.BounceU.com to get the full effect). Others use red as an accent color—that's what I did when I designed the Creative Apple Scrampers site shown in Figure 2–3. As you can see, apart from the apple, the majority of the site is white, clean, and simple.

Figure 2–1. Sites for children often use lots of red.

Figure 2–2. Red makes a site festive.

Figure 2–3. In general, use red in moderation.

So, as you see, there are sites that use red to great effect as a primary color or accent color, as it is a bright, fun color that complements a playful company theme. Still, for the most part, I suggest using red only to draw attention to a particular item or area of your blog or post, say to highlight a promotion.

I've done some research into what different colors mean and I'm going to discuss this below. I'll also present some samples and recommendations. Do keep in mind that colors may have different meanings to you and your culture, and that, of course, should take precedence. What follows can help you set a mood, but really it's just for fun!

- *Black* is the color of authority and power.

  However, blogs that have a totally black background and white or light text are hard to read and should be used only in special cases. On the other hand, it's just fine to use a black background the way artist John Mayer does on his blog (www.JohnMayer.com/blog); the center is still white with dark text (Figure 2–4).

Figure 2–4. Good use of a black background

- *Red*, an intense color, gets your heart racing. This color is definitely an attention-getter!

  Use this color if you want to draw your visitor's attention to a particular area of your blog, such as a red "NEW" button to draw customers to a new product highlighted in your blog's sidebar.

- *Blue* is the most popular color. It is both corporate and peaceful, and evokes truth, wisdom, and tranquility.

  When I had Michelle Laycock (`www.laycockdesigns.com`) give my "Blogs By Heather" (`www.blogsbyheather.com`) a makeover, I asked for something that looked more business-y instead of crafty. Originally, I had the design match my "Hand Stamped By Heather" blog (stamping and paper crafting; `www.HandStampedByHeather.com`), which is Victorian in style. I love roses and the vintage look, so both blogs used the same look. As my business grew and my needs changed, I wanted a more corporate look—but still wanted to keep a little of my personality. So she recommended shades of blue and I think it fits my profession perfectly. And we added a curve/wavy look for some fun and a little pink in the banner for femininity. I've received many compliments on the new look!

- *Green*. This color is easiest on the eye and symbolizes nature. It is a calming, refreshing color. Of course, green makes some people think of money, and reminds others of the saying "green with envy."

- *Purple* is the color of royalty and symbolizes wealth, luxury, and sophistication. To some it also represents femininity and romance.

- *Pink* is playful and delicate, as Figure 2–5 shows.

- *Brown* symbolizes reliability, friendliness, and genuineness.

- *Orange* can be seasonal (summer or Halloween) but it's also an attention-getter. It's not quite as powerful as red, but still bright and in-your-face.

- *Gray* represents formality.

- *Yellow* is optimistic and cheerful, but supposedly the hardest for the eye to take in so try not to overuse it.

For more insights into the meaning and use of color, check out `www.infoplease.com/spot/colors1.html` and `www.desktoppub.about.com/cs/color/a/symbolism.htm`.

Figure 2–5. Use pink for a light, feminine look (`www.vkdesigncompany.com`)

Using Fonts

Each blog platform comes with a set of fonts you can choose from, typically fonts that are very common and popular in a variety of applications (Georgia, Times New Roman, Arial, and Verdana, for example). There is a reason for this. These fonts are standard, generic, but most important, they are easy to read! Many bloggers want to use other fonts, perhaps those that match their banner, for example. Although you can do this, and we'll discuss that shortly, you should take caution. While some fonts may be coordinated with your graphics, and you may really like them, if they are not easy to read, they won't serve your purpose. If a visitor can't read your blog, they will not stay on it and will not come back—and you could lose a potential customer.

Whatever font you choose for your posts, be sure it's not too small. You don't want your readers to have to take out a pair of glasses just to read your blog! In general, a 10- or 12–point font works very well.

Until recently, if you wanted to display a custom font on your site, you had to do this by using the font in a program like Photoshop and then saving it as an image (a .JPG, .PNG, .GIF, or .TIFF file, for example). In Figure 2–6, you'll notice that Connie Babbert (`www.inkspiredtreasures.com`) uses a nice font in her sidebars for the titles and buttons (Email me, Subscribe, and About me). The words are actually images with additional images (snowflakes) that complement her banner. This use of a custom font enhances the overall blog design. However, such a font (with the swirls) would not enhance the readability of the posts and so should not be used for all the text on a blog.

Figure 2–6. Creating text with graphics

Many bloggers continue to use graphics as headings. However, an application called Typekit (www.typekit.com) can make using fancy fonts much easier. You can install Typekit on any blog platform (or traditional web site) that allows CSS (Cascade Style Sheet) customization, and it's free for one site with fewer than 25,000 page views per month. You can view other pricing plans (www.typekit.com/plans), which depend on the number of custom fonts you want to use, the number of blogs or sites you need them for, and the number of page views your site receives per month (we'll discuss visitor tracking in Chapter 8). The Ballot Bucks (www.ballotbucks.org) site has Typekit installed (Figure 2–7), and you'll find more examples at Typekit's gallery www.typekit.com/gallery.

Figure 2–7. A Typekit example

Blogger users will also find some unique free fonts at www.kevinandamanda.com/fonts, along with instruction on how to install them. Tonya Dailey asked me to install one of the fonts from Kevin and Amanda's site on her Blogger blog (www.tonyadaileyblog.com/), as shown in Figure 2–8.

Figure 2–8. Custom fonts installed on Blogger

Organization

We've spent a little time talking about the look of your blog; now let's think about its organization. First we'll discuss how to organize and place information on your blog, especially to emphasize a current promotion. Then we'll note the importance of focusing on one theme or overall topic for your blog. Next we'll review house cleaning techniques for your blog; how to unclutter your blog's sidebars so your blog does not become too busy. Lastly, we'll review image use and misuse, and recommended layout and design tips.

Organize Information

One of the things that frustrates blog readers most is not being able to find what they're looking for quickly. And not only do you want your visitors to be able to hone in on the information they need, you equally want them to discover the information *you* want them to see (such as a featured item for sale or the date and time of an upcoming event.

Categorizing (or labeling) your posts allow visitors to quickly find topics of interest. When visitors come to your blog, you don't want them to have to scroll through dozens of posts to find an article of interest—and risk losing them as potential customers or loyal followers. Categories give your readers a way to search your blog by topic, like a table of contents or a site map. You will learn how to do this in the next chapter when we see how to set up a blog with Blogger, TypePad, and WordPress.

A basic rule of thumb for making sure your blog followers find what you want them to find is to put this information at the top of your blog, on the opening screen, the part you see without having to scroll. That's the prime real estate on your blog! This is where you want to display a current promotion or upcoming event in a featured post or as an advertisement in your sidebar.

Separate Blogs

Know when to separate! You may have a main blog; mine, for example, focuses on blog development and how-to tutorials. But you may also have a part-time job or hobby like me and want to blog about that as well. I'm also a Stampin' Up! Demonstrator and enjoy making—and blogging about—handmade cards and projects. Take my advice—don't try to run both your business and your hobby from one blog. Develop and maintain a separate blog for each. Each blog should have a main purpose and primary focus. Of course, you can link from one to the other to help promote and drive traffic to each. If you mix content and try running both business and leisure pursuits from one blog, you'll eventually lose your following. I would most definitely lose my blog development followers if I started posting about how to make a handmade card and the supplies I used to make it. In the next chapter, you learn how to create a blog, and you can then simply create one for each business, hobby, story or event.

Unclutter Your Sidebars

Neat, uncluttered sidebars are becoming a popular trend in blogging, and people often ask me how they can do this. After blogging for years, your list of categories can become very, very long and take up a lot of room in your sidebar. One idea is to convert these into to a drop-down list and immediately save a lot of space. Another is to remove the Facebook Like Box and Twitter Updates, which take up lots of sidebar space, and replace them with simple icons linking to your Facebook page and Twitter account.

To reduce the amount of clutter and information on your sidebar, I recommend the following:

- *Image Size:* Make images in your sidebars smaller (no more than 125 pixels wide) and keep them the same size, for neatness and consistency.

- *Image Alignment:* If you are centering images, keep them all centered. All images should have the same formatting and alignment, as well as be the same size.

- *Use Pages:* Blogger, TypePad, and WordPress all have a "Pages" feature that lets you put content on a separate page, so take some of the items off your sidebar and move them to a different page. If you are selling products, for example, you can list one or two featured products in your sidebar and then have a "click to view more" link to a page that lists all your products, pricing, and payment options. Similarly, if you are hosting a special event you may have an image in the sidebar promoting the event, but you can put all the event details and payment options on a separate page.

- *Create a Navigation Bar or Drop-down Menu:* If you end up creating several pages, you can use a menu (navigation bar) to link to different areas of your site. You can create a link to a Products page, for example, from the menu and eliminate the need to have any products listed in your sidebar at all. You can also use a drop-down menu to directly link to files or PDFs. In Figure 2–9, under the Catalogs menu there are submenu items listed that are direct links to files rather than pages.

  Drop-down menus keep your blog organized and the sidebars clean and neat, not to mention providing easy access to pages and other important information.

Figure 2–9. *Drop-down menus help keep things neat and easy to access.*

Layout Design Tips

Now let's consider the placement of images on your blog. Of course you want to create a blog that is nice to look at and that portrays your business, event, or theme. Images can help you do that. However, you do not want your blog's design to distract your visitors from its content and purpose, and images can do that as well.

Here's a list of popular ways images are used to enhance a blog's appearance. Figure 2–10 (www.craftysassystamper.com/) shows many of them. In most cases you would not install all of these elements, as your blog would look busy and cluttered and, even worse, take forever to load!

- *Banner:* this is the blog header or image that appears at the top of your blog.

- *Background:* this is an image that can be placed behind the text on your blog instead of just using a color.

- *Post signature:* this is a special signature at the end of a post; some people like to use these to make a post personal, unique, and attractive.

- *Post Header:* this is an image that can be used before the text in the Post Title area or sit beneath the Post Title.

- *Post Footer:* this is an image you can place between posts to act as a separator.

- *Category/Sidebar Separators:* these images reside in your sidebar and can be used if you want a specific font and graphic instead of the default font and color set in your blog's design settings.

- *Blog Footer:* this is an image that sits at the bottom of your blog. It matches the design of rest of the blog and may have a closing in a font that matches the banner's font, something like "Thanks for visiting!" or "Have a great day! Thanks for stopping by!"

- *Buttons:* these are images that visitors can click on, such as for Online Ordering, Email Me, Classes & Events, etc.

You can use a combination of these graphics to build a custom blog look, but remember—if you use too many images, it takes away from your blog's content and message. Again, graphics are meant to enhance your blog, not bury its content. Keep it simple. More is not necessarily better. In thinking simple, a popular trend right now is using a lot of "white" in the design, creating a very clean and neat look.

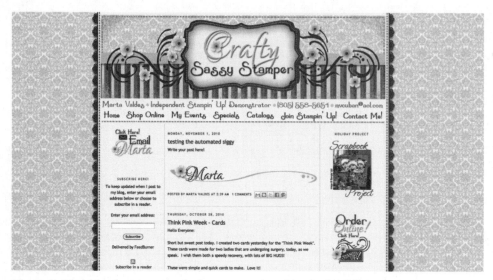

Figure 2–10. A blog layout example that uses various images for different purposes.

Images and Animation

As noted earlier, images in your sidebar should be small (but readable) and consistent in size. And the same goes for your banner and your blog posts. Too often, while viewing people's blogs, I have encountered images that are too large—either they don't fit in the posting area or the blog banner is so long that it takes up half the screen. Chapter 4 is dedicated to working with images and videos, so we'll look at these issues in more detail there.

Animated GIFs on a blog are attention-grabbing and great to use if you are promoting a service, item, or upcoming event. However, too much animation is distracting. Have you ever visited a blog or web site where everything is moving and you have no idea where to look first? You don't want your visitors to feel that way when coming to your site. So use animation, but keep it to a minimum. If you visit my blog, www.BlogsByHeather.com, one of the first things you'll notice is the flashing button about upcoming webinars to the left of the first post; because it is animated but also because of its position, it will be seen quickly and easily by new or returning blog followers.

Screen Resolution

In the simplest terms, screen resolution is how many pixels make up the image you see on your computer screen, which is reflected in how much of a blog's page you see on your screen. When computers have a high resolution (say, 1920 x 1200), you can see more of an image, although objects appear smaller. If the resolution is lower, you can better see the objects on your screen, but you won't be able to see as much in the browser window (unless you have a large monitor). I mention this because it is important from a design perspective. You want to design your blog graphics so that the majority, if not all, your blog visitors can see your blog without having to scroll. (Keep in mind that if you visit a blog where you can't see the entire site, you can use the Ctrl key (or Command key on a Mac) and the hyphen key to zoom in.

Browser Differences

Be sure to look at your blog in all of the popular browsers: Mozilla Firefox, Internet Explorer, Apple Safari, and Google Chrome. Unfortunately, browsers handle and interpret CSS code differently, so if you are doing CSS customization on your blog, you'll have to make sure your work looks good in the different browsers. All of your visitors should see the same thing. I recommend using Adobe BrowserLab—a free, fast and easy way to do cross-browser testing. Visit `https://browserlab.adobe.com`.

Blog Design Templates

Don't worry—you don't have to be, or hire, a graphic designer to have a beautiful blog! There are many free templates you can get online. Typepad (`www.typepad.com/`) has a large gallery with a wide variety of templates to choose from. Among the many sites you can find online for free Blogger and WordPress templates, here are a few recommendations:

- `http://bTemplates.com` organizes its free Blogger and WordPress templates in a number of different ways, including the number of columns, style, color, width, and those most viewed (Figure 2–11).

- `www.bloggertemplatesfree.com` offers beautiful, free Blogger templates (Figure 2–12).

- `www.thecutestblogontheblock.com` provides backgrounds for Blogger, WordPress, MySpace and Twitter, as well as banners, and accessories like animated buttons (Figure 2–13).

- `www.wordpress2u.com` delivers free and premium WordPress templates compatible with WordPress 2.7 – 2.9, and widget-ready (Figure 2–14).

Figure 2–11. A bTemplates example

Figure 2–12. A BloggerTemplatesFree example

Figure 2–13. *The Cutest Blog on the Block background example*

Figure 2–14. *A WordPress2U example*

Summary

In this chapter we continued to discuss blog design and layout. We reviewed color, fonts, and organization, and provided some design and layout tips. In short, you want to keep your blog uncluttered by reducing sidebar images, using pages, and creating a menu or navigation bar. Remember to position important items and promotions at the top of your blog!

We noted the importance of screen resolution and browser testing, and suggested some design template resources for you to explore. You want to be sure all your visitors can read your blog with ease, without having to scroll, and that it looks the same in any web browser.

In Chapter 3 you will set up your blog! Now that you have a name, know what you want to write about, and have some idea how you want it to look, it's time to start implementing your vision! We'll discuss which blogging platform is best for your personal or business needs based on your purpose, the functionality you need, and your budget.

CHAPTER 3

■ ■ ■

Let's Blog

In the last chapter we discussed many of the elements you'll use to design your blog, such as color, font, and images, and how to best organize and lay out your blog so visitors can find what they need. We took a look at many blogs that demonstrated a unique use of color or featured certain image elements. We examined a variety of layouts for business and personal use and noted a few blog templates you can find online to apply to your blog's design.

Now you'll get your hands dirty! You will actually begin blogging: you'll learn how to create a new blog, understand the different areas of your blog, and create your first blog post.

The first step is deciding which blog platform to use—but how do you know which is right for you? Is one better than another? How much do they cost? What can each blog platform do? What are their limitations? We'll review a few of the most popular platforms to help you determine which best suits your particular blogging goals and needs, as well as your budget.

Which Blog Platform Should You Use?

This is the million dollar question and, of course, there's no one right answer. What is good for me may not be best suited for you. Let's discuss the three most popular platforms, Blogger, TypePad, and WordPress.com and weigh the important factors such as cost, ease of use, scalability, support, and available features.

Cost

With the economy struggling, many are interested in free blogging services. Blogger and WordPress are very popular and that may be the number one reason why. They are free and loaded with features and functionality.

TypePad's free version, TypePad Micro, is very, very limited, allowing you to choose from among only three different templates. And the only areas you can customize are the banner and background image (depending on which template you select). Moreover, it has a storage max of 3GB. For example, my personal blog, with 268 posts and 463 pictures, uses 30MB of storage. Basically, the only thing you can do is post. And while posting is the main purpose of having a blog, most bloggers do want to personalize their blog. Honestly, I do not recommend TypePad Micro. You should use Blogger or WordPress, or instead go with one of TypePad's professional packages (Plus, Unlimited, or Premium). TypePad offers a free two-week trial for any of these packages, then charges a monthly fee (or you can save two months if you pay for a year upfront); the fee depends on which package you choose. If you'll eventually want a custom design like mine, www.BlogsByHeather.com, with a custom background and full customization control, you'll need the Unlimited package, which is $14.95 USD a month. However, you can always start with the Plus package ($8.95 USD a month) and upgrade later.

The free version of WordPress.com has a lot of functionality. However, to do more advanced customization to your blog's theme, you have to purchase the Cascading Style Sheet (CSS) upgrade for

$14.97 a year. Registering a domain is $5 and then mapping it to your blog (discussed in Chapter 6) is $12; mapping a blog in Blogger and TypePad is free. WordPress.com also comes with only 3GB of free storage space. If you need more, you can purchase a Space Upgrade by paying a yearly fee of from $19.97 for 5GB, up to $289.97 for an extra 100GB. The Space Upgrade also allows you to add audio files. If you like, you can pay another $59.97 a year for the VideoPress upgrade, which lets you upload and embed videos directly onto your blog). In Blogger and TypePad, you can insert an image, audio, or video in a post without having to purchase an upgrade.

In comparison, Blogger's free storage space is very limited at 1GB, though upgrading to 20GB is only $5 USD a year. And Blogger allows you to customize your banner, background, posts, footers (just about any aspect of your blog) for free! You have complete control of your blog, its elements, and functionality, and you can easily customize your blog using HTML and CSS code if you want.

Ease of Use

So Blogger is free and allows full customization, but is it easy to use? Absolutely. Of the three platforms we'll be reviewing throughout this book, Blogger is the easiest, especially for those without any prior blogging experience. Not only is it easy to create a blog, you'll find you can begin posting immediately, and use the toolbar to quickly insert an image and format text. And it's very easy to change your blog's layout, template, color scheme and more. Blogger is very user-friendly and easy to follow.

WordPress is also easy to use and navigate using the tools available in the free version. However, once you have to upgrade (CSS Upgrade) to do advanced customization, it is not so easy to figure out where and how to customize your blog (using CSS code) which we'll review in Chapter 10.

While the for-pay version of TypePad has some features that the others don't (which we'll discuss shortly), it can be harder to use in that it may take many more steps to accomplish certain tasks, such as adding an image to your blog's sidebar. Here are the steps for adding an image in all three platforms:

- In Blogger, you click on Design from the Dashboard, then on Page Elements, and then on Add a Gadget. Choose Picture gadget and Browse to upload a picture from your computer. Save Changes and you're done.

- In TypePad (you can only do this in Plus or higher versions), you first go to the Library drop-down and choose the File Manager. You click Browse to choose the file from your computer, then Upload to upload the file. Next, right-click on the new file name (as it is now listed in File Manager) and choose Copy Shortcut or Copy Link. Then go to the Library drop-down and choose Typelists. Then click Create a New Typelist. Then add a title and the type of Typelist. Then click the Create New Typelist button. In the Add New Typelist area, skip the label and in the Notes area write the code `<img src="<path to file>">` (where `<path to file>` is the pasted URL from the copied file location of the newly uploaded image). Next click Save Changes. Then, since it's a new typelist, you have to click Publish. Now click on the check box next to your blog's name and click Save Changes. And you're finally done. Did I lose you along the way?

- In WordPress, from the Dashboard you click on Media, then on Add New. Then click on Select Files and locate the image on your computer. Click Open, copy the file URL and click Save All Changes. On the left, from the Dashboard, click on Appearance, then Widgets. Click and drag a Text Widget to the sidebar. Enter a title and in the large text box write the code `<img src="<path to file>">` (where `<path to file>` is the URL you copied from the Media File Manager). Now click Save and then Close. As you can see, it's not as quick in WordPress as the 1-2-3 Blogger method, but it's still much simpler than in TypePad.

In my opinion, Blogger and WordPress are easier to learn than TypePad.

Scalability

As your blog grows, your business grows, your needs grow, which platform will grow with you and handle all your business or blogging needs? The good news is they all do! If your blog grows significantly, however, chances are good you'll eventually be paying. As noted earlier, you'll run out of free storage space with Blogger faster than with TypePad or WordPress. But additional space in Blogger is affordable, and you can create as many blogs as you'd like under one account. In contrast, TypePad lets you create up to four blogs at the Plus level and you'll need to pay $14.95 USD a month if you want to be able to create unlimited blogs.

Using the paid versions of TypePad the storage space is unlimited, but there is a restriction on the amount you can upload per month: 150 MB maximum for Plus users, 1000MB for Unlimited users, and 2000MB for Premium users.

WordPress also provides many ways to upgrade, such as allowing unlimited users for $29.97 a year.

As you can see, there many factors to consider regarding scalability—storage space, upload limits, number of authors, and so forth—but any of these platforms should allow your blog to grow along with your needs.

Help

People often forget how important it is to be able to get help—when you're starting your blog, when you want to upgrade, when you run into problems. Is help or documentation available? What kind? Do you have to pay?

None of these platforms have wonderful phone support. TypePad is a paid service but you don't get "real" support unless you have the Premium package ($29.95 a month). Blogger and WordPress are free and don't have phone support. Blogger probably has the weakest help section although you can quickly find a lot of help on the Internet. In fact, when I run into any Blogger problems, I typically just do a Google search before even looking through Blogger Help. In contrast, WordPress is known for its plentiful documentation.

Features

Blogger used to lag behind in its features in comparison to TypePad and WordPress, but that's no longer the case. It now has wonderful new features and its functionality continues to improve. Here are some of its newest useful features.

- Pages. In addition to creating posts in your blog, you can maintain separate, standalone pages. Pages are like traditional web site pages used for sharing information about you (About Me page) or your services (Our Services page). Many people use Pages to showcase products, setting up a Page for each category or type of product they are selling. If you look at my site, `www.BlogsByHeather.com`, in the left sidebar you'll see how I use Pages to detail the different services I offer, as well as for testimonials.

- Share Buttons. These are the buttons often found at the bottom on a post that allow you to quickly "share" your post with Google Buzz, Facebook, and Twitter, for example.

- Popular Posts. This feature ranks and displays your blog's most popular posts in your sidebar.

- Stats. This lets you see data about your blog, such as the number of visitors.

- Both TypePad and WordPress let you share posts, track visitor activity, use a Pages feature, and more. And they've always had a template gallery while Blogger used to have only a handful of layouts to choose from. Now, with its new Template Designer, Blogger offers its users a wonderful set of templates that can be customized as well.

Two features Blogger lacks (and hopefully will someday include) are a "Feature This Post" ability, which allows a user to quickly choose a given post to be "featured" and therefore remain at the top of the blog as the first post, and a built-in file manager. Yes, of course there are work-arounds, but they are just that—not built-in features. In TypePad, you can also set a "page" as the Front Page of your blog to serve as a traditional home page that doesn't show a list of your posts.

TypePad and WordPress both have a file manager you can use to easily upload PDFs, images, or other documents you want to share with your blog readers or customers. In Blogger, you have to use another application to do so, such as Google Docs (docs.google.com). Yes, it's free but you still have to go to another application to manage documents (it's another account to manage) instead of having it right there inside your blog's Dashboard, easily and quickly accessible.

Another feature loved by TypePad and WordPress users is the ability to password-protect a blog. In Blogger, there is something similar under Permissions, but it requires you to manually invite those users who can view your blog instead of simply setting a password.

One of the biggest drawbacks of using WordPress (the free version) is that it doesn't allow or properly convert JavaScript code. For example, many bloggers want to add a Sign Up for My Newsletter box to their blog to allow people to subscribe to their newsletter through Constant Contact (an e-mail marketing concern). However, as I know from personal experience, WordPress allows you to paste in the code provided by Constant Contact, but it doesn't work and is automatically modified by WordPress. Still, you can often find another way to do things, such as using a text link or creating an image to be used as a link to the sign up form. JavaScript can be used in TypePad and Blogger without a problem.

Another Blogger issue is page formatting when inserting PayPal buttons (which we cover later in this book when we discuss setting up a blog store). Even when using the updated editor, when you insert code from PayPal and paste it into a Blogger post or page, extra space is added. The HTML code has to then be manually tweaked to look like it would in TypePad or WordPress.

And inserting images into your blog posts and pages and placing them where you want is easier in TypePad and WordPress, even with Blogger's updated editor. As noted earlier, though, adding images to your sidebar with Blogger is much faster and easier.

In a Nutshell

If you are on a tight budget or creating a blog for a fundraising event or a school project, Blogger is free, powerful, and easy to use. It is loaded with lots of functionality—without the cost!

If you are developing a blog for business or professional use and you anticipate you'll need of more than ten pages, I recommend TypePad and WordPress as there is no limit on the number of pages you can create, and they keep the HTML code structured within the page nicely where Blogger requires tweaking.

TypePad and WordPress are also more suitable if you are going to be sharing a lot of documents with your customers or blog readers. Blogger doesn't have this capability built-in.

Naming Your Blog

Although we discussed this in Chapter 1, it's worth mentioning again. No matter which platform you choose, before you actually create a blog, you need to think of a name for it. The reason for belaboring the point is that though you can change your blog name later, on some platforms it's a big deal to do so (you may lose all your images, for example). So, it is important to take the time to think about a name before getting started.

In the next section, we'll set up blogs using Blogger, TypePad, and WordPress. When you set up a new blog in these platforms, they each prompt you to enter a blog name. Of course, you don't have to set up three blogs if you'd rather not. I'm going through the process of creating a new blog with each platform so you can get some idea of what each is like, to help you determine which blog platform is right for you.

Using Blogger

As we discussed, Blogger is extremely powerful in that you have full control of your blog, its design, and functionality. You can quickly take it from a simple, brand-new blog to a fully customized, professional-looking site without having to purchase any additional upgrades. What it lacks in features (which is not much), it makes up for by delivering a high-quality blogging platform at no cost.

With Blogger you can create a blog within a few minutes and be on your way! Blogger is owned by Google, so when you create a new blog you'll be prompted to create a new Google account or use an existing one. Then you'll be asked for a Blog Title and address (your blog's URL) and to choose a template—and you're done!

After you set up your new Blogger blog, we'll review the Dashboard, create a new post, and view your blog to verify what your readers will see.

EXERCISE—CREATE A NEW BLOG

In this exercise, you will create a new Blogger blog:

1. With your browser open, go to www.blogger.com.

2. This brings you to Blogger's home page, as shown in Figure 3–1.

Figure 3–1. Blogger's home page

3. Click the Get Started button.

4. On the next screen, create a new Google account (see Figure 3–2).

■ **Note** If you already have a Google account, go back to Blogger's home page (`www.Blogger.com`) and enter your Google username and password and click Sign In.

Figure 3–2. *Creating a Google account*

5. Enter an e-mail address and retype it to verify it's correct.

6. Enter a password of at least eight characters. It is good practice to use a password that contains upper and lowercase letters, punctuation marks, and numbers, or create an acronym. This makes it more difficult for an unauthorized user to access your blog. For example, it is not a good idea to use your name as your password unless it's garbled. After you are finished typing your potential password, Google displays the password's strength—weak, fair, good, or strong. Keep experimenting until you enter a strong password. Then retype to verify.

7. Enter a display name and birthday.

8. Enter the characters in the Word Verification box. Don't worry if you get it wrong on the first try: The letters and words are meant to be difficult to read. Google Blogger is using CAPTCHA (Completely Automated Public Turing test to tell Computers and Humans Apart), a program used to generate distorted characters for you to type in. A human can pass this sort of test; a computer can't. Using CAPTCHA helps prevent spam on blogs and web sites.

9. Check the Acceptance of Terms and click Continue.

10. On the next screen, enter a blog title and the URL as (see Figure 3–3). Click Check Availability and if the name you chose is already taken, keep trying until you find an available one that still suits your interests. Click Continue when ready.

Figure 3–3. Name your blog

11. Now choose a Template; the selection that you are shown is only a sample of the many new designs and options available in the Template Designer. Our example uses the Simple design template. You can always choose another design later using the Template Designer.

12. Click Continue.

13. You have now created your first blog; click the Start Blogging button.

14. You will receive an e-mail from Google to verify your account. Make sure you verify your Blogger account by clicking the link in the e-mail. You will have limited functionality until your account is verified.

When you've completed the setup process, you are directed to the New Post area. However, we won't create a post just yet. Instead, we'll review the elements of your screen (the Dashboard), which is what you typically see when you log into Blogger. After that, we'll walk through an example of creating a new post with an image and simple formatting.

Examining the Dashboard

From the New Post area, click Dashboard in the upper-right corner of your screen. The Dashboard serves as a menu, or a way for you to navigate to different areas of your blog depending on the task at hand (see Figure 3–4).

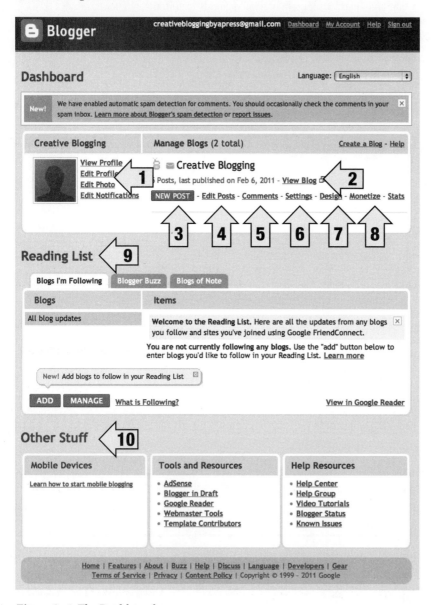

Figure 3–4. The Dashboard

Now let's take a brief look at the important options available on the Dashboard. We will briefly review each option (in the following list), while other areas will be discussed in more detail later in the book.

1. Profile
2. View Blog
3. New Post
4. Edit Posts
5. Comments
6. Settings
7. Design
8. Monetize
9. Reading list
10. Other stuff

Profile

This section is where you enter the information about yourself that you'd like to share with readers of your blog (a form of an "About Me" page). You can enter your name, e-mail address, birthday, sex, physical location (city, state, and country), interests, and a mini biography. There's also a place to upload your picture. This profile image will be shown on your blog's sidebar (when you insert the Profile gadget).

■ **Note** We've created one blog so far, but if we decided to create more than one blog under this Google account, we would see a list of all the blogs in the Dashboard, all with the same options beneath them (View Blog, New Post, Edit Posts, Settings, Design and Monetize). In our example, Creative Blogging is the blog name listed in the Dashboard (see Figure 3–4).

View Blog

Click the View Blog link to open and view your blog in a browser window. We will do this shortly, after creating a new post.

New Post

When you click New Post from the Dashboard, a screen appears where you can enter a new post. Generally you start by entering a title, then you write some content in the large text box. You can then categorize your post by entering what Blogger calls a Label, and, finally, you click Publish Post to make it viewable to the world.

Edit Posts

Sometimes you'll need to edit an existing post or simply delete one. To do this, click on Edit Posts from the Dashboard to see a list of your posts (most recent first). To edit a post, click the Edit link next to that post. To delete it, click the Delete button located to the right of the post.

Comments

At times you may receive spam-like comments or those that you may not wish to appear on your site for some reason of another. You can come to this area, Comments, and view all the comments left on your blog. You can quickly and easily select those you want to delete if necessary.

Settings

In this section of the Dashboard, you can set up formatting preferences, your preferred date/time format, how your blog archives posts, how you'll manage comments, and or set up a custom name.

In addition, you can protect your blog by inviting only those readers you want to allow to view your blog. You can also configure mobile settings so you can post from your mobile phone or e-mail.

You want to be sure you are using the new Updated Editor in Blogger. While viewing Settings, go to the Basic tab, scroll to the bottom under Global, and click Updated Editor. Click Latest Features to review in detail all the new and improved features. You'll definitely want to set this up at the start because of the new image handling functionality. Many users have mentioned in forums that they've had difficulty inserting images where they would like. Now you can insert images exactly where you like, and if you want to move an image, you can drag and drop until it pleases you. We will see how to insert an image when we create a new post in the next exercise.

Design

This is where you can have some fun designing your blog. Using the Template Designer, you can choose different colors for various elements of your blog, as well as which fonts to use (from the selection available), insert a background image, modify the layout (where sidebars are placed), and adjust column widths.

You can also drag and drop page elements. You do this in the Page Elements option and you can add sidebar items for your blog (Add a Gadget), including a visitor counter, slideshow, picture, and links to other blogs and web sites you like. In Chapter 5 we review many popular and useful gadgets for your blog (regardless of what platform you choose).

The Edit HTML area is where you can customize the design and layout of your blog. For example, you can convert a two-column blog to a three-column format, and you can use CSS to adjust spacing and margins, colors and borders, and more.

Monetize

Blogger has a built-in feature to quickly add Google AdSense to your blog. In brief, Google AdSense adds content-related ads to your blog in the sidebar or under posts.

Reading Lists

When you visit other Blogger blogs, you can choose to become a "follower" (which is like subscribing to a blog). Any blogs you choose to "follow" would then appear in this section under Blogs I'm Following.

Other Stuff

This section of the Dashboard has links to Blogger help and tools and resources, like Picasa Web Albums which you'll learn more about in the next chapter.

Create Your First Post

Posting is what blogging is all about. A post can consist of text, pictures, video, and more. Remember to include a Label to help organize and categorize your posts.

EXERCISE—CREATING A POST

It is finally time to create your first post, which will include inserting an image.

1. From the Dashboard, click New Post.

2. On the New Post screen, shown in Figure 3–5, enter a Title. This should very briefly describe what your post is about. For this example, enter "Welcome to my blog!"

3. The large text box is where you can enter actual post. For example, type "I am excited to be sharing this new venture with you…" and write a little more about yourself or your company, and what you plan to bring readers—tips, advice, products for sale, a service, etc.

Figure 3–5. Creating a new post

4. Next, click the Insert Image button on the toolbar (it's the button to the right of the blue word "Link").

5. Then click Choose Files to select an image from your computer. When you click the Choose Files button, a window pops up that lets you search for an image to insert.

6. When you find the one you want, click Open and you'll see it displayed in the Add Images window as shown in Figure 3–6.

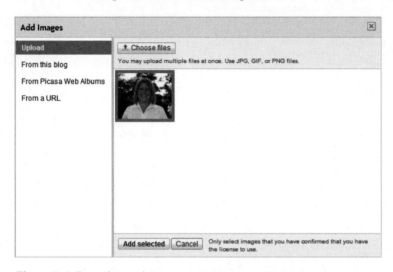

Figure 3–6. *Inserting an image*

7. Click on the Add Selected button and the image is inserted into your blog post, centered.

8. Click on the image to see the options for modifying the image layout (a new feature of the Updated Editor), as shown in Figure 3–7.

9. In the lower-right-hand corner, you'll see the Labels text box, I entered "Announcements, Creative Blogging" to categorize this post. Notice that I've separated words or phrases with a comma. You can assign more than one label to a post.

Figure 3–7. Image options

10. Click Publish Post if you're ready to publish the post. You can also click Post Options, and under Labels on the right you'll see Post Date and Time. Use this to schedule a post to be published at a future date and time (this is very useful, for example, if you are going on vacation and want to prepare posts ahead of time and schedule them to be delivered while you're away).

    If you want to save the post as a draft and not publish it, click Save Now. Then click to create a new post or another area of your blog. You may need to save a post as a draft if you need to research more information or if the post is not completed.

11. Click View Post to view your new post (see Figure 3–8).

■ **Note** You can use Labels to categorize your posts. This lets your readers quickly find posts of interest without having to search through your entire blog.

Figure 3–8. Viewing your post

In the last exercise, we created a post, published it, and viewed it. When viewing your blog while logged in, you'll notice the small wrench/screwdriver tools on your blog (see Figure 3–8). These only show when you're logged in. Many applications use a pencil to symbolize editing. Blogger uses a wrench-like symbol for this. While you are logged in and viewing your blog, you can click any wrench/tool to quickly and easily edit that particular area of your blog. Elements in your blog are called gadgets, and most of the gadgets we'll be installing throughout this book will be located in the sidebar.

Also notice the Post a Comment area, where readers can leave a response to your post. Readers don't see this box on the main blog page when they first come to your blog. They'll only see this area when they select a specific post by clicking the title of the post (if that's how you've configured the Comments settings).

In viewing your post, notice there are default gadgets already in your sidebar, including About Me, Followers, and Archives. Later in this book we'll see how to add a gadget.

Using TypePad

I enjoy TypePad for the many reasons I've already mentioned, such as unlimited page creation, its built-in file manager, and its "Feature This Post" capability. And I especially love its large template gallery. With TypePad, you can create a professional-looking blog right out of the box.

TypePad formats pages better than Blogger, especially if you're using PayPal buttons, Google Checkout buttons, or other merchant payment buttons. Blogger adds a bunch of extra space and you have to manually edit the HTML code to fix it. TypePad keeps the original formatting intact.

Furthermore, as you will see, TypePad has a large Dashboard with lots of settings and features. The flip side of this is that the many different options can make it harder to find what you're looking for!

In the next exercise we create a new TypePad account, using the Unlimited version. As noted earlier, the free TypePad Micro is too limited. I've selected the Unlimited package as it has the more practical features we need, including the CSS code and customization features we'll use in this book. TypePad offers a free two-week trial for any of its packages.

After setting up a new account, we'll look at the Dashboard and briefly discuss each of the elements as we did with Blogger. We'll finish this "Using TypePad" section by creating a new post.

EXERCISE—SET UP A TYPEPAD BLOG

In this exercise you will set up a new TypePad blog in just a few minutes. As with other applications, when you create a new account, you'll be prompted to enter a username, e-mail address, password, and so forth.

1. Go to www.typepad.com. TypePad's home page shown in Figure 3–9.

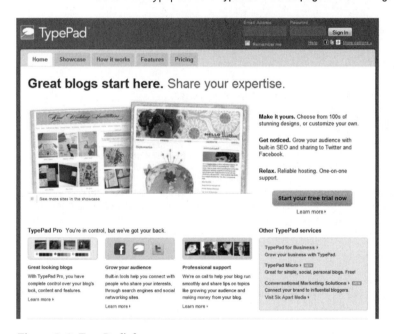

Figure 3–9. TypePad's home page

2. Click on Start Your Free Trial Now.

3. Click Sign Up under Unlimited.

4. In the next step, Create an Account (Figure 3–10), enter a URL for your blog, an e-mail address, password, display name, your gender (or decline to answer that), and whether you want to receive TypePad newsletters and notices.

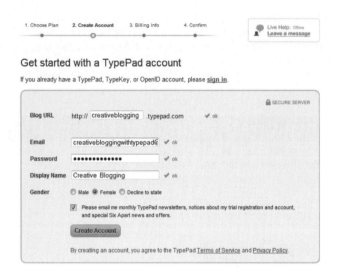

Figure 3–10. Creating a TypePad account

5. Click Create Account and proceed to step 3 of the setup process.

6. Enter your billing information (although you will not be charged for two weeks) and click Continue.

7. On the next screen, confirm your information (URL, e-mail address, and billing information) and click Continue and Start Your Blog.

After completing the setup, you are brought to a new screen prompting you to write your first post or design your blog (see Figure 3–11). You can enter or modify your blog's title here as well, and check off "Publicize this blog on search engines and my TypePad profile."

Figure 3–11. A new TypePad blog

Design

As we did in the previous Using Blogger section, let's first choose a template. Click Design Your Blog to choose a theme for your new blog. In doing so, you enter the Design tab of the Dashboard, the area in TypePad where you can begin customizing the design of your blog (see Figure 3–12). In the next exercise, though, we'll simply choose a template.

Figure 3–12. *Starting the design process*

EXERCISE—CHOOSE A THEME

Now you'll see how quickly you can make your new TypePad blog look the way you want. It's just a matter of choosing a theme—the hardest part is browsing all the choices and making a decision!

1. From the Design tab, click on Choose a Theme. The TypePad gallery is categorized or you can click on All to browse through all of the themes.

2. When you find a design you like, click Choose.

3. With many templates you can choose a color. For example, I chose the Baron template and then Blue.

4. Check to apply the design to your blog, then click Save Changes.

You are done selecting a new template, but you're still in the Design area of your new TypePad blog.

Examining the Dashboard

To begin, and to see what you typically see when you login to TypePad, click on Dashboard from the top menu (see Figure 3–13).

Figure 3–13. The TypePad Dashboard

Let's take a look at the elements of the Dashboard so you can get to know the TypePad interface. You can return to the Dashboard at any time by clicking "Dashboard" from the top menu bar. I will discuss the following Dashboard elements:

1. Quick Compose

2. Manage My Blog

> Stats
> Design
> Settings
> Compose
> Posts
> Comments

3.   Recent Activity

4.   Blogs

5.   Library

6.   Account

7.   Help

Quick Compose

This is a fairly new feature and pretty cool if you just want to quickly post a message without accessing the toolbar for formatting and inserting links, etc. (as you see in Figure 3–14 in the New Post screen), but you do have the two buttons to quickly insert an image or a video.

Manage My Blog

This area allows you to quickly access many elements of your blog in a menu-like format, including Stats, Design, Settings, Compose, Posts, and Comments. Notice there is a View Blog button that opens your blog in a new window.

Stats

This feature allows you to view the number of posts, comments, page views, and recent referrers. The number of page views often gets confused with the number of visits or visitors. When someone accesses your blog, that's a visit. It's also a page view for any page that person goes to. If that same visitor is inactive on a blog for a period of time (normally a half hour), then when they click on a page (either the same one or a new page), it counts as a new visit. That visitor may click on many pages during that one visit to your blog, and those are all page views.

Design

We just used this feature to choose a theme for our new blog. Since we are using the Unlimited package, you'll notice other options such as Custom CSS (only available in the Unlimited and Premium packages). The Content area allows you to see a visual layout of your blog's elements and the Layout lets you select, for example, a three-column layout with a left and right sidebar.

You can change your theme at any time, but I've found a glitch: when you do, the elements of your blog shift. You then have to go to Design ➤ Content, and then drag and drop the blog elements back where you want them. Don't forget to Save Changes.

With the Plus level and higher, you have the ability to install a custom header (banner image) and to set the colors for your links, post title, sidebar title, post text, etc. in what's called the Theme Builder.

So when you have time, come back to this area of the Dashboard and experiment with changing your blog's layout.

Settings

This is where you come to configure the different elements of your blog, including Basics, Categories, and Posts. In Basics you can set or change your blog's title and description, and choose to password-protect your blog.

Under Categories, you can remove TypePad's default categories and build a new list of your own. This list of categories is shown in the sidebar area of the New Post screen under Categories and will save you the step of clicking "Add a New Category" when composing a new post.

In the Posts settings, you can set the date/time format for posts, set a page to be the Front Page of your blog, or set how many posts to display before the previous/next navigation buttons are shown.

Compose

Clicking this option from the Manage My Blog area takes you to the New Post screen. You can then click the Compose drop-down (again, see Figure 3–14) and choose Page if you want to instead create a new page.

Posts

When you click this option, a screen with all your posts is displayed so you can select one to edit or delete. Or you can again click Compose at the top to create a new post or page.

Comments

As you begin to blog, your visitors will start posting comments. As the author, you are automatically notified when someone posts a comment to your blog. If you find spam or an unwanted comment, you can click on Comments from Manage My Blog and then select which comments to delete or move to spam.

Recent Activity

In this area you will see news posted from TypePad about a new feature for example, or a recent comment posted on your blog by a visitor, or recent posts by those who follow you on TypePad.

Blogs

At the top of your screen, to the right of Dashboard, there is a drop-down menu named Blogs that allows you to select which blog you'd like to work on (if you later have more than one) or to Add a Blog. In the Plus package, you can have up to four blogs under one account and in the Unlimited and Premium versions, you can have unlimited blogs.

Library

The TypePad Library helps you manage your files and media using File Manager, Photo Albums, and TypeLists. You can create a number of galleries for your blog, and you can easily share documents (files) with your customers or blog visitors from within your blog, without have to find or pay for another document or image storage service. For many, this is a huge advantage over Blogger.

Account

If you are looking for a specific setting and don't find it under Settings, it is probably under Account. Here you can enter or update billing information and your About Me profile, set up other accounts (such as Facebook and Twitter so you can then click on them in the New Post screen to have your post feed into your Facebook Wall and Twitter account), or map a custom domain to your TypePad blog. A custom domain is the personalized URL you want visitors to see for your blog URL. For example, I purchased and use the custom domain www.BlogsByHeather.com and mapped it to my TypePad blog, www.heatherporto.TypePad.com.

Help

If you're looking for help on a specific topic, click Help and then search the Knowledgebase. Or you can use this wonderful site for more direct help help.sixapart.com/tp/us/overview.html. TypePad does update its knowledgebase often.

Create Your First Post

As you can see in Figure 3–14, the New Post screen is different from Blogger's, but what we can do there is similar, as you'll see in the next exercise: creating a post, inserting an image, and adding a category. Moreover, TypePad lets you set up keywords, which gives it a step up in search engine optimization.

Figure 3–14. TypePad's New Post screen

EXERCISE—COMPOSE A NEW POST

In this exercise you'll create a new post.

1. From the Dashboard, click Compose to display the New Post screen, as shown in Figure 3–14.

2. Enter a post title such as "Welcome to my blog!"

3. In the Body area, begin typing the text of your post.

4. Click the Insert Image button (which is the tiny image icon you'll see on the Rich Text toolbar. This brings up the screen shown in Figure 3–15.

Figure 3–15. Inserting an image

5. Click Browse to locate an image on your computer.

6. Click Custom under Set image options. This lets you choose to float images to the left or right, as well as change the size of the image to be inserted.

7. Click Insert Image. The image is then inserted on the left. To center, click the image and then click the Center justification button on the toolbar.

That's the easy part and very similar to both Blogger and WordPress. However, we're not done.

In Blogger, you categorize the post using Labels. In TypePad, there is a default list of Categories, which you can see on the right in Figure 3–14. However, these categories generally don't suit business needs, so, on the fly you can create a new category.

8. Click Add a New Category in the right sidebar.

9. In the small Create Category window that appears, enter a category such as Announcements. Click the Create button to add it to your list.

10. Click the Add a New Category again if you want to add another category, such as "Blogger Tips," and again click the Create button.

11. So you've added two new categories that will now always be available on your Categories list, and they are already selected. If you want this post to stay at the top of your blog for a period of time, click the check box next to Feature This Post.

12. Next, let's add some keywords to the bottom Keywords section of your blog, separated by a comma. In my example I used "creative blogging, blogger tips, blogger help."

13. I always copy the keywords and paste them into the Technorati Tags area (which will be used when people search www.Technorati.com).

14. Now you are finally ready to click Publish to save and publish your post.

15. At the top you'll see a message that the post is published. Click the hyperlink to View Your Post (see Figure 3–16).

If you want to schedule a post to be published at a future date, from the Status drop-down you can click Publish On and choose a date and time.

If you just want to save the post as a draft (and not publish it immediately), click on Draft from the Status drop-down.

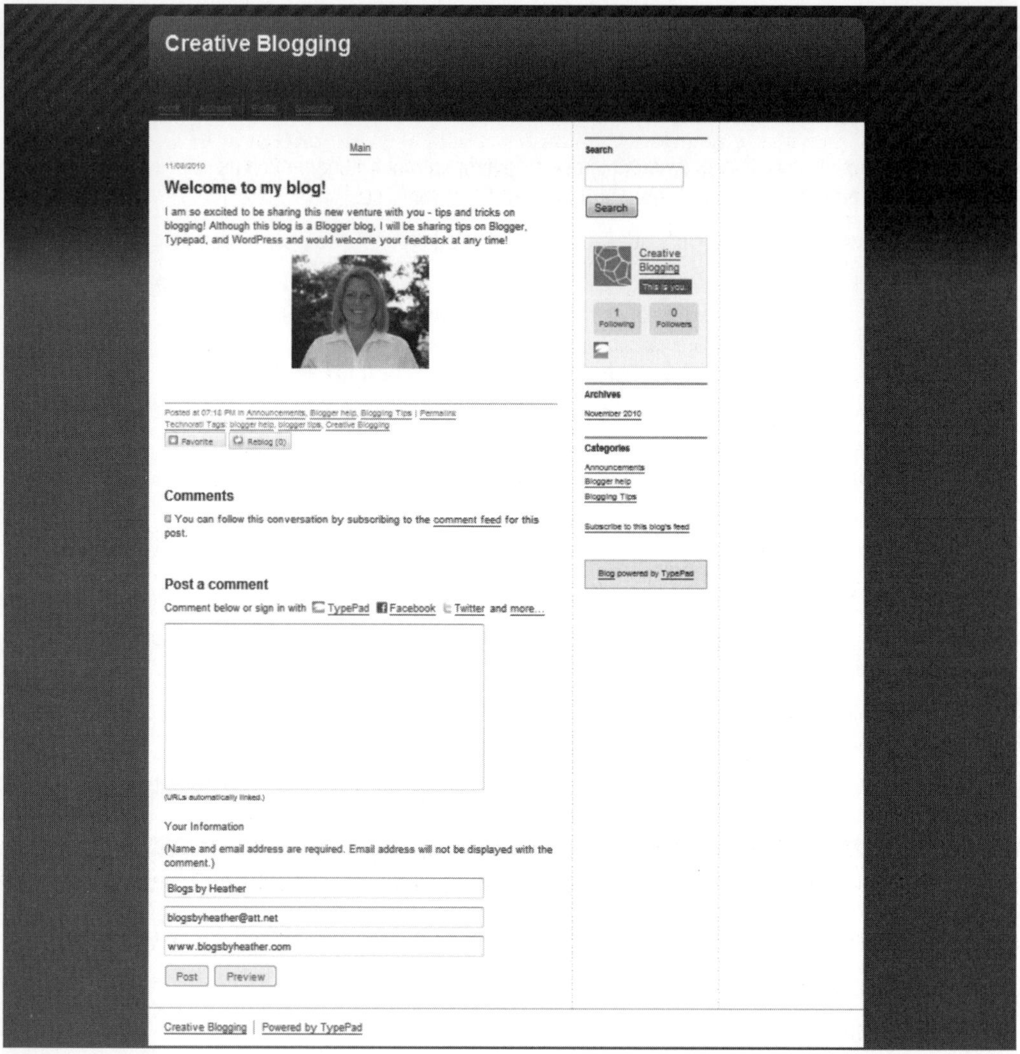

Figure 3–16. *View TypePad post*

As you can see, there's an area under the post where visitors can leave a comment (and where they can enter their name, e-mail, and web site address). Notice that a few gadgets have been added to your sidebar based on the template chosen (in this example, I used the Baron template).

Also notice that the default navigation bar shows up under the Blog banner/title area, as well as a Search box in the upper right corner.

You are now on your way to blogging with TypePad!

Using WordPress

Many of my business associates and customers enjoy working with WordPress. It is well-organized and easy to navigate. The Dashboard may appear busy, but you'll find it's well-structured so you can find what you're looking for. WordPress's Dashboard runs along the left side and is composed of many sections (drop-down boxes) that expand when clicked. We'll discuss the following Dashboard features (as highlighted in Figure 3-20) in a bit. First let's create a WordPress blog.

1. Dashboard
2. Upgrades
3. Posts
4. Media
5. Links
6. Pages
7. Comments
8. Feedbacks
9. Ratings
10. Polls
11. Appearance
12. Users
13. Tools
14. Settings

EXERCISE—CREATING A WORDPRESS.COM BLOG

In this exercise we will create a WordPress.com blog similar to those we created in Blogger and TypePad.

1. Go to www.WordPress.com (shown in Figure 3–17).
2. Click on the Sign Up Now button.

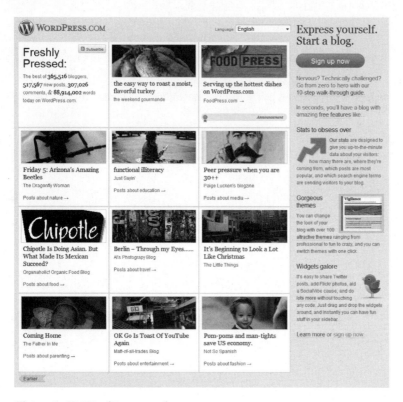

Figure 3–17. WordPress.com home page

3. Complete the information on the sign-up form (see Figure 3–18).

WORDPRESS.COM

Home Sign Up Features News About Us Advanced

Get your own WordPress.com account in seconds

Fill out this one-step form and you'll be blogging seconds later!

Blog Address

[   ] .wordpress.com

Want your own domain?

Choose a wordpress.com address or get your own URL with a custom domain name. (?)

Sign up for just a username.

Username

[   ]

At least 4 characters.
Lowercase letters and numbers only.

Password

[   ]

Confirm

[   ]

Use a mix of upper and lowercase characters to create a strong password.

If your password isn't strong enough, you won't be able to continue with signup.

E-mail Address

[   ]

We send *important* administration notices to this address.

Sign up →

You agree to the fascinating terms of service by submitting this form.

AN **AUTOMATTIC** CREATION

About Us • Terms of Service • Privacy

Figure 3–18. Sign up for a WordPress blog

4. Start with the address you want for your blog. WordPress also checks to see if that domain is available as well, so you may get a message beneath the URL that the domain is also available for a price. (I received a message that creativebloggingwithWordPress.com was available for $17 a year.) You don't have to set up a custom domain if you don't want to, or you can do it later. We discuss custom domains later in this book.

5. Next enter your desired username. It will default to the blog name you previously entered.

6. Enter a password and then again in the box below to confirm the password.

7. Enter a valid e-mail address.

8. Click Sign Up.

9. You will then see a message that an e-mail will be sent to the address highlighted within the next 30 minutes so you can activate your account. If you don't activate it within two days, you'll have to sign up again.

10. On the next screen, enter your First Name, Last Name, and About Yourself.

11. Click Save Profile.

12. Once you activate your account (via the email WordPress sent) you will then see another screen (shown in Figure 3–19) with a message "Your account is now active!"

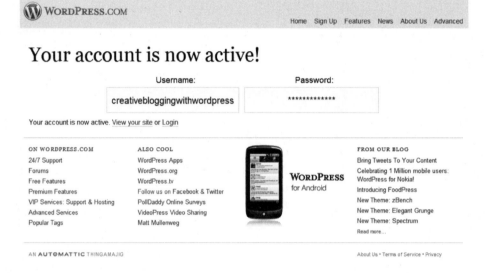

Figure 3–19. Account activated

13. Click Login and sign in using the username and password you previously set up.

When you log in, you will see WordPress's dashboard, similar to what's shown in Figure 3–20. To get to your blog's dashboard, go to the My Blog menu at the top of the screen and click on My Dashboard.

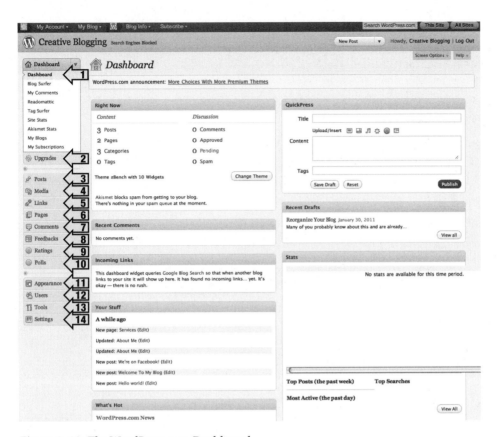

Figure 3–20. *The WordPress.com Dashboard*

Design

Unlike Blogger, WordPress doesn't have you choose a design template, or theme, during the initial setup process. So, as we did with TypePad, in the next exercise we'll choose a theme and modify the Site Title.

Like TypePad, WordPress has many themes to choose from and they are customizable; you can install a custom header in many of them, customize the menus and backgrounds, edit CSS code, and more. (As we noted earlier, in TypePad you can't edit CSS code unless you have the Unlimited package; and, of course, this is free in Blogger.)

EXERCISE—CHOOSING A THEME

At present, we are in the Dashboard, and we can quickly choose a theme for our blog.

1. From the Dashboard, click on Appearance.

2. You should see Manage Themes, but if not, click on Themes on the left sidebar under Appearance.

3. You can now preview all the 100+ available themes.

4. My example uses a simple theme called zBench.

5. When you find a theme you like, click Activate.

6. From the top menu bar, click on My Blog to view your blog (see Figure 3–21).

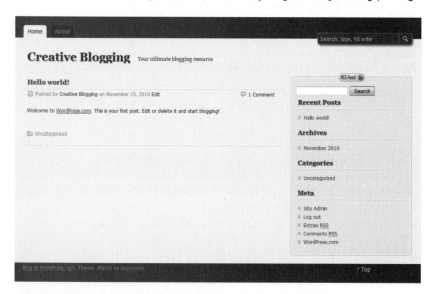

Figure 3–21. WordPress blog with zBench Theme

7. Next, from the left sidebar, go to Settings and modify the Site Title and Tag Line (not all themes have a Tag Line).

8. Then click Save Changes.

In the following section, we'll take a look at all the different elements of the WordPress Dashboard (shown in Figure 3–20).

Examining the Dashboard

Of the three platforms, WordPress has the largest Dashboard, but it is well-organized into categories (on the left), and is easy to navigate. In the main area, the large open area under the word "Dashboard," you'll find the following areas.

Right Now

This quickly lets you know how many posts you've created, how many pages are set up, how many categories have been added, as well as how many comments have been posted. In addition, it displays what theme is currently installed, how many widgets you have (mostly in the sidebar and known also as sidebar items), and if any messages are being blocked as spam.

Recent Comments

Here you'll find recent comments, but you can also click View All to see all the comments on your blog.

Incoming Links

This widget queries Google Blog Search to see if there's any incoming traffic, links from the search engine to your blog.

Your Stuff

This section shows the current work, such as a new post, page, or comment. It also displays the post title, page title, or who posted the comment. Right Now, in contrast, simply displays numbers (stats).

What's Hot

This displays new posts from WordPress.com News, top WordPress.com blogs, top posts around WordPress.com, fastest growing WordPress blogs, and latest posts.

QuickPress

This feature is very similar to TypePad's Quick Post feature. It allows you to quickly post to your blog, and you can insert an image and use tags, but you can't format text or add categories. You can publish a post right then and there.

Recent Drafts

This shows recent drafts— posts that are saved but not published; they are not live or viewable on your blog.

Stats

This very useful area reports daily, weekly, or monthly visits to your blog in a bar graph, as well the sites that link to your blog and which posts and pages on your site received the most views. This is a popular feature as people want to know how much traffic their blog is getting, from whom (the referrer), which keywords helped (search engine results), as well as which are the most popular posts or most popular searches.

On the left side, again you see the Dashboard menu at the top (in a drop-down), and many options, categorized, to help you manage and customize your blog's posts, layout, and functionality.

Dashboard

This Dashboard submenu shows many options related to following your favorite blogs, tags, top posts, subscriptions, and even friends on Twitter. You'll also find some additional Site Stats, such as Search Engine Terms and Clicks, and Akismet Stats, which lets you keep track of spam.

Upgrades

This displays a list of available upgrades and pricing (such a VideoPress for $59.97 a year), and lets you add a domain.

Posts

Here you can add a new post, view all existing posts, and manage Categories and Post Tags. This means you can enter a list of Categories and Post Tags in this area, instead of having to create them on the fly when composing a new post.

Media

This displays all the images inserted into your posts, and you can upload (Add New) images to the Media Library. In future posts, you can then select an image from the Image Library instead of uploading from your computer.

Links

This section displays a current blogroll links list, but more importantly, it allows you to build your own lists to add to your sidebar.

Pages

This area of the Dashboard allows you to manage pages on your blog. These Pages are similar to the ones we discussed for Blogger and TypePad, and they appear on the menu bar (depending on the selected WordPress theme).

Comments

You can view all the comments on your blog in this section, whether approved, pending, marked as spam, or deleted.

Feedbacks

In this area you can view and manage any information entered through a form posted in your blog; such as using or inserting a contact form from the toolbar when creating a WordPress post. Any information entered in that contact form would be available for review in this Feedbacks section of the Dashboard.

Ratings

You can choose to allow visitors to rate your post, pages, or comments (using votes and number of stars). This is similar to the ratings you see of books on Amazon, for example.

Polls

You can create polls on your blog, if you create an account with PollDaddy.com.

Appearance

This is probably the most popular area after Posts, and it's where you can select themes, create menus, add widgets, change your blog's background or header, edit CSS, and more to modify your blog's layout.

Users

This is a wonderful feature that lets you add users to your site, like another author. Some bloggers like to have guest bloggers write posts for them, and in WordPress this is easy to do.

Tools

Here you can import posts from another WordPress blog, a Blogger blog, or export your blog. You can also delete your site.

Settings

This is where you configure general settings for your blog, such as post settings, notifications, domain or privacy/site visibility settings.

   You'll also find, at the very top of your screen, a task bar with drop-down menus that allow you to quickly navigate to certain useful areas.

My Account

This menu lets you update your profile, follow your subscriptions, track comments, start a QuickPress post, get support, or log out of WordPress. There is also an option to go to the Global Dashboard. This is the Dashboard on the left sidebar that, when pressed, displays all Your Stuff, What's Hot, and other news-related items.

My Blog

This menu contains quick links to your blog, such as the Dashboard, and others related to your blog and Dashboard, such as Site Stats, manage comments, go to a new post, and register a blog (which means to create an additional blog). There is also a Read Blog option that is equivalent to a View Blog action. It lets you quickly and easily view your blog within the WordPress main screen, not opened in a new browser window.

Blog Info

This is an interesting feature. You can use the Search WordPress.com search box at the right to find other WordPress blogs. Then you can use this Blog Info menu to report them as spam or as mature (having adult content), for example, or to find a random post in a blog, or to create a short link (a hyperlink) to the blog.

Subscribe

This allows you to subscribe to a blog that you are viewing within WordPress.

Search WordPress.com

This lets you search other WordPress.com blogs in combination with the All Sites button, which searches all WordPress.com blogs. This Site searches your own blog, the default if you type in the search box and press Return.

Create Your First Post

In this exercise, we'll create a new WordPress post, much like the ones we created in Blogger and TypePad, with an image and text. WordPress has a feature that Blogger and TypePad don't have, called Post Tags, which serve as another way of categorizing your posts (though some people view tags as keywords or phrases.

Like the other platforms, WordPress has a formatting toolbar to assist in formatting your post's content, as well as Categories to allow you to categorize or group your posts.

EXERCISE—ADD NEW POST

In this exercise, we will create a WordPress post.

1. In the left sidebar, go to Posts, click the drop-down, and choose Add New (see Figure 3–22).

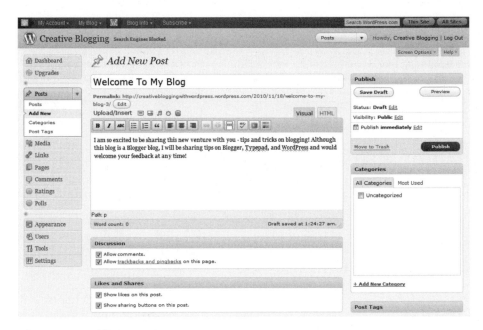

Figure 3–22. *Adding a new post*

2. Enter the title of your post in the first text box, such as "Welcome to My Blog!"

3. In the post body area, type in some content for your post.

4. Click on the Add an Image button (the first button above the toolbar to the right of "Upload/Insert".

5. Click on Select Files to add an image (or media) from your computer.

6. From the pop-up, select a file to upload.

7. When you've chosen an image, click Open and you'll see it as a thumbnail in the Add an Image window, where you may also add additional information, as well as specify the size and alignment (see Figure 3–23).

Add an Image

From Computer   From URL   Media Library

Add media files from your computer

Allowed file types: jpg, jpeg, png, gif, pdf, doc, ppt, odt, pptx, docx, pps, ppsx, xls, xlsx.

Choose files to upload   (Select Files)   (Cancel Upload)

Maximum upload file size: 1GB

You are using the Flash uploader. Problems? Try the Browser uploader instead.

3 GB upload space remaining. You can upload mp3, m4a, wav, ogg audio files and increase your available space with a Space Upgrade. You can upload videos and embed them directly on your blog with a Video Upgrade.

File name: heatherwrightporto-color.jpg

File type: image/jpeg

Upload date: November 18, 2010

Dimensions: 1447 × 1152

(Edit Image)

Title	*	HeatherWrightPorto-Color
Alternate Text		Heather Wright-Porto
		Alt text for the image, e.g. "The Mona Lisa"
Caption		
Description		
Link URL		http://creativebloggingwithwordpress.files.wordpress.com/2010/11/hea
		(None) (File URL) (Post URL)
		Enter a link URL or click above for presets.
Alignment		◉ ■ None ○ ■ Left ◉ ■ Center ○ ■ Right
Size		○ **Thumbnail** *(150 × 119)* ◉ **Medium** *(300 × 238)* ○ **Large** *(1024 × 815)* ○ **Full Size** *(630 × 501)*

(Insert into Post) Delete

(Save all changes)

Figure 3–23. The Add an Image screen with a file uploaded

8. In this example, I chose size Medium and Center alignment.

9. Click Insert into Post.

As we've discussed, it's useful to add a category (or categories) to allow visitors to quickly find areas of interest on your blog without having to scroll through pages of old posts.

10. Since this is a new blog, there are no categories set up yet so, under Categories on the right, click on Add New Category. A little text box appears underneath as shown in Figure 3–24.

11. Enter a category name and click the Add New Category button and it will be added to the Categories box and checked.

12. You can continue adding categories (one at a time) following the same steps.

You can take it one step further using Post Tags, which help you to further categorize your posts. For example, suppose I write a post about how to create a new post in WordPress. I can then put it in a category called Blog Tips and add a few post tags, such as Blogger, Insert an Image, and Add a New Post.

Categories and Post Tags are not required, but they are recommended to increase your blog's visibility and chances of being found by search engines. And, of course, they help your blog readers search your site.

13. Click on Publish.

14. Click on View Post to see what your new post looks like live (shown in Figure 3–25).

If you wish to save the post as a draft, for example if you need to finish the post later to insert images you still have on your camera, then instead of clicking Publish, click on the Save Draft button.

Additionally, if you need to schedule a post to publish on a later date, perhaps when you go on vacation, click on Edit next to Publish Immediately and set a date and time, and click OK.

In Figure 3–22, you can see that there's a formatting toolbar in the Add New Post screen. This allows you to format text, such as making it bold, modifying alignment, or changing font size.

Additionally, if you need to later modify a post, on the left sidebar under the Posts drop-down, click on Posts and all your posts will be listed. You can put your mouse over the Post Title and click Edit.

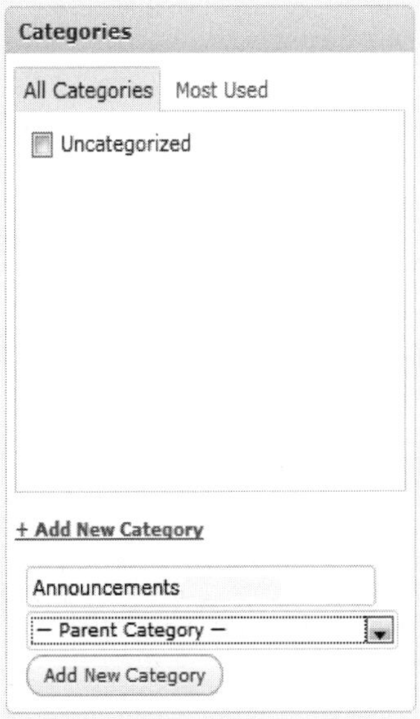

Figure 3–24. Adding a new category

Figure 3–25. Viewing a post

Summary

How are you doing? Have you decided which blog platform is right for you? In this chapter we reviewed how to set up a blog with Blogger, TypePad, and WordPress.com, and examined the elements you see on each Dashboard and created a post on each platform. They are similar but each has its own set of desirable features.

Blogger is a very popular. It is free but very powerful and, most of all, easy to use and navigate. You can create posts with images, text, videos, audio, hyperlinks and more, choose from a new and improved Template Designer, customize a blog's layout and design using HTML and CSS code, or map a domain. Blogger also has a Pages feature you can use to set up an online store, describe each of your services, create a custom About Me page, and more. It has all the bells and whistles without the cost.

TypePad is not as popular as Blogger and WordPress but that doesn't mean it isn't a good platform. It has a very good knowledgebase and a trouble ticket system to allow you to ask questions of the TypePad team. It has the same abilities as Blogger but costs $14.95 a month if you want to add a custom background or modify the CSS code. However, it does have a few very likeable features that Blogger does not have, such as Feature This Post, password-protected blogs, and a built-in file manager. You can also create photo albums from within TypePad, instead of having to use an external program. (Blogger uses an external free program called Picasa Web Album, part of Google's free family of products). TypePad also handles image placement better than Blogger within a post, and handles HTML code formatting better when inserting external HTML code from a third party like PayPal.

WordPress basically has the advantages of both. It is free like Blogger, but also has many of the desired built-in features of TypePad such as a file manager and media library. Its Dashboard is loaded and can be overwhelming at first, but is very organized and categorized to help you find what you need.

It has hundreds of themes to choose from, is customizable in that you can change a header and/or background (depending on the selected theme), and add CSS (when you purchase the CSS Upgrade).

In deciding what platform is best for you, you'll have to consider your budget, the ease of use, available help, and functionality (features). Even more important is what you intend to do with your blog. If you are on a tight budget or want a blog that is easy to use, I highly recommend Blogger. If your main purpose is to sell items on your blog and use your blog as an online store, then I recommend TypePad or WordPress due to the way they handle the HTML formatting from inserted PayPal or other payment buttons.

Regardless of which platform you choose, the good news is this book will cover blogging topics broadly and conceptually and provide instruction for each platform, so the topics discussed can be applied to Blogger, TypePad or WordPress. So what are you waiting for? Let's blog!

The next chapter focuses on working with images and video—how to take pictures and videos from your camera and video recorder, load them to your computer, and then how to install them on your blog and into your blog posts.

CHAPTER 4

■ ■ ■

More Than Text

Congratulations! You've created a blog using Blogger, TypePad, or WordPress (or all three!) and created your first post. Your blog will consist mostly of posts—it is what blogging is all about—sharing your story or experience, business services, or other valuable information. And, of course, that's what I'll stress throughout this book—that posting is very important, and posting regularly and consistently is even more so. But there's more to blogging than just text. To make your blog really compelling, you'll want to add images and even video. That's a difficult next step for many people. But don't worry. In this chapter you'll learn how to work with images and videos and how to get them uploaded to your blog.

We'll see how to take pictures for the web, how to resize them for your blog, and add a watermark. We'll also review the sizes recommended for different elements of your blog (such as the banner and sidebar) and discuss the options of taking pictures to use later or creating images of your own using a program like Photoshop.

Did you know you could also take snapshots of your screen? Yes, you can—of all or part of your screen, using a very cool tool. I can't wait to share it with you later in the chapter! In the end, regardless of how you take or create images to use on your blog, you'll see how to get them from wherever they are to wherever you want them, and you'll understand where the images are stored.

For those who are interested in adding video to their blogs, we'll discuss how to get your home videos from your video recorder to your computer and then uploaded and embedded into a blog post. For that exercise we'll be using the popular FLIP video recorder (www.TheFlip.com). And we'll see another trick: you can create videos by capturing and recording actions on your computer screen! That's right! You can record what you are doing on your computer to share with technical support staff or to create your own set of video tutorials! We'll see how to upload those videos to YouTube to share with the world, as well as how to place them on your blog.

Working with Images

Even if you don't think of images when you start a blog, chances are good that sooner or later you'll want to add some—images of a product you're featuring on sale, pictures of your family, your children, something you've made or of somewhere you've visited. You can do this in your blog and we did so in Chapter 3 when creating our first post. But to make the most of the pictures you take, there are a few things to keep in mind.

Many of us use digital cameras and when we take the camera out of the box, we just leave the default settings and start taking pictures. When we then download the images to a computer, we see they are very large. If you are simply going to print your pictures, that's not a problem at all. However, if you are going to upload them to your blog, size does matter!

Of course, there are probably many other adjustments you'll want to make, such as removing red-eye, adjusting contrast levels (if a picture is too dark) or color balance (if picture is too yellow, for example), but these fall outside the scope of this book. However, I'll provide links to some helpful photo editing sites. In this chapter, we'll concentrate on creating and sizing your photos to get them to fit properly into your blog's layout.

First, I want to take a moment to show you a few of the different types of images I have on my own business and personal blogs, and how they were created (see Figures 4–1 and 4–2). Some were taken with my Canon EOS Digital Rebel XT; some were created by my designer, Michelle Laycock, in Photoshop; others I created myself using Photoshop or with a screen capture software called ScreenHunter, which we'll discuss shortly. Table 1-1 describes the images called out in Figures 4–1 and 4–2.

Although I will certainly mention Photoshop and the way I used it to create or edit images, we won't get into the ins and outs of using it here. Given its popularity, though, you'll have no trouble finding more information on the Web.

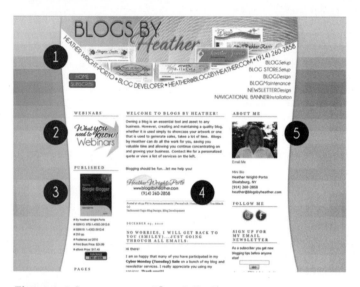

Figure 4–1. Images on www.BlogsByHeather.com

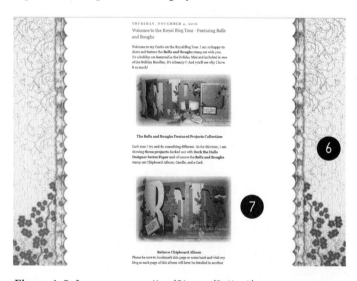

Figure 4–2. Images on www.HandStampedByHeather.com

Table 4–1. Notes on the Images Called Out in Figures 4–1 and 4–2

Element	Notes
1. Banner	My "Blogs By Heather" banner was created in Photoshop by my designer, Michelle Laycock, and is 950px (pixels) wide. I modified the image and sliced it to create an image map, making different areas of the banner clickable (such as Home, Subscribe, Blog Setup, Blog Store Setup, etc.) and to link to other pages on my blog.
2. Animated GIF	I created this image, "What you need to know Webinars" in Photoshop and used its Animation window. I made the width of the image 180px, so it would fit within my blog's sidebar.
3. Beginning Google Blogger	I took a snapshot of the cover of my book from the Apress web site, www.Apress.com. For this image, and all screenshots you see in this book, I used ScreenHunter, a free screen capture program (for PC users) we'll discuss in this chapter, or Capture Me (for Mac users).
4. Post Signature	This is an image designed in Photoshop to coordinate with my banner that I can insert at the bottom of posts (when desired).
5. About Me	This picture was taken with my Canon EOS Digital Rebel XT, then converted to a grayscale image in Photoshop, and resized to 180px wide to fit within the sidebar.
6. Background	This is my personal blog where I showcase some of the hand-stamped projects I create. The floral, scalloped background image was created in Photoshop.
7. Watermark	I took this photo of the "Believe" album with my digital camera, edited and resized it in Photoshop, and then applied a watermark (bottom right corner of the photo). A watermark is a faint image you should put on your artwork or images to protect them, as well as simply to put your "stamp" on them. We'll discuss how to create a watermark later in this chapter.

Taking Pictures

Before taking any pictures with your camera, I highly recommend you read the manual! I know it's a bit tedious and time-consuming, but knowing what settings to use and when really makes a difference! Still, you don't need to be an expert. Most digital cameras have default settings for many different situations. For example, my camera has settings (called Basic Zones) for Portrait, Landscape, Sports, Night Portrait, Close-up, and Flash-Off. If I want to take a picture of my lovely kids, I'd use Portrait if they were posed or sitting still, or Sports for an action shot. I normally use the Auto-Flash, which means the camera will detect the light level and use the flash when needed.

The setting that's probably most important to you as a blogger is image size. The higher the setting, the more pixels that are used to create an image. The larger the image is, the larger the file size and the more space used on your camera's memory card. I use the high setting if I am taking a picture that I will later crop (reducing the number of pixels) and customize, or that I want to print beautifully as an 8x10 photo (and not look blurred, unclear, or pixilated). So I recommend keeping your image size "large" for shooting, but then you will need to resize them for your blog. We'll discuss this more in a bit.

■ **Note** Natural light is best when taking photos! Open the blinds! Let the sunshine in or even better, take pictures outside on a beautiful sunny day.

Saving Pictures

I am often asked "How do I get the pictures from my camera onto my blog?" First, though, you have to get them from your camera to your computer. Although some of the specifics for doing this are different for each digital camera, the general approach is pretty similar for most. Of course, you'll want to follow the instructions that come with your camera. You may find a quick-start guide that can help, or you can look at the manual.

Your camera probably came with a CD containing software you can use to extract the images from your camera and save them on your computer. Be sure to run the setup and install the software. Typically, the software includes some sort of utility that lets you select the images you want to transfer, as well as some type of image browser or viewer (see the example in Figure 4–3) with a few image editing options that let you crop, remove red-eye, or add effects.

To get the images from the camera to the computer, you generally use a USB cable, which typically comes with your digital camera as well. When you connect the cable to your camera and computer, the installed utility will open to let you select the images to transfer, and then opens them in the installed image manager/browser. For example, after images from my camera transfer, a program called ZoomBrowserEX opens and displays them, as shown in Figure 4–3.

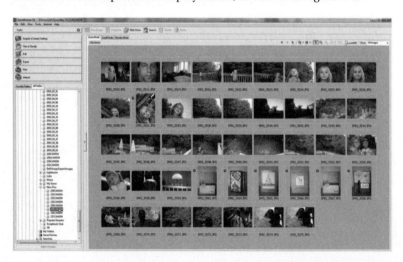

Figure 4–3. ZoomBrowserEX for the Canon EOS Digital Rebel XT

Your situation might be a bit different. It may be that you connect the USB cable and then open Windows Explorer or My Computer (on a PC) and see an additional drive (usually E:, F: or G:). You then open that drive and any folder that appears until you see all the images on your camera. Then you copy and paste the images between folders, from your camera to your computer, just as you would any other files on your computer (see Figure 4–4).

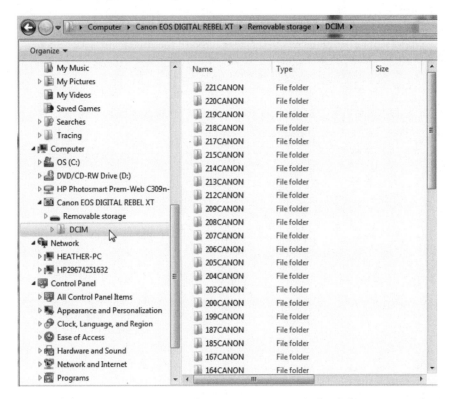

Figure 4–4. Windows Explorer with my Canon EOS Digital Rebel XT connected

Similarly, with some cameras when you connect the USB cable, the LCD panel on the digital camera changes and prompts you about transferring images to your computer. By selecting OK, the new drive letter appears in My Computer and your images are available.

In the next section, we'll discuss what sizes your images should be for your blog, and then later how to resize them and add a watermark.

Creating Images

There are many popular programs to help you create images for your blog, like Photoshop or Photoshop Elements, or free programs like GIMP (for the PC (www.gimp.org/windows/) and Mac (www.gimp.org/macintosh/), or those that come preinstalled on new computers (such as MS Paint on the PC). No matter which you choose, there are a few guidelines to follow for creating images for your blog. We'll discuss the recommended size of images for your blog, depending on whether you are creating images to put in your sidebar, your posts, or a custom header. Then we'll review image resolution and color mode, as well as how to save images and which image formats to use.

Image Size

Although Blogger, TypePad, and WordPress each have different templates and themes to work with, for the most part the sizes for the sidebars and posting areas are consistent. As shown in Table 4–2, images created for the sidebar should be about180px wide to start. This could be a picture of you, a company badge or logo, or images to be used as sidebar headings, as shown in Figure 4–5.

■ **Note** Any third-party gadgets you'd like to include on your sidebar, such as a calendar or slide show, should also be sized to approximately 180px wide to fit within your sidebar.

Figure 4–5. Sidebar headings on luvtostamp.blogspot.com

Table 4–2. Recommended Image Sizes for Blog Elements

Element	Size (pixels)	Notes
Sidebar	150 – 200	Images for sidebars should be about 180px wide for most blogs as sidebar width is usually 200px. Some templates have narrower sidebars, so you may need a smaller width of 125px.
Post	400	For Blogger, TypePad, and WordPress, the width of the main posting column varies, but an image width of 400px will fit most templates and themes.
Banner	700 – 960+	When you insert a custom banner into your blog's layout, the width will vary depending on the template you choose in Blogger, TypePad, or WordPress. In Blogger, if you use a custom 2-column layout, the banner image should be 700-720px wide; for a custom 3-column layout, it should be 900-920px. . If you use the Template Designer, the banners may be as wide as 950px. In WordPress, the theme you use will state the recommended banner size. In TypePad, if you're using Theme Builder, for a 3-column format, 870px is best, while 670px is best for a 2-column layout. The banner (TypePad) in Figure 4–1 is 950px wide; the banner in Figure 4–2 (Blogger) is 890px wide.
Background	Variable	For the background, if you are going to use a tiled or repeated image, it can really be any size. It depends on the image you're using or the look you are trying to achieve. There is no right or wrong size to use for this type of background image. Do keep in mind that larger images will, of course, cause your page to load slower.
Static Background	Variable	Take a look again at Figure 4–1 and Figure 4–2 and notice the background in each blog. You can see a white center with a design on either side. This large central image is referred to as a Static Background. An image used like this has to be large enough to let the sidebar(s) and main posting area fit in the center. Note that the white (center) of my background is actually part of the one large image that makes up the background. They are no separate images on the left or on the right. As noted, the size will vary depending on how wide your main posting area is and the width of your sidebar(s). You'll want it wide enough to serve as the center of the static background image, plus an additional 200-300 pixels on each side to allow for the actual background design (such as the blue waves in Figure 4–1 or the vintage scallop floral in Figure 4–2). Again, note that larger images take longer to download and may result in a slower page load time.

If you plan on using other images in your posting area, such as a Post Signature like the one shown at the bottom of the post in Figure 4–1 or "Rachel" shown in Figure 4–6, or an image to separate posts (known as a Post Separator or Post Footer as shown in Figure 4–6). Keep in mind that they also have to fit within the post area width (400px wide or less is recommended).

Figure 4–6. *Post Separator on www.RachelStampsHappy.Blogspot.com*

Image Resolution and Color Mode

When you create images for your blog, you want the images to be as small as possible, so they load faster and also so they won't take up as much storage space. As we discussed in Chapter 3, each blog platform offers a limited amount of storage space. Therefore, when creating images in an image editing program (such as Photoshop), use a low resolution of 72 ppi (pixels per inch) and color mode RGB (Red Green Blue). Keep in mind that your blog will be seen only via a monitor that can display only up to 72ppi and different colors using a combination of RGB. When it's time to save your image, look for a "Save for Web" option. Use that setting and save your image as a JPG, GIF, or PNG. Use the PNG and GIF formats if your image has transparent areas. You must also use the GIF image type if you create an animated (moving) image. Note that if you've used layers (artwork placed over other pieces of artwork) in Photoshop or other imaging software) be sure to "flatten" the image first, which merges the layers and results in a smaller file size.

■ **Note** If you're creating images for print, set the resolution at 300-600dpi (dots per inch) and the color mode to CMYK (Cyan Magenta Yellow Black).

Taking Snapshots

Many images you see throughout this book were taken with one of my favorite applications, called ScreenHunter. This is a screen-capturing program for PC users; it's very easy to use and, best of all, it's free. You can download it at `www.wisdom-soft.com/products/screenhunter_free.htm`. I also use a Mac and a similar program called Capture Me, which like ScreenHunter can capture parts (or all) of your screen and save it to a file or to the Clipboard.

It can be very helpful to be able to capture an image from the screen of your computer. When I needed an image of the cover of my book, *Beginning Google Blogger*, for my blog's sidebar (shown in Figure 4–1), I went to www.Apress.com and captured the image using ScreenHunter. I often use this program when working with customers' banners or other blog graphics that they want modified or resized, especially if they don't have the original artwork files. I open their blog or web site and copy any graphics they'd like me to work on. You can also use this program (or Capture Me or iGrab for the Mac) to take a snapshot of part of a PDF document you are viewing or a product you'll be featuring from your supplier's website. The possibilities and uses are endless. However, please keep in mind these snapshots are not your originals or your property to profit from, resell, or distribute without permission.

ScreenHunter

Let's get started. Go to the ScreenHunter web site to download a free copy of ScreenHunter and install it on your PC. Click on Download, then Just Download. Under Free Programs, click on SetupScreenHunterFree.exe and save it to your computer. Then double-click the file to run the installation. When it's finished, open the program (see Figure 4–7). We'll review the available options and, in the next exercise, we'll take a snapshot and go through a quick example of capturing just a portion of the screen.

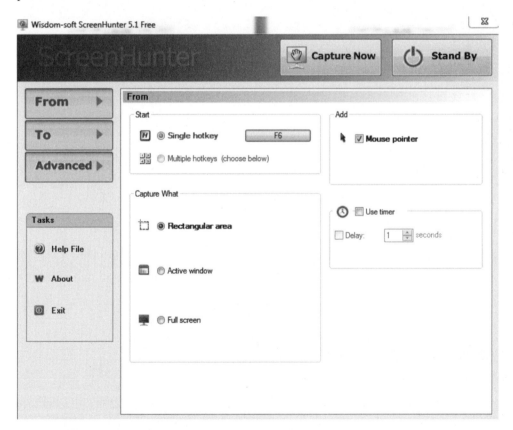

Figure 4–7. The main ScreenHunter screen

■ **Note** If you are using a Mac and need to capture a screen shot, use Command+Shift+3. If you need to capture a portion of your screen, use Command+Shift+4 and crosshairs will appear, and you can then click and drag a rectangle to capture the area of interest. When using either set of commands, the image captured is saved in PNG format as an image on your desktop.

Note that F6 is the "hot key" that triggers the application (brings up the crosshairs, which you'll click and drag to select the area of the screen to capture. In the Capture What section, choose Rectangle Area. With this option you can actually capture a portion of your screen or the entire screen.

In Figure 4–8, note that I've clicked on the To button and chosen the Clipboard option, which means the screenshot will be copied to the Clipboard, just as if you performed a Copy. Then you can open up Microsoft Word, Photoshop, or another program and paste in the screenshot as you would anything copied to the Clipboard.

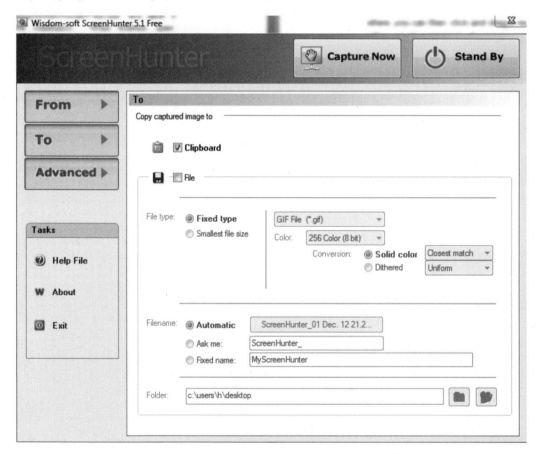

Figure 4–8. Choosing the Clipboard option in ScreenHunter

You could as well click on File, which would save the screenshot to your computer in the specified image format (such as GIF, BMP, or JPG) and color mode, to the location and filename selected.

So are you ready to give it a try? Open up a PDF or go to a site where you want to capture part of the document or screen. In this exercise, we'll use ScreenHunter to capture part of your screen and then copy it into a Microsoft Word document.

EXERCISE – USING SCREENHUNTER

To perform this exercise, open ScreenHunter, Microsoft Word, and a PDF document or a web site (whichever you'd like, to capture a portion of the document or screen).

1. With either the PDF or the web site open on your screen, press F6 on your keyboard.

2. When the red crosshairs appear, click and drag your mouse until a rectangle covers the area you wish to select.

3. When you release your mouse, the image is copied to your Clipboard (in this example).

4. Go to Microsoft Word, and use the Paste command to insert the image into a document.

5. Voilà! You're done!

Note that the "x" in the upper right corner of the ScreenHunter window doesn't actually close the program; it just lets it run in the background. To actually close the application, open it and click Exit (the last option on the left sidebar).

Capture Me

If you are using a Mac and want to use a program like ScreenHunter, Capture Me is a good choice. Go to www.chimoosoft.com/products/captureme/ to download Capture Me, then drag the icon to your Applications folder. Open the Applications folder and click on the new Capture Me icon to install the program. When it's done, open the program (see Figure 4–9). Let's try using Capture Me to capture just a portion of your screen.

In Figure 4–9, notice the Capture Me menu bar at the top and then the partially transparent rectangular box in the middle of the screen. If you want to capture just a portion of the screen, you move that box and resize it (using the sizer in the bottom right corner), placing it around the area you want to capture. Then click inside the rectangle and you've captured the image!

Next you can go to the File Menu and save the image either to your desktop or to a specific folder on your computer. You can also go to the Edit Menu and choose Copy and then open a new file in Word or Photoshop (or other desired program) and Paste the screen capture. It's that simple!

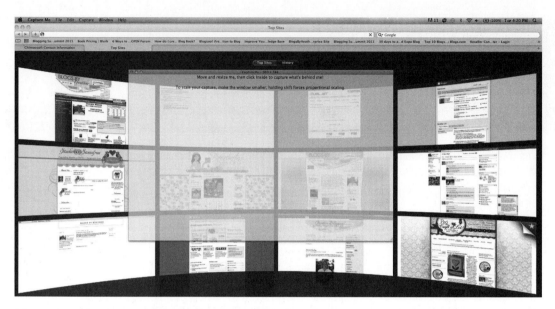

Figure 4–9. *The Capture Me main screen*

Free Resizing and Watermark Programs

Now that you have taken pictures, created your own images using Photoshop or other image editing application, or captured screenshots, you may need to resize these images to fit in your blog's sidebar (180px width recommended) or posting area (400px width recommended). I know not everyone owns Photoshop, so I have used and can recommend a free program for PCs called FastStone. For the Mac, you can use iWatermark. FastStone is primarily used to resize images; however, you can also use it to add a watermark (if it is your creation), and it has some other light photo-editing tools as well. (Don't add your watermark to an image that is not yours, such as a snapshot of another web site.)

Go to the FastStone web site (`www.faststone.org`), click on Download, then download FastStone Photo Resizer 3.0 (the .exe file). Run the setup and go through the installation process. Mac users can download iWatermark from `http://www.apple.com/downloads/macosx/imaging_3d/iwatermark.html`. Then drag iWatermark.dmg to the Applications folder and install. In the next exercise we'll resize an image and apply a watermark.

A watermark is typically a partially transparent image (normally a PNG or GIF file) that is placed somewhere on your artwork to designate ownership and keep others from copying and profiting from your work. Figure 4–10 shows a watermark applied to a solid background, while Figure 4–11 shows a watermark applied to an actual piece of artwork (photo taken with my camera). Below are a few tutorials to help you create a watermark (or you can have one professionally made):

- Photoshop: www.blogsbyheather.com/2008/11/how-to-create-a-watermark-in-photoshop.html

- Photoshop Elements: http://kurtisamundson.com/resources/watermark

- GIMP: www.websbyamy.com/wptutorials/WatermarkGimp.html

- iWatermark: www.laycockdesigns.com/watermarks/iwatermark-tutorial/

Figure 4–10. *Watermark sample on solid background*

Figure 4–11. *Watermark sample on artwork*

EXERCISE – USING FASTSTONE PHOTO RESIZER

In this exercise we will resize an existing photo on your computer, as well as apply a watermark (if you have one).

1. Open FastStone Photo Resizer (see Figure 4–12).

2. Use the file navigator to locate one of your images (on the left).

3. Click the image to select it, then click the Add button to move it to the Input List on the right. Although you can select multiple files, start with just one to familiarize yourself with the program. Note that your images may be of varying sizes and wouldn't be resized with the same settings.

4. View the settings at the bottom right, as shown in Figure 4–13.

5. Select an Output Format (the image file format).

6. Choose an Output Folder. This is a folder you should create on your computer to store the edited, resized versions of the images (so you'll always have the originals as backups).

7. Check Preview so you'll see a preview of the selected image.

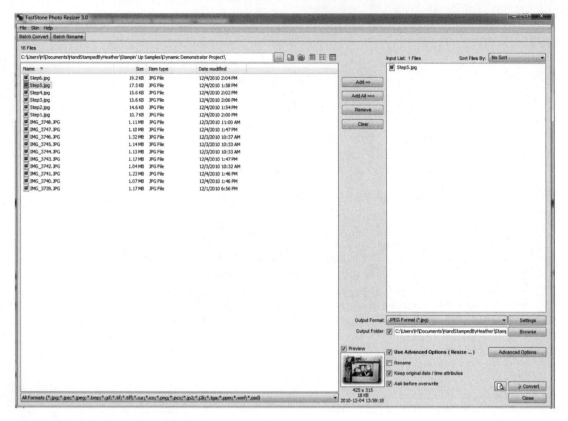

Figure 4–12. FastStone Photo Resizer

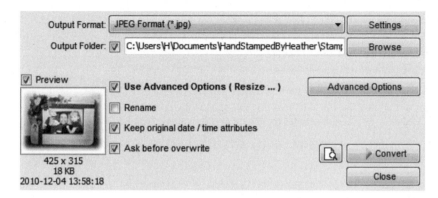

Figure 4–13. *Setting options for FastStone Photo Resizer*

8. Check Use Advanced Options, as we will be using these options.

9. Check both the Keep original date/time attributes and the Ask before overwrite boxes.

10. Click the Advanced Options button, then click on the first tab, Resize (see Figure 4–14).

11. Be sure to check the Resize box in the upper left corner.

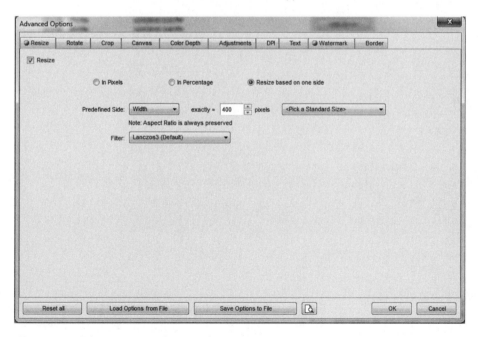

Figure 4–14. *The Resize window in Advanced Options*

12. Here, you can choose to resize your photo in Pixels, Percentage, or Resize based on one side. Let's use the last option and specify 400px (as you would to use the image in the main posting area of your blog).

13. Select Predefined size (width) and then the exact width to use, 400 pixels in this example.

14. Then take a look at the other available options such as Cropping, Adjustments, or Border. Under Adjustments you can convert the image to grayscale or sepia!

15. Let's continue with adding the watermark. Click on the Watermark tab to show the window in Figure 4–15).

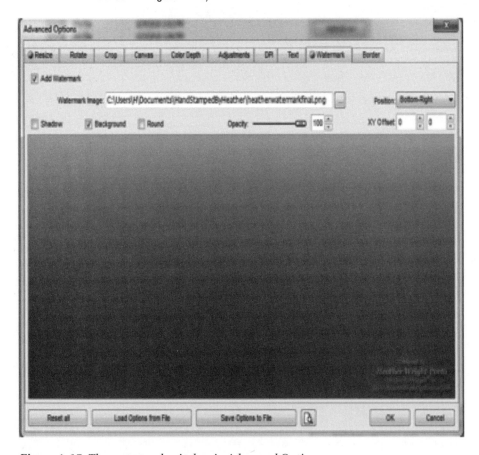

Figure 4–15. The watermark window in Advanced Options

16. Check the Add Watermark box (upper left).

17. Select your watermark image.

18. Choose a location where you'd like the watermark to be placed in your, usually the Bottom-Right, as in my sample.

19. Click OK and you are returned to the main window (see Figure 4–12).

20. Click the Convert button. You'll see another window appear, showing the images converted (we just did one).

21. Click Done.

22. Continue with other files or click Close to exit the program.

Again, check out the other tabs in the Advanced Options. There is more to this program than we can review here, but it's definitely worth your time to investigate and experiment! Have fun!

EXERCISE – RESIZE AND APPLY WATERMARK WITH IWATERMARK

For Mac users, use iWatermark to resize an image and apply a watermark.

1. Open iWatermark (see Figure 4–16).

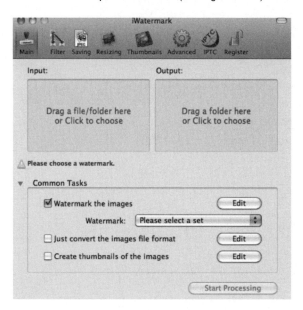

Figure 4–16. The iWatermark opening screen

2. On the left, in the Input box, click to select an image from your computer.

3. On the right, in the Output box, click to select a folder to save the watermarked image to.

4. Select "Watermark the images" and click Edit. You'll see a screen like the one shown in Figure 4–17.

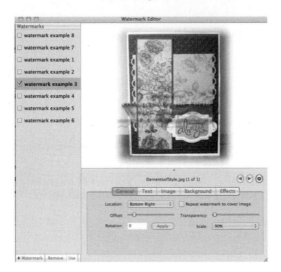

Figure 4–17. *The Watermark Editor*

5. Click General to select the location.

6. Click Text to write your own text or to delete any text if you are going to apply a watermark image.

7. Click Image to choose a watermark image from your computer.

8. Close the window and you are back at the screen in Figure 4–15.

9. Click Resizing if you want to resize your picture. You'll see the screen shown in Figure 4–18.

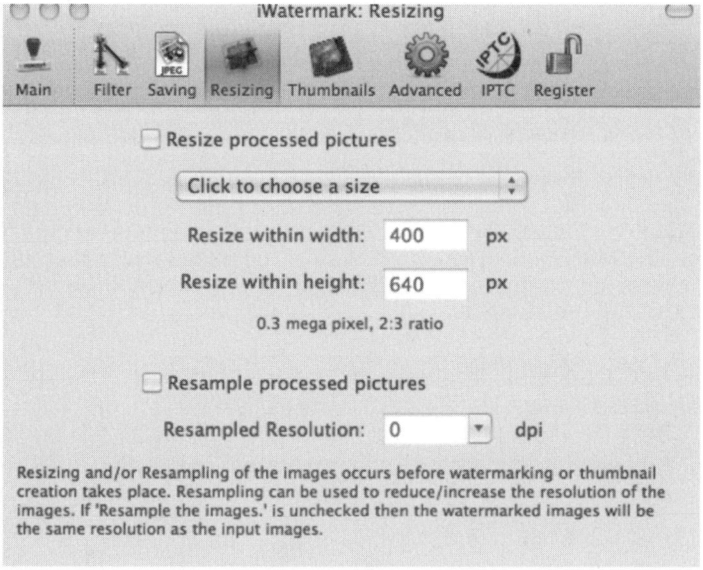

Figure 4–18. *Resizing with iWatermark*

10. Resize within width. I set it to 400 to be sure it fits inside the posting area of my blog.

11. Click Main.

12. Click Start Processing.

You're finished. Note that you get no message that says it's been saved or processed, but the watermarked image is now in the output folder you selected.

Storing Images

Whether you know it or not, when you insert an image into a post on your blog (regardless of which platform you use), it's being stored "somewhere." I want to take a few minutes to review the "where" in this somewhere, and why you may need additional storage.

Let's begin with Blogger. As we noted in the last chapter, Blogger can do many things, but it lacks a built-in file manager to store images, documents, and other files. TypePad has one. WordPress has one. So what does Blogger do? Blogger uses another free Google application called Picasa Web Album (picasaweb.google.com) to store images from your blog. Basically, any image used in your Blogger blog is stored in Picasa Web Album.

Figure 4–19 shows what I see when I log into my Google account for my Blogger blog (www.HandStampedByHeather.com). The albums created by Blogger and used by a Blogger blog display the Blogger icon, the orange "B," so you can that this account has two Blogger blogs (Heather's Testing Area and Welcome to Hand Stamped By Heather).

■ **Note** Anyone can use Picasa Web Album for free with a Google account. You don't have to have a Blogger blog, or any blog for that matter. If you are using Gmail, you can log into Picasa Web Album (`picasaweb.google.com`) with that username and password and begin creating free photo albums.

Picasa Web Album is very easy to use, as you'll see in the next exercise. You can quickly and easily insert images into your existing Blogger Picasa Web Album (which stores all of your blog's images as well as any you manually insert) or create a new album (to store additional images for your blog or business, or to create a personal album to share with family and friends).

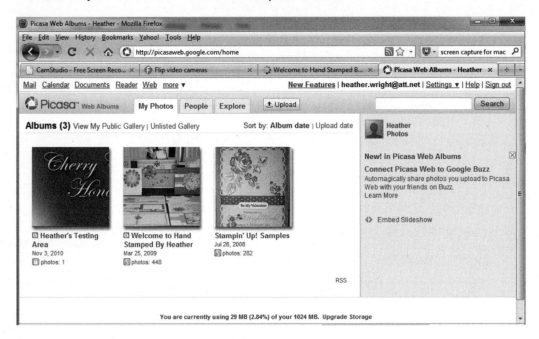

Figure 4–19. My albums stored in Picasa Web Album

■ **Note** Remember that Blogger has a storage limit of 1024MB (1G). I am using 29 MB—2.85% of my available storage space.

EXERCISE – USING PICASA WEB ALBUM

In this exercise, we'll see how to insert and delete images in a Picasa Web Album.

1. Click on the Blogger album with your blog's name (for me, this is Welcome to Hand Stamped By Heather) to open it. You'll see something similar to what's shown in Figure 4–20.

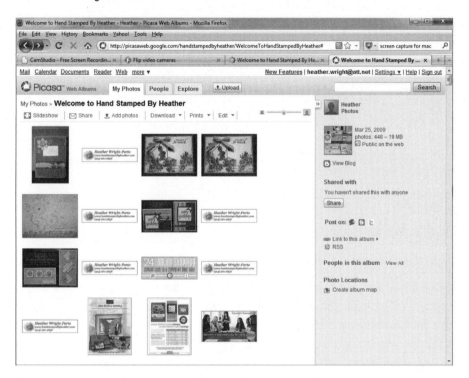

Figure 4–20. The Welcome to Hand Stamped By Heather Picasa Web Album

2. All the images currently in the album are displayed. If you want to add photos to this album, click the Add Photos button. A dialog box like the one in Figure 4–21 appears where you can upload (at most) five at a time.

Figure 4–21. *Uploading Photos in Picasa*

3. Click the Browse button to select an image to upload from your computer.

4. When you finish selecting images, click Start Upload and they are added to the end your album.

5. And that's all there is to uploading images to an existing album.

■ **Note** If you delete an image from a Blogger Picasa Web Album, you may accidentally remove an image from an existing, live post and therefore a red x "missing image" placeholder will appear in the post instead. So be careful when deleting images. It's a good idea to delete them from your blog first, then from the album. (Yes, the album holds all copies of inserted images, even those deleted from your blog. In Figure 4–20 you can see the number of "signatures" I have in my album—with my name "Heather Wright-Porto" and the small rose to the left)!

If you do need to delete an image, click on the image, then click the Edit button, and finally click on Delete This Photo. Again, be cautious when deleting images that may be on your blog already!

If you'd like to create a new album, instead of clicking Add Photos, click the Upload button; then click on Create a New Album, give it a name (Title) and click Continue. The dialog box you saw in Figure 4–21 will appear and you can upload images as you did previously.

You can close Picasa Web Album but your Google account is still open, so if you like, you can go back to www.Blogger.com and continue working on your blog.

In the next section, we'll try out the TypePad and WordPress file managers. First, though, I'd like to mention two other photo storage sites that I personally use and recommend: Google Sites and Photobucket.

At times, I need to store very large background files—images I create for a blog's background. Blogger doesn't have a file manager and this type of file can't be referenced in Picasa Web Album. I can't use a Picture Gadget for these large files, and Photobucket actually shrinks them. Google Sites (http://sites.google.com) is one site I've used (via a recommendation from my designer, Michelle Laycock) that is free and stores the images without any problems.

I do use PhotoBucket (www.PhotoBucket.com) a lot to store animated GIFs for my Blogger blog. I had problems with Blogger displaying an animated GIF using the Picture Gadget, so I had to find another solution, another place to store the image and then reference it (link to it) from my blog.

Again, I use these sites as additional storage when working with Blogger blogs, due to the lack of a file manager. In TypePad and WordPress, I haven't had any issues with image size or using animated GIFs.

Inserting Images in a Sidebar

You already know how to insert an image into a post. In this section I want to show you how to insert an image into your blog's sidebar and bring this "Working with Images" section together—from taking pictures and creating images, to resizing them, and now to actually put an image into your blog's sidebar and link it to a post or page in your Blogger, TypePad or WordPress blog.

Before we begin,

1. Resize your image to approximately 180px wide.

2. Create a post the image will later link to when placed in the sidebar.

3. Get the URL of the page or post to link to (right-click on the Post Title and click Copy Shortcut or Copy Link Location).

Let's quickly review how each platform refers to items in the blog layout. In Blogger an item is called a gadget; in TypePad it is called a typelist; and in WordPress it is called a widget.

EXERCISE – INSTALLING AN IMAGE LINK TO A SIDEBAR

I will show you how to add an image link to your blog's sidebar—that is, an image on your sidebar that links to a post on your blog. For example, you could display a picture of a new product you are offering (or other featured item for sale), and have it link to a post on your blog that contains more information about that item or sale.

You can also use this technique to create a custom About Me page in which you insert an image of yourself in the sidebar and have it link to a page you've written about yourself, the services you provide, or about your company or organization. Creating a page is very similar to creating a post. We cover pages later in this book when we discuss how to set up a blog store (Chapter 9).

Using Blogger

Of the three platforms we are reviewing in this book, Blogger has the easiest and quickest method for inserting an image into a blog's sidebar and having it link to "somewhere," such as a post on your blog. This image will be stored in the Picasa Web Album that Blogger is using to host all the images on your blog.

1. Log in to Blogger.

2. From the Dashboard, click Design.

3. From the Page Elements tab, click on Add a Gadget (on your left or right sidebar).

4. From the list of available gadgets, choose Picture (see Figure 4–22).

Picture

Add a picture from your computer or from somewhere else on the web.

By Blogger

Figure 4–22. Adding a Picture gadget

5. In the Configure Image window that appears (Figure 4–23), enter the Title and a caption if desired (text that appears below the image). In the Link text box, paste in the address (URL) of the post you previously noted (in my example it's `http://www.handstampedbyheather.com/2010/02/parisian-breeze-card-kit.html`).

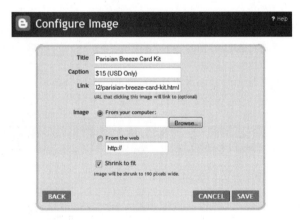

Figure 4–23. Linking to an image

6. Next, click on the Browse button to upload a picture from your computer.

7. Find the image on your computer and click Open. You'll see a preview in the Configure Image window as shown in Figure 4–24.

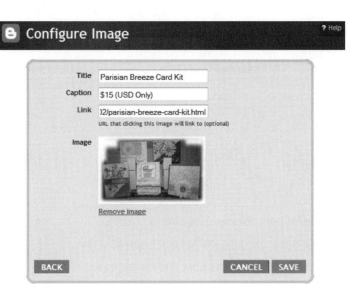

Figure 4–24. *A preview of the image*

8. Click Save and the gadget now appears in your sidebar in the Page Elements layout and is also live on your blog.

9. The image is currently at the top of your sidebar. Drag and drop it wherever you'd like it on your blog. If you change the location, click Save on the Page Elements screen to save the new location of the gadget.

10. You're done!

Using TypePad

TypePad doesn't have a Picture Gadget like Blogger, but it does have a built-in file manager as shown in Figure 4–25. We will upload an image file to the File Manager and then copy the link to that file to insert the image into the sidebar (a TypeList).

1. Log in to TypePad.

2. From the Dashboard, click on the Library menu and choose File Manager. You'll first need to upload the image you want to use in the sidebar because TypePad doesn't have a "Picture" type of TypeList.

Figure 4–25. The TypePad File Manager

3. Click the Browse button and locate the image on your computer.

4. Click Open and the path will appear in the text box to the left of the Browse button.

5. Click Upload to add the file to the left (where you'll see a list of other images and files you may have uploaded).

6. Right-click on the file and choose Copy Link Location (or Copy Shortcut depending on your browser and whether you are using a Mac or PC. I am using Mozilla Firefox and have a PC.) See Figure 4–26.

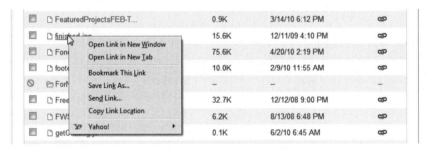

Figure 4–26. TypePad File Manager, Context Menu

7. Save this link as you will need it (http://heatherporto.TypePad.com/finished.jpg in my example).

8. Next, you need to create a new TypeList. From the Library menu, click on TypeLists.

9. Click on Add a TypeList.

10. Choose Notes as the Type. The Notes TypeList is most commonly used as it can hold any HTML or JavaScript code. We'll use it in this case to insert an image to link to a post in your blog.

11. Enter a Title for the TypeList (sidebar item) such as Featured Project.

12. Click on Create New TypeList.

13. Enter a Label, such as the name of the product or item, or you can leave it blank.

14. In the Notes area is where you will enter HTML code very similar to mine (see Figure 4–27):

```
<a href="http://heatherporto.TypePad.com/parisian-breeze.html">
<img src="http://heatherporto.TypePad.com/finished.jpg"></a>
```

where HREF is the location of your page or post on YOUR blog, and where SRC is the location of the image in the File Manager (the link location you copied).

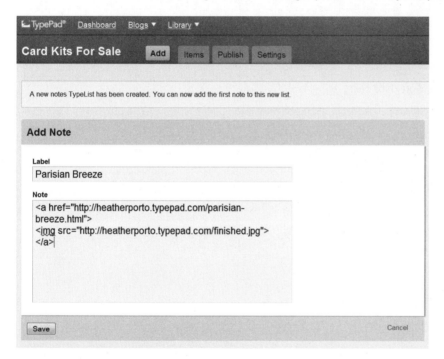

Figure 4–27. A Notes TypeList in TypePad

15. Click on Save.

16. Since this is a new TypeList, you must click on Publish to have it appear on your blog. Once you've created and published a TypeList, you can modify it as you please; you don't have to publish it again and again. You do this only done once when you create a new TypeList.

17. Click the Publish tab.

18. Click a check mark next to your blog's name.

19. Click Save Changes.

20. Click on Organize Content (the text link to the right).

21. Click on Content. Now you are in the layout of your blog and the newly added TypeList appears on the bottom of one of your sidebars.

22. Click and drag it wherever you'd like it to appear in your layout.

23. Click Save Changes.

24. View your blog and you're finished.

Using WordPress

Like TypePad, WordPress has a built-in file manager to store all sorts of documents. In this exercise we'll be using it to store an image of a featured item for sale. So, as with TypePad, we'll first upload the image to the Media Library and then use the address (URL) of the uploaded image to insert the image into the sidebar.

1. Log into your WordPress blog.

2. From the Dashboard, click Media, then Add New.

3. Click Select Files and locate the image on your computer. Click Open.

4. A thumbnail/preview appears where you can enter a Title and Alternate Text (which is used in case the image can't be shown, and it also helps with search engine optimization). See Figure 4–28.

Figure 4–28. WordPress File Manager

5. Copy the File URL.

6. Click Save All Changes.

7. Now you are ready to add it to your sidebar. On the left, click Appearance.

8. Click Widgets.

9. Click on a Text Widget and drag it to your sidebar. Drag the Text Widget, which can hold text or HTML code.)

10. Enter a Title (see Figure 4–29).

11. Enter code like this:

```
<a
href="http://creativebloggingwithwordpress.files.wordpress.com/2010/
11/Parisian-Breeze.html">
<img
src="http://creativebloggingwithwordpress.files.wordpress.com/2010/1
1/heatherwrightporto-color.jpg">
</a>
```

where you will replace the HREF with the URL of your blog post, and the SRC with the File URL you just copied above.

12. Click on Save and you're finished.

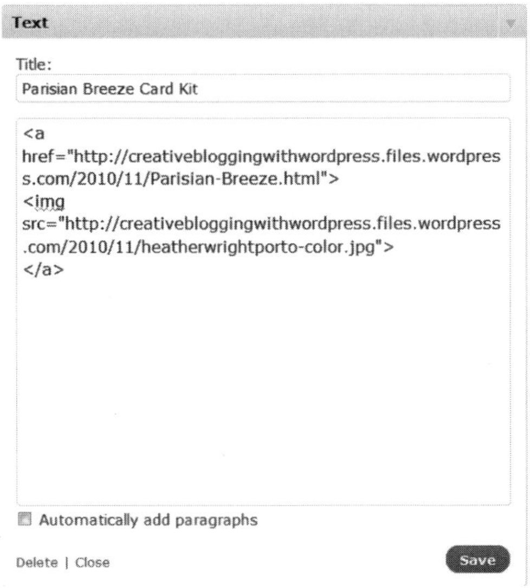

Text

Title:

Parisian Breeze Card Kit

```
<a
href="http://creativebloggingwithwordpress.files.wordpres
s.com/2010/11/Parisian-Breeze.html">
<img
src="http://creativebloggingwithwordpress.files.wordpress
.com/2010/11/heatherwrightporto-color.jpg">
</a>
```

☐ Automatically add paragraphs

Delete | Close   Save

Figure 4–29. WordPress Text Widget

In the end, you'll have a picture in your sidebar that, when clicked, will go to the post you created with more details about that product on sale or featured project, as shown in Figure 4–30 (the Parisian Breeze Card Kit).

Figure 4–30. Parisian Breeze Card Kit sidebar image added

At this point, you know a lot more than most about working with images, what sizes they should be depending on where they'll appear in your blog, how to resize them for free and add a watermark for protection, and most importantly, how to insert an image into your blog's sidebar and have it link to another area of your blog! Congrats! Next, we'll be working with videos.

Using Video

Just as many bloggers enjoy sharing pictures with their followers, many also want to share videos. In this section, we'll look at some applications and processes related to video, and how to get your video uploaded to YouTube and to your blog.

Embedding YouTube video into your blog is so easy, and what's even better is that since the video is stored on YouTube, you are not using up any storage space on your blog. Although we will be using YouTube, you can also directly insert video into your blogs (with an extra upgrade charge if using

WordPress), but again that will take up space. Furthermore, YouTube has a high volume of traffic, so it doesn't hurt to use it to help increase your online presence.

We're going to use the very popular FLIP video recorder. I got one for Christmas two years ago and I love it! It actually looks like a camera, is compact, and mine stores up to two hours of video. Now there are many cool new versions of the FLIP (UltraHD, MinoHD, SlideHD). Check them out at www.TheFlip.com if you're looking for a video recorder that is affordable, easy to use, and just as easy when it comes to moving videos from the recorder to your computer!

Then we'll use a screen recorder, a different way of creating videos that you can also upload to YouTube. This is a good way to create how-to videos or to share a step-by-step process with support staff when seeking help.

In the upcoming exercises we will be uploading both types of videos to YouTube, so you'll need to create a YouTube account if you don't already have one; or you can use your Google account.

EXERCISE – CREATING A YOUTUBE ACCOUNT

In this exercise we'll create a new YouTube account. However, if you already have a Google account, you can skip this step and use it later to sign in to YouTube.

1. Go to www.YouTube.com.

2. Click the Create Account button.

3. Enter the information shown in Figure 4–31 (Email Address, Username, Postal Code, Date of Birth, and Gender).

4. Click the I Accept button to accept YouTube's and Google's Terms of Service.

5. Complete the account creation form shown in Figure 4–32.

6. Click the Create My New Account button.

7. Note your account information. At this point you are now logged into your new YouTube/Google account.

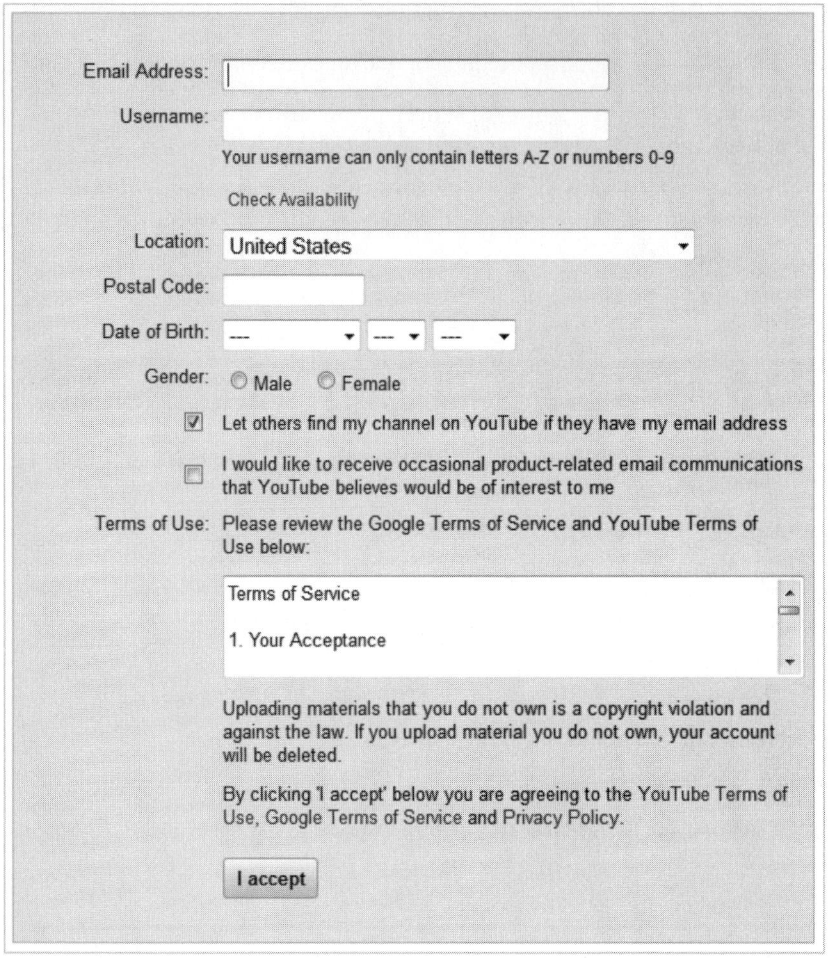

Email Address: [   ]

Username: [   ]

Your username can only contain letters A-Z or numbers 0-9

Check Availability

Location: United States ▼

Postal Code: [   ]

Date of Birth: [--- ▼] [--- ▼] [--- ▼]

Gender: ○ Male ○ Female

☑ Let others find my channel on YouTube if they have my email address

☐ I would like to receive occasional product-related email communications that YouTube believes would be of interest to me

Terms of Use: Please review the Google Terms of Service and YouTube Terms of Use below:

Terms of Service

1. Your Acceptance

Uploading materials that you do not own is a copyright violation and against the law. If you upload material you do not own, your account will be deleted.

By clicking 'I accept' below you are agreeing to the YouTube Terms of Use, Google Terms of Service and Privacy Policy.

[I accept]

Figure 4–31. Creating a Google/YouTube Account

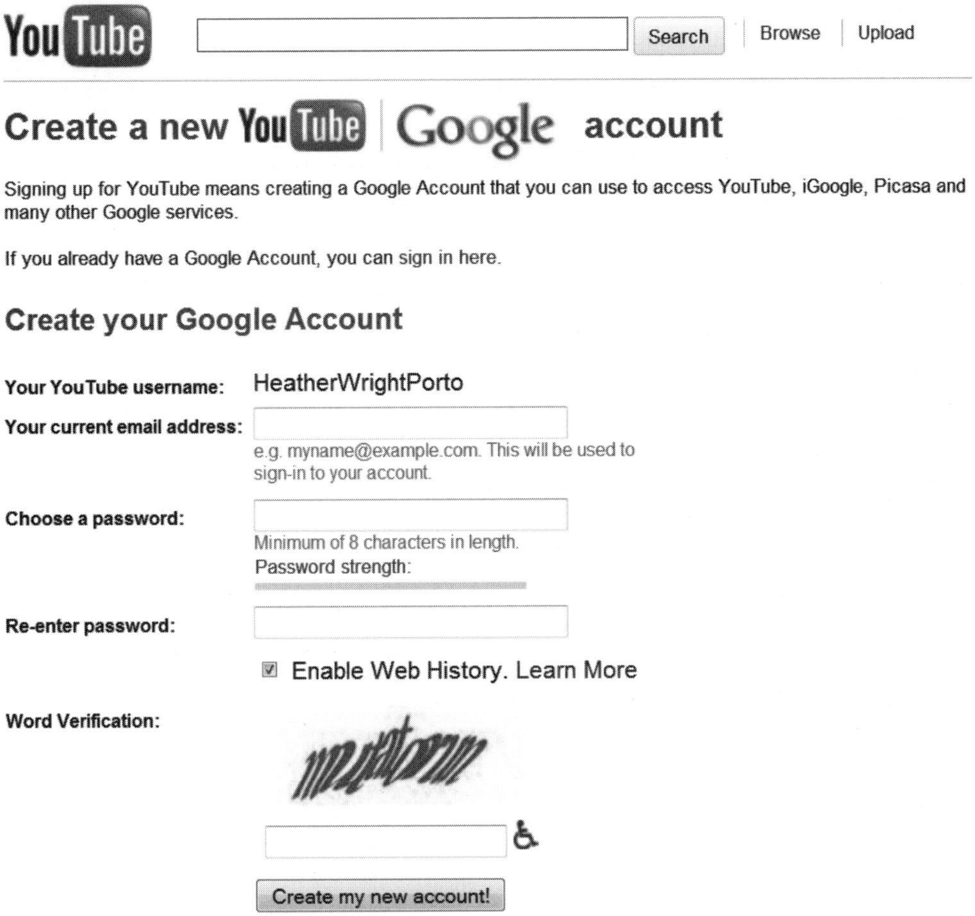

YouTube
Search
Browse
Upload
Create a new YouTube Google account
Signing up for YouTube means creating a Google Account that you can use to access YouTube, iGoogle, Picasa and many other Google services.
If you already have a Google Account, you can sign in here.
Create your Google Account
Your YouTube username:
HeatherWrightPorto
Your current email address:
e.g. myname@example.com. This will be used to sign-in to your account.
Choose a password:
Minimum of 8 characters in length.
Password strength:
Re-enter password:
Enable Web History. Learn More
Word Verification:
Create my new account!

Figure 4–32. Completing Google account setup

Downloading Video

After taking a video with the FLIP, you'll want to download it to your computer, and it couldn't be easier. As soon as I plugged in my FLIP (via a USB cable), it was installed instantly and appeared as drive E: on my computer (see Figure 4–33). There is no additional software needed. You can then select which videos to copy to your computer. You can drag and drop them or select them, and copy and paste them as you would any other files using Windows Explorer or My Computer. They are downloaded as MP4 files.

Editing Video

Candid videos are great, but you may wish you could remove that moment when the vase was knocked over, the phone rang, or the baby started crying! If you're using a PC, you can use Movie Maker to do this; on a Mac, you can use iMovie. In Windows 7, the application is called Windows Live Movie Maker; see Figure 4–34. There it shows our quick visit with Santa this year and the frames that make up the video. I will be removing the first three frames as the first frame shows the last family leaving Santa and the second frame shows us walking up to Santa. I want the video to start just when we are seated near Santa. Next, we'll add music to the video, "Jingle Bells." Lastly, we'll upload the video directly to YouTube, right from Window Live Movie Maker or iMovie.

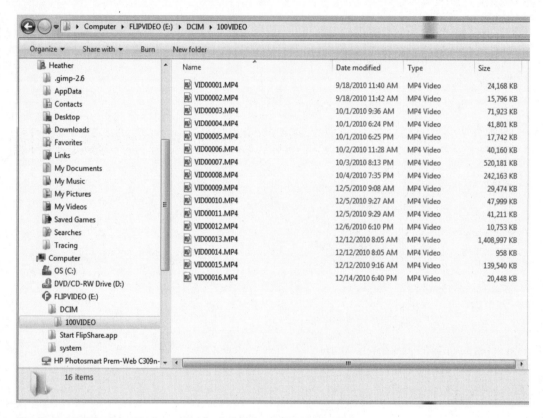

Figure 4–33. Windows Explorer Displaying Drive E: (FLIPVIDEO)

***Figure 4–34.** Windows Live Movie Maker (Windows 7)*

EXERCISE – EDITING VIDEO USING WINDOWS LIVE MOVIE MAKER

So you've downloaded the videos to your computer and you've opened Windows Live Movie Maker (Programs➤All Programs➤Windows Live➤Windows Live Movie Maker).

1. Click in the middle of the screen where it says "Drag videos and photos here or click to browse for them."

2. The Browse window opens and you can select one of your videos (see Figure 4–33).

3. For my example, I want to remove the first three frames, so I will set the Start Point at the fourth frame.

4. Select the fourth frame.

5. Go to the Edit menu and click the Set Start Point button (the first three frames just vanish).

6. Next, we'll add music.

7. Click on Home.

8. Click the Add Music button on the toolbar.

9. Click Add Music from the submenu to apply music to the entire video.

10. Locate the music file on your computer, such as an MP3 file, and click Open.

11. Play the video by clicking the arrow (the play button) beneath the main video window (on the left).

12. You can even publish this new, edited video right to YouTube.

13. Click the Project menu (upper left corner), then Publish movie, then Publish on YouTube, as shown in Figure 4–35.

Figure 4–35. *Choose to Publish on YouTube*

14. You will be prompted to log in to YouTube.

15. Another YouTube window will appear where you'll complete information about the movie (video) you are uploading (see Figure 4–36).

Figure 4–36. Describing your movie before publishing on YouTube

16. Click Publish.

17. Wait until the file is uploaded (this may take several minutes). Please note that you may need to remove the music from the video before uploading (right-click on the Music bar above the video frames and click Remove).

18. Click View Online, but if you get an error message when you get to YouTube, processing may not be complete. Allow time for processing and then try again.

19. For now, close MovieMaker by clicking the Project drop-down menu and choosing Exit.

EXERCISE – EDITING VIDEO USING IMOVIE

Now we'll use iMovie to edit a video; in my case, it'll be the holiday video just used in the Windows Live Movie Maker example.

1. Drag and drop a video into iMovie or go to the File Menu and choose Import➤Movies.

2. From the browser that opens, select a video and click Import.

3. The video is imported into Events.The frames from your video will appear as shown in Figure 4–37.

Figure 4–37. iMovie Events

4. Select any frames you want to delete and click the Delete key on your keyboard.

5. Select all the remaining frames (Command + A) and drag them up to the Projects window.

6. Now you can publish it to YouTube.

7. Click Share and then YouTube.

8. Enter your YouTube Account (by clicking Add) and Password, and the Category and Title (and a Description and Tags if you like), and select the size as shown in Figure 4–38.

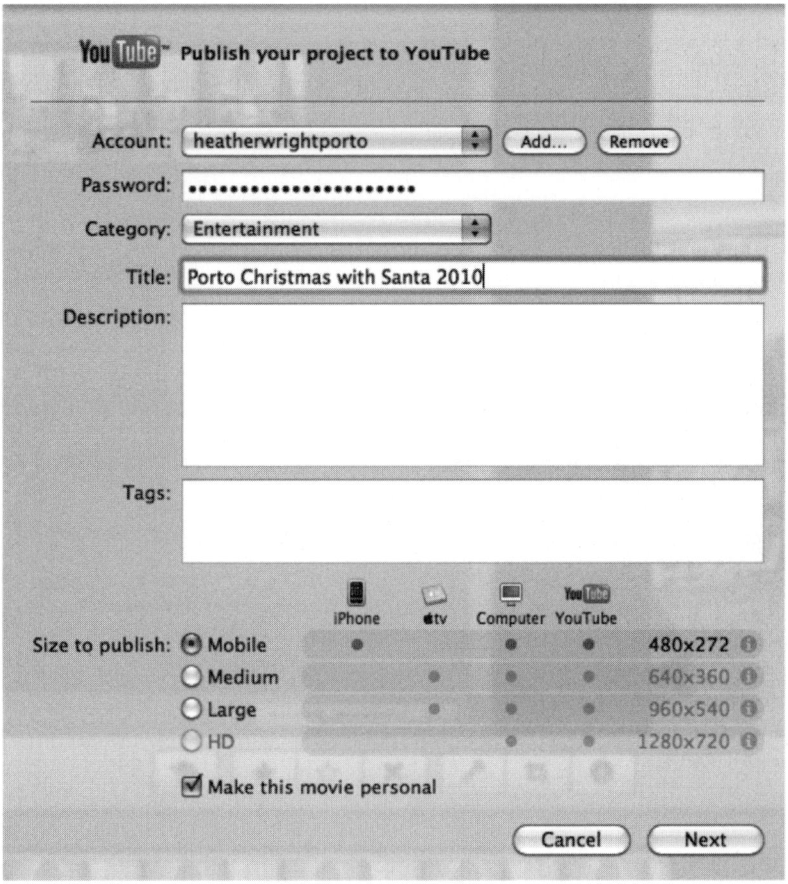

Figure 4–38. Publishing to YouTube with iMovie

9. If you want to make your video public, uncheck "Make this movie personal."

10. Click on Next.

11. Read the YouTube Terms of Service.

12. Click Publish.

13. After the movie is published, the Title Bar changes to "Publish to YouTube."

You project changes are saved automatically. You can quit/exit iMovie at any time.

Using a Screen Recorder

As mentioned previously, you can also make videos that record what takes place on your computer screen. These videos are helpful if you want to share step-by-step instruction with your students, if you want to simply share your computer expertise in a video, or are trying to help technical support staff troubleshoot a computer problem you are having.

We'll be using a free program called CamStudio (for Windows). To download the application, go to www.CamStudio.org and click on `CamStudio20.exe` under the title Download Links (towards the middle of the page). Save the file to your computer (if you're using Windows 7, it will be stored in your Downloads folder). Then simply double-click the executable file (`CamStudio20.exe`) to step through the installation process. It only takes a few seconds!

For Mac users, we'll experiment with Capture It, which you can download from `www.apple.com/downloads/macosx/video/captureit.html`, then drag it to the Applications folder and install. It doesn't even take a minute!

In the following exercise, we'll record our first video using these screen recording applications. Let's have some fun!

EXERCISE – USING CAMSTUDIO

In this exercise we'll record and capture your screen movements. In doing so, CamStudio creates a video—an AVI file.

1. Find the CamStudio shortcut on your desktop (blue square logo) and double-click to open the program (see Figure 4–39).

Figure 4–39. The CamStudio opening screen

2. When you are ready to begin recording, click the red circle. To pause, click the double gray vertical bars, and click the blue square to stop.

3. In this example, we will record how to insert a YouTube video into a Blogger post. There will be no sound in this example; however, you can record audio as well if you have a microphone connected to your computer.

a. Go to Options and select which audio option you'd like to use. In this case we won't be recording any audio, which is the default.

4. Before starting, go to the Region menu and select Full Screen (you can select another option if that best suits the area you'd like to record).

5. Now, we'll begin recording. Click on the red circle.

6. For my example, I'll go to my YouTube channel (www.youtube.com/user/HeatherWrightPorto) and select the Visit with Santa 2010 video.

7. Right-click on the video and choose "Copy embed html" from the shortcut menu.

8. Open a new browser window (which leaves the YouTube window open).

9. Go to Blogger and log in.

10. From the Dashboard, click New Post.

11. Add a Title.

12. Add text in the post body.

13. Switch to the Edit HTML view (if you are currently in Compose view).

14. Right-click and Paste or use Ctrl+V to paste in the HTML code copied from YouTube.

15. Notice the width is set to 600px, which is too large to fit in most posts so we'll modify it to be 400px wide and 244px high. This is done in two places in the code (bolded in the sample below).

```
<object style="height: 244px; width: 400px;">
<param name="movie" value="http://www.youtube.com/v/u1ilOM6PvUc?version=3">
<param name="allowFullScreen" value="true">
<param name="allowScriptAccess" value="always">
<embed src="http://www.youtube.com/v/u1ilOM6PvUc?version=3" type="application/x-
shockwave-flash" allowfullscreen="true" allowScriptAccess="always" width="400"
height="244"></object>
```

16. Click Compose to go back to that view. You will not see the actual video preview until the post is published.

17. Enter a Label to categorize your post.

18. Click Publish to save and publish your post.

19. Click View Post to view the video live on your blog, as shown in Figure 4–40.

Figure 4–40. Viewing a post with a YouTube video embedded

20. Go back to CamStudio and click the blue square to stop the recording.

21. You will be prompted to save the file to your computer in AVI format. In my example, the file name is EmbedYouTube-Blogger.avi.

22. When the file is saved, the CamStudio Player opens and you can watch your new screen recording!

23. Click the black arrow (Play) to begin reviewing your video.

24. Click File, then Exit to exit the Player.

25. Do it again (File, then Exit) to close CamStudio.

EXERCISE – SCREEN RECORDING USING CAPTURE IT

If you're a Mac user, you'll enjoy using Capture It to record screen video.

1. Open Capture It and click the Record button.

2. Uncheck "Record audio from" if you don't want to record sound.

3. Uncheck "Keep raw files (cividx files)" if you simply want to keep the encoded, finished movie files (.mov format).

4. When ready, click the fourth button on the toolbox shown at the bottom of Figure 4–41.

Figure 4–41. Capture It Record preferences

5. The recording begins. You can record the creation of a blog post as we did in the Cam Studio example, or demonstrate a problem you are having.

6. When you're done, click the blue check mark that appears on the toolbox when you begin recording.

7. When the recording is finished, the encoding automatically begins. This takes a few minutes but you can do other things while it processes.

8. When the processing is complete, Capture It will save the movie (an .mov file) to your desktop and you can then play it.

Experiment and have fun. In the next exercise, you'll learn how to upload the video to YouTube.

Earlier we saw how to embed your YouTube video in Blogger, and the process is very similar for both TypePad (where "Compose" is "Rich Text") and WordPress (where the "Edit HTML" tab is simply named "HTML" and the "Compose" tab is called "Visual"). Other than the naming of the tabs, the instructions are the same.

1. In YouTube, right-click your video and choose Copy Embed HTML.

2. Create a new post.

3. While in Edit HTML (Blogger and TypePad) or HTML (WordPress), paste in the code from YouTube.

4. Modify the dimensions to fit inside your posting area (width to 400px and height to 244px, for example).

5. Click Compose (Blogger) or Rich Text (TypePad) or Visual (WordPress) to visually look at your post.

6. Categorize your post.

7. Publish.

Uploading to YouTube

At this point we have the screen recording saved on our computer. Next, we will manually upload it to YouTube, instead of publishing it to YouTube from within an application.

EXERCISE – UPLOADING VIDEOS TO YOUTUBE

If you want to simply upload videos to YouTube without any editing, this is the exercise for you!

1. Go to www.YouTube.com and click Sign In.

2. Enter your Google account username and password and click Sign In.

3. Click the Upload link at the top.

4. Click the Upload button.

   Note that you can AutoShare your uploads with your other accounts, such as Facebook, Twitter, MySpace, etc. We discuss social networking in Chapter 8.

5. Select the file(s) you want to upload, such as the one we recorded using CamStudio.

6. Click Open and another window opens where you can see the progress of your video being uploaded. You can enter other information such as a Title and Description (see Figure 4–42).

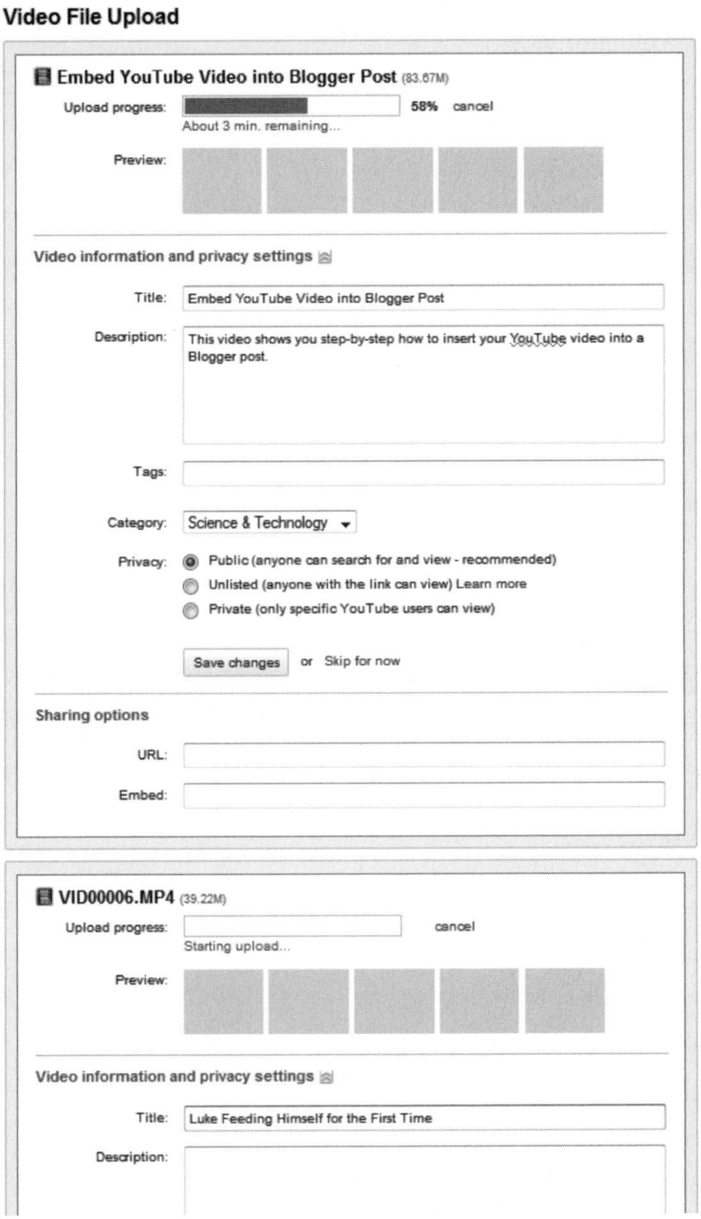

Video File Upload

▣ Embed YouTube Video into Blogger Post (83.67M)

Upload progress: ████████████ **58%** cancel
About 3 min. remaining...

Preview: ▢ ▢ ▢ ▢ ▢

Video information and privacy settings ▣

Title: Embed YouTube Video into Blogger Post

Description: This video shows you step-by-step how to insert your YouTube video into a
Blogger post.

Tags:

Category: Science & Technology ▾

Privacy: ◉ Public (anyone can search for and view - recommended)
◯ Unlisted (anyone with the link can view) Learn more
◯ Private (only specific YouTube users can view)

Save changes or Skip for now

Sharing options

URL:

Embed:

▣ VID00006.MP4 (39.22M)

Upload progress: cancel
Starting upload...

Preview: ▢ ▢ ▢ ▢ ▢

Video information and privacy settings ▣

Title: Luke Feeding Himself for the First Time

Description:

Figure 4–42. Uploading a video file to YouTube

7. When the video is finished uploading, you'll see a green check mark and a preview
   as shown in Figure 4–43.

Video File Upload

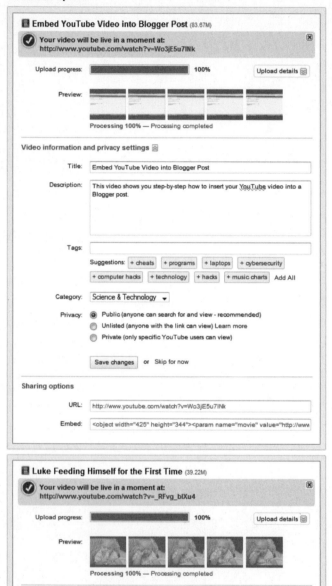

Figure 4–43. *YouTube upload complete*

8. To go to your channel and view all your videos, click on your Account Name (menu) and then choose My Channel as shown in Figure 4–44.

Figure 4–44. YouTube Account drop-down menu

Add Video Bar to Sidebar

You should post videos to your blog if you want your followers to see them. However, another way to showcase your YouTube videos is to insert a video bar into your sidebar, which shows your most recent videos—and gives your readers quick access to them!

Figure 4–45 shows a sample video bar, horizontal view, not in a sidebar. We are going to create a vertical gadget to be placed in your sidebar.

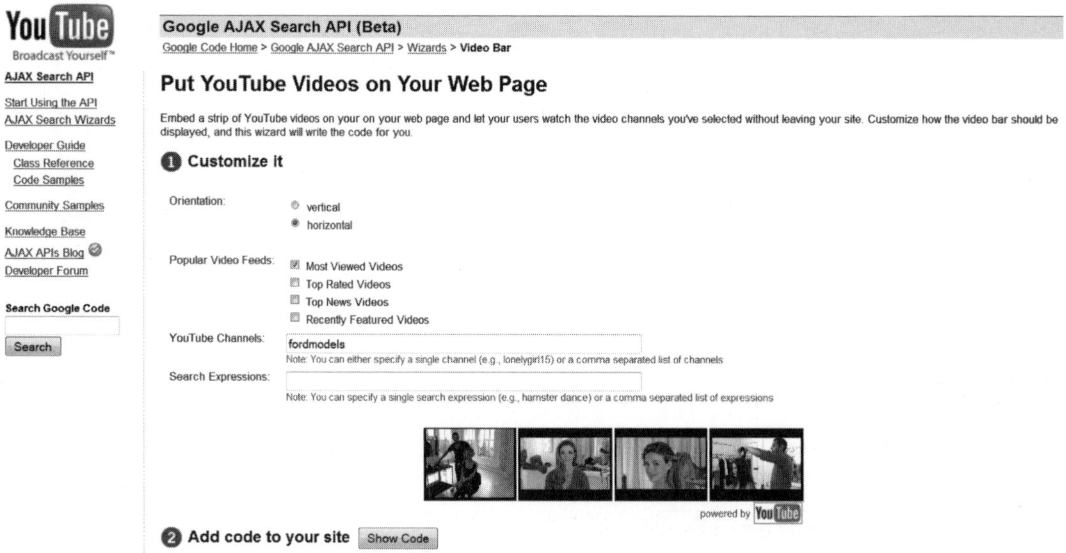

Figure 4–45. A sample video bar

EXERCISE – INSERT VIDEO BAR

In this exercise we'll see how to insert a video bar into the sidebar of your Blogger or TypePad blog. This is an example of code that can't be inserted or used in the free WordPress.com version. (Remember back in Chapter 3 we reviewed the pros and cons of each platform, and one of the limitations of the free WordPress.com version was the inability to use certain HTML and JavaScript code.)

1. Go to www.google.com/uds/solutions/wizards/videobar.html (the page shown in Figure 4–45).

2. In Step 1 (Customize It), choose Vertical.

3. Uncheck Most Viewed Videos.

4. In the YouTube Channels text box, type in the name of your YouTube channel (this is the YouTube username you created earlier (refer back to Figure 4–32).

5. The preview of your videos should now appear on the right as a vertical bar as in Figure 4–46.

Figure 4–46. A vertical video bar

6. Then click the Show Code button and a text box will appear below it with all the code you need to select and copy.

7. Paste the code into your sidebar.

Using Blogger

1. From the Dashboard, go to Design➤Page Elements.

2. Click on Add a Gadget.

3. Choose HTML/JavaScript.

4. Enter "I'm on YouTube" as a Title (or whatever you like.) See Figure 4–47.

Figure 4–47. Adding code for a video bar in Blogger

5. Paste the code in the large Content box.

6. Click Save.

7. Drag and drop the video bar where you'd like it to appear in the sidebar.

8. Click Save Changes and you're done.

Using TypePad

1. Under Manage My Blog, click on Design.

2. Click on Content. You are now looking at a visual layout of your blog.

3. In the middle box (Modules), click on Embed Your Own HTML.

4. On the right (under Details), click on the Add This Module button.

5. A Custom HTML window appears as shown in Figure 4–48.

Figure 4–48. Custom HTML module in TypePad

6. Enter the Label (which is a title).

7. In the HTML text box, paste in the code for the video bar.

8. Click OK.

9. Drag and drop the module where you want it in the sidebar.

10. Click Save Changes and you're done.

If you try to add this in a WordPress.com blog using a Text Widget, it will not work. See Figure 4–49 which shows the inserted "I'm on YouTube" widget, but not as a video bar. What you see instead is just a bunch of code. This will work on other (paid) WordPress blogs, such as those hosted by www.WebsByAmy.com. You can find more documentation and an explanation here: www.en.support.wordpress.com/code/.

Figure 4–49. A nonfunctional widget in WordPress

Summary

I hope I have answered many of the questions you had regarding how to get your images from camera or video recorder onto your computer, and then how to upload and insert them into your blog posts or in the sidebar. Although I know we don't all have the same camera and not everyone owns the FLIP (yet!), I really hope you'll give it a try using whatever hardware you have. You can do it! Go have some fun—try those screen capturing programs, create your own videos, and snap all the pictures you want!

In the next chapter, Advanced Blog Design, we'll continue the discussion of imaging as we install a custom banner into our blogs, then change our blog's theme or color scheme to coordinate with the new banner.

■ ■ ■

Advanced Blog Design

In Chapter 2, we briefly discussed the layout and design of your blog with regard to organization, recommended fonts and colors, and image size and placement. I also presented samples of design templates that can be found on the Web for Blogger and WordPress, as well as those in Blogger's template designer, in WordPress themes, and those that can be used in TypePad. Here, we will bring that discussion back to life and walk through the steps of customizing your blog's design. We will install a custom banner—that is, a banner you created, or took a picture of, or had a professional graphic designer prepare for you. Then, to complement the new banner, we'll adjust your blog's color scheme to coordinate with the new banner, and make any other changes necessary (such as adjusting column widths).

Blogger, TypePad, and WordPress all have design elements that are customizable. In the following exercises we'll review Blogger's Template Designer, Typepad's Theme Builder, and WordPress's Appearance section. You'll find that all of them are easy to use and you can give a new look to your blog in minutes!

Blogger's Template Designer

Blogger released its Template Designer in the summer of 2010, and it is a wonderful new addition! We will use the Template Designer to customize the color scheme, adjust column widths accordingly (depending on the size of the banner), and to install a background image. In Chapter 4, when working with images and video, we reviewed the standard sizes for many blog elements, such as the banner and background. When we look at CSS basics in Chapter 10, we'll discuss how to further adjust background image settings.

Before adjusting anything, however, the first step is to install your custom banner, then you can adjust the width accordingly. We do this outside the Template Designer, in the Design area of your blog. You should have the image for your custom banner ready. Since, in this example, the banner will take the place of a title and description, your image should include a title and perhaps some information about your blog's purpose. Also, remember in Chapter 3 we chose the Simple (Blue) template. It's still in use, but we will be changing the blog design throughout this chapter in the upcoming exercises.

EXERCISE – INSTALLING A BANNER

We'll do this part in the Design area of your blog, not in the Template Designer.

1. Login to Blogger.

2. From the Dashboard, click on Design, and then Page Elements.

3. In Page Elements, at the top, you'll see an area that says "(header)." Click Edit and the Configure Header window appears as shown in Figure 5–1.

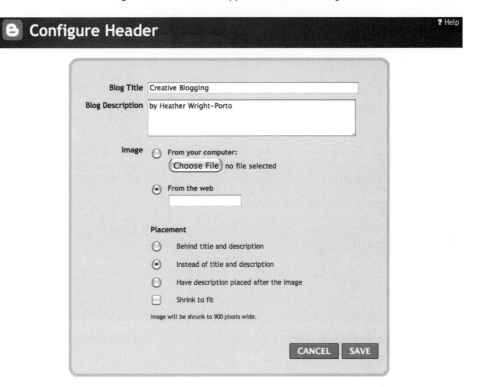

Figure 5–1. The Configure Header screen

4. Click the Browse button to find the image on your computer you want use as the banner for your blog. Select the image and click Open.

5. You'll see the image as a preview in the Configure Header window.

6. Click "Instead of title and description" and then click Save.

7. Click View Blog (see Figure 5–2) to view your new banner, but keep in mind you will be adjusting other elements of your blog to complement this new banner.

Figure 5–2. Viewing the new banner in Blogger

Templates, Adjustments, and Advanced Settings

Although we won't be discussing every element of Blogger's Template Designer, I encourage you to experiment with all the different options. Notice, in Figure 5–2, the right side of the banner is truncated (where the phone number doesn't display completely). Also, the current Simple (blue) clashes with the new banner design. Luckily, the new Template Designer makes it easy to adjust the blog's column widths to fit your banner and desired blog appearance. And we'll change the blog template and modify the color scheme to coordinate with the colors of the banner.

EXERCISE – USING THE TEMPLATE DESIGNER

In this exercise, we'll walk through the steps to modify your blog's layout using the Template Designer: we'll change the template, adjust the widths, and set new colors to suit your new banner.

1. From the Dashboard, click on Design.

2. Click on Template Designer (see Figure 5–3).

Figure 5–3. Templates in Blogger's Template Designer

3. Notice, at the top, the Simple template is still highlighted. In this example, I've selected the last sample under Simple, the white template with gray lettering.

4. Click on Adjust Widths.

5. Since my banner is 950px wide. I set the Entire Blog width to 980 (see Figure 5–4) and left the Right Sidebar setting alone. This setting may differ for you depending on the width of your banner. For my example with the chosen Blogger template, the banner showed completely and correctly when I set the width to 980px. Any lower and the phone number was truncated; any higher and the banner was no longer centered. Note that, by setting these two widths, the main column width automatically adjusts appropriately. So it's easy to play around with the settings in the Blogger Template Designer and set them as you need.

Figure 5–4. Adjusting widths in Blogger Template Designer

Next, we'll adjust some of the colors. For example, we'll make the post title in this example blue to make it stand out from the rest of the gray, and we'll also change the links color to the same blue (hexadecimal code #7491AF), as shown in Figure 5–5. Of course, not everyone will see your blog exactly as you wish. Most modern computers use the 24- to 32-bit color setting, which displays over 16 million colors. However, some older computers use only a 16-bit color spectrum, and some even older computers (very, very old) may have only an 8-bit color setting and can only display 256 colors.

6. Click on Advanced.

7. From the list on the left, click on Links (Figure 5–5).

Figure 5–5. Advanced settings in Blogger Template Designer

8.   Notice that I changed the three different colors related to links: Link Color, Visited Color, and Hover Color. I made Link Color and Visited Color the same (blue, #7491AF) and chose a dark gray (#333333) for the Hover Color (the color the text changes to if your mouse is placed over the link). Some users don't know the difference between a link and a visited link (one that has been clicked), so I generally keep them the same color; but I do think it'is a good idea to have the Hover color be different so if people move their mouse over the link, it changes color and is more noticeable.

9.   Now we'll change the Background color to the same blue as the links.

10. Click on Backgrounds, then set the Outer Background to a color of your choice (in my example, as shown in Figure 5–6, I chose the same blue). Feel free to experiment with the color and font settings in this Advanced tab.

11. When you're finished, click on Apply To Blog (the orange button in the upper right corner) to apply all the new settings to your blog.

12. Click on Back to Blogger to exit the Template Designer and return to the Design area of the Blogger layout.

13. Click View Blog to see the changes live.

Figure 5–6. Viewing the blog at www.CreativeBloggingByApress.Blogspot.com

I do hope you continue to experiment with the Blogger Template Designer as it has many options to help you customize your blog without any coding. If you are interested in coding and learning HTML and CSS, however, then read on. It's coming up later in this book!

One last suggestion is to change the Navbar setting in the Design area to Transparent Light or Transparent Dark. You can change the color if you want. Click Edit on the Navbar element, choose a color that best complements your blog, then click Save. The default is blue, which may not match your design. Other colors include Black, Silver, or Tan. But if you are looking to coordinate the Navbar with your blog design, Transparent Light or Transparent Dark simply fades or darkens the color of your blog, keeping it within the same color family (hue).

TypePad's Theme Builder

TypePad uses a Theme Builder that, like Blogger's Template Designer, allows you to customize your blog's design and layout. Unlike with Blogger, though, it is all done in the same place, as you'll see in our next exercise. The resulting TypePad blog will look much like what you see in Figure 5–6, in that the banner is the same (just resized to a width of 670px to fit in the new Typepad layout), and the post title, link colors, and background color will be the same blue. Of course, you will choose colors that compliment your own new banner.

EXERCISE – USING THEME BUILDER

In this exercise, we'll be installing a custom banner and adjusting column widths and color settings. TypePad's Theme Builder has more options than Blogger's Template Designer, but we'll try to keep the exercises similar.

1. From the Dashboard, click Design and then click the Choose a Theme button.

2. Under the Themes area in the top left, click on Customizable.

3. From the options available, click on Theme Builder.

4. Click the Choose button (see Figure 5–7).

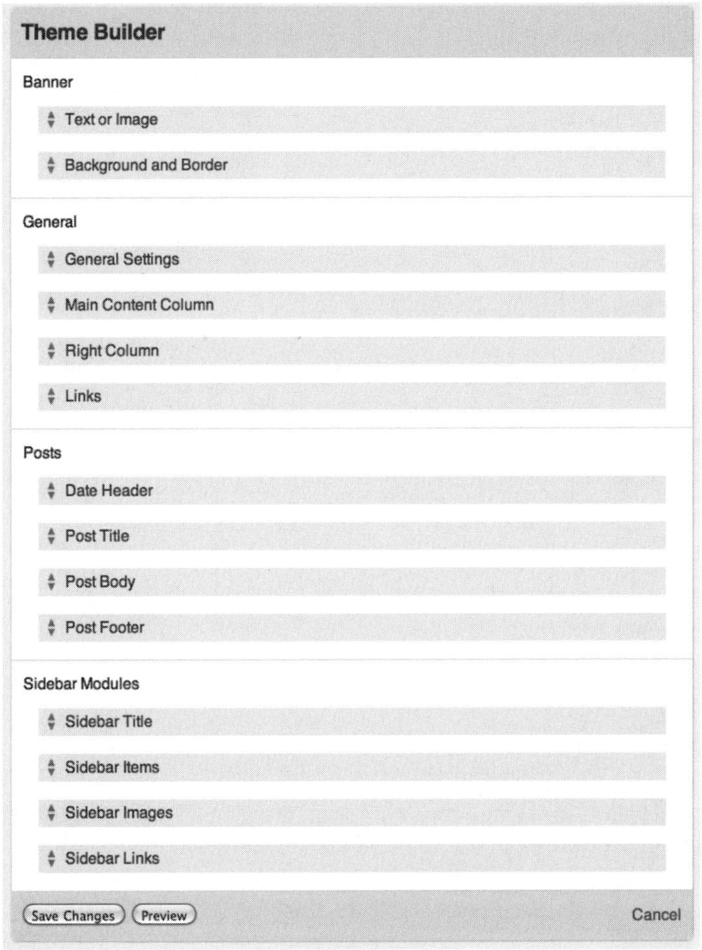

Theme Builder

Banner
- ⬍ Text or Image
- ⬍ Background and Border

General
- ⬍ General Settings
- ⬍ Main Content Column
- ⬍ Right Column
- ⬍ Links

Posts
- ⬍ Date Header
- ⬍ Post Title
- ⬍ Post Body
- ⬍ Post Footer

Sidebar Modules
- ⬍ Sidebar Title
- ⬍ Sidebar Items
- ⬍ Sidebar Images
- ⬍ Sidebar Links

(Save Changes) (Preview)   Cancel

Figure 5–7. The TypePad Theme Builder

We'll start with the installation of the new banner.

5. Click on Text or Image under the Banner area.

6. Select Image.

7. Click the Browse button to find the custom banner image on your computer. Select it and click Open.

8. Click on Background and Border under the same Banner area (see Figure 5–8).

Banner

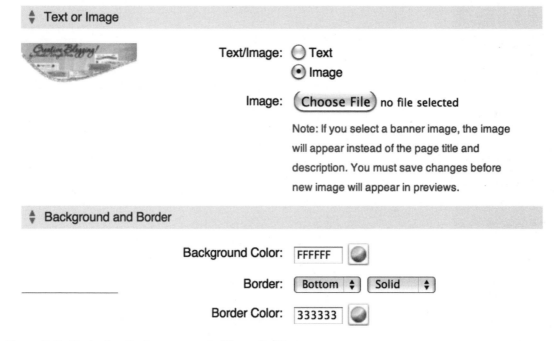

Figure 5–8., Designing the banner area in Theme Builder

9. In my example, I set the Background Color (of the banner area only) to white (#FFFFFF), set the Border to Bottom and Solid; and chose a medium gray (#333333) for the Border Color.

Next we'll customize the General area, including colors for the links.

10. Click on General➤General Settings and set the Background Color to one that coordinates with your new banner. In my example, I used the same blue (#7491AF) as in the previous example. See Figure 5–9.

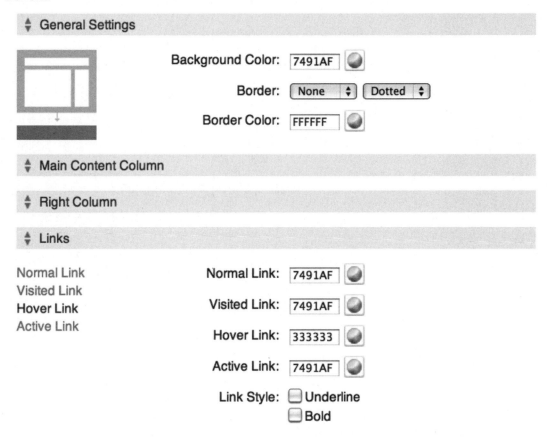

Figure 5–9. Theme Builder's General settings

11. I also set the Border to None (so the border color and type doesn't matter).

12. Under Main Content Column, I increased the Center Column width from 400px to 500px.

13. I made no changes to the Right Column, though you can if you wish.

14. Under Links, I again used the same blue of the Background Color (under General Settings) as the main link color. And I set the Hover Link color to a medium gray (#333333).

Next, let's format some post settings. Under the Posts area, I changed the Post Title color and font settings as shown in Figure 5–10.

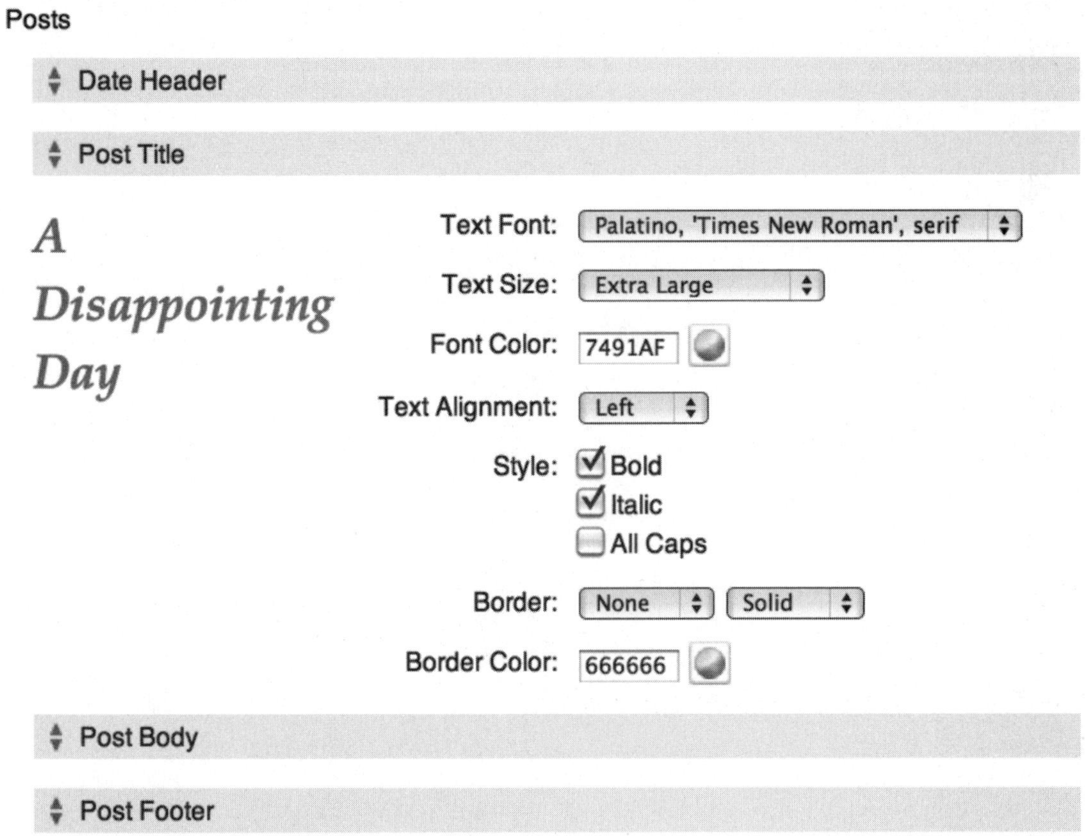

Posts

⬍ Date Header

⬍ Post Title

A Disappointing Day

Text Font: Palatino, 'Times New Roman', serif ⬍

Text Size: Extra Large ⬍

Font Color: 7491AF ⬤

Text Alignment: Left ⬍

Style: ☑ Bold
☑ Italic
☐ All Caps

Border: None ⬍ Solid ⬍

Border Color: 666666 ⬤

⬍ Post Body

⬍ Post Footer

Figure 5–10. *Theme Builder, Posts Area in Typepad*

15. I changed the Text Font to Palatino, the Text Size to Extra Large, the Font Color to 7491AF (the same blue), and the Style to include Bold and Italic.

16. Go ahead and experiment with the other Post settings, such as for Date Header, Post Body, or Post Footer.

Now let's look at the Sidebar Modules, where I changed the link colors to match those in the General Settings, as shown in Figure 5–11.

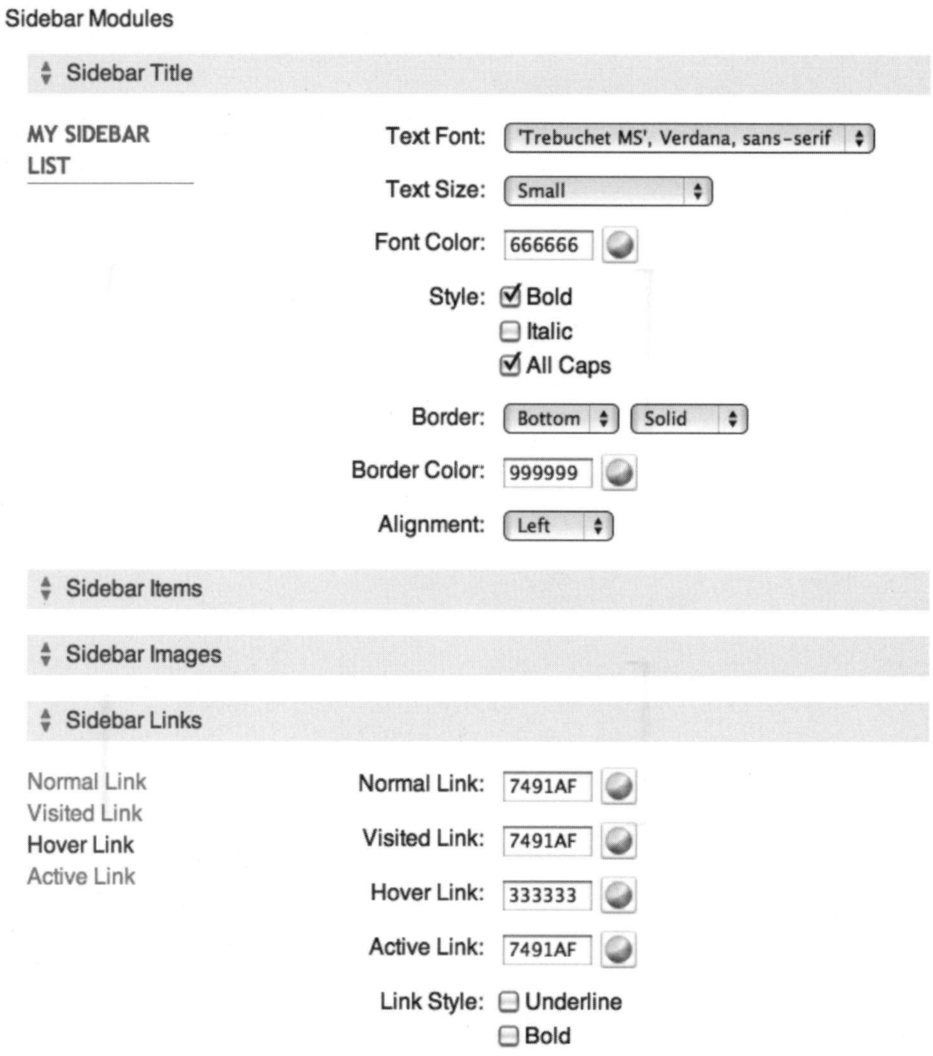

Sidebar Modules

Figure 5–11. Setting link colors in Theme Builder's Sidebar Modules area

17. In my example, I changed the Text Size in the Sidebar Title to Small as I thought Extra Small was too hard to read. You might want to do the same in Sidebar Items.

18. In Sidebar Links I changed the link colors to match those of the General Settings, using the same blue and dark gray.

19. Under Link Style I removed the Bold and Underline.

20. After you have finished customizing the different elements, click on Apply This Design to Creative Blogging (of course, the name of the blog will be your blog's name, not Creative Blogging). You only have to click this once because we just changed the design to Theme Builder from the original template chosen back in Chapter 3 when you first created your TypePad blog.

21. Click on Save Changes (which you should do every time you make any design changes).

22. Click View Blog to look at your new layout (see Figure 5–12).

Figure 5–12. *Viewing the blog after Theme Builder changes*

If you want to make any other changes, you are still in Theme Builder and can simply click on one of the headings again, such as General Settings. After making any changes, remember to click on Save Changes.

You can also change the number of columns in your blog and where they appear on the layout (to the right, to the left, one sidebar on each side) in the Layouts area under Design. In the Content area is where you see a visual representation of your blog (similar to Blogger's Page Elements screen). There you can drag and drop elements to a new location. Be sure to click Save Changes if you do change Layout or Content settings. We will use the Custom CSS area later in this book and you will learn how to use CSS to customize your blog further, in ways you can't with the Theme Builder. Note that you will only see the Custom CSS area if you are using the TypePad Unlimited or higher package.

The WordPress Appearance Menu

In WordPress, you can change elements of the theme you chose under the Appearance menu in the Dashboard. The options available to be modified differ from theme to theme. I used the zBench theme in my example.

Although it's easy to install a new banner and change the background color in WordPress, the results are a little unpredictable and may be misleading until you click Visit Your Site while experimenting.

Unfortunately, WordPress doesn't have as many noncoding options as the other two platforms. In fact, there are just a few limited options under the Appearance menu. Much customization has to be done in CSS (such as post title, link colors, and column widths), which requires an upgrade ($14.97 USD a year). Nevertheless, in the next exercise, we will customize the look of your WordPress blog using the Appearance menu!

EXERCISE – USING WORDPRESS'S APPEARANCE

In this exercise, you will install a banner and adjust your blog's background color.

1. After logging into WordPress, click on My Blog Menu, then Dashboard.

2. From the Dashboard, click on Appearance (on the left).

3. Click on Header to install a new banner. For the template I chose for this example, the banner size is defined as 960x200px. (So if you are using WordPress and plan to have a custom banner designed by a graphic designer, be sure to check this area for the dimension needed for whatever theme/template you choose.)

4. Click Browse, select the banner file from your computer, and click Open.

5. Click Upload.

6. In my example I chose No under the Header Text area as my custom banner has text (the Blog Title) in the actual image. You could choose Yes and then simply upload a background image for the banner. See Figure 5–13.

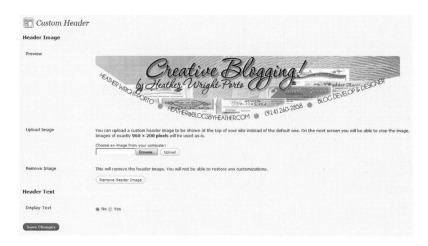

Figure 5–13. Custom Header in WordPress Appearance

7. Click Save Changes. Your banner is installed. Next we'll change the background color of your blog as we did in Blogger and Typepad.

8. Under Appearance, click on Background. Here you can install a custom background image; however, we'll do that later in this book.

9. Under Display Options I entered the hexadecimal color code for the blue I've been using (shown in Figure 5–14). You can also click on the Select a Color text link to use a color wheel, or you can get the color value from your designer.

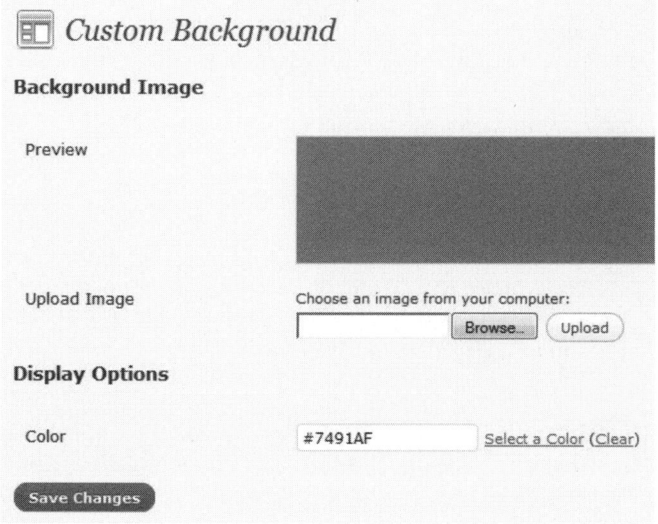

Custom Background

Background Image

Preview

Upload Image
Choose an image from your computer:
[   ] (Browse...) (Upload)

Display Options

Color
[#7491AF] Select a Color ([Clear])

(Save Changes)

Figure 5–14. Custom Background in WordPress Appearance

10. Click Save Changes.

11. Click Visit Your Site (at the top). Notice in Figure 5–15 that with the zBench template I was using, this color change does not work—it changes the entire body of the template, not just the background area. Therefore, I'll set the background color back to white, shown in Figure 5–16. One thing you can do to overcome this limitation is to download the P2 theme by Automattic (`http://p2theme.com/`). With P2 you can change the background color just as you've seen with Blogger and TypePad where the main posting and sidebar areas stay white.

Figure 5–15. Background Color applied in WordPress Appearance

Figure 5–16. *Custom Background removed in WordPress Appearance*

Again, please note that, depending on the template chosen, the background may or may not look as desired when you click Visit Your Site, and the options available under Custom Background may differ by Theme chosen as well.

Later in this book we will see how to customize a template, like the one I chose, using CSS code instead of choosing another template.

I would like to encourage you to experiment with different themes, and then to revisit the Header and Background areas under Appearance to see how the options and settings change. Not all templates allow you to add a custom banner, while others do but use different sizes.

Summary

I really hope you had fun experimenting with the design of your blog and installing a new look! Each platform allows for some customization, and we installed a custom banner on each of them. You may design your own banner, hire a professional graphic designer, find an online source, or take a picture to use in your banner. No matter which you choose, a custom banner goes a long way toward making your blog look just as you want.

In Blogger, you add a banner in the Design area of the blog under Page Elements, not in the Template Designer. However, we used the Template Designer to change the color scheme (the color of the Post Title and Links as well as the Background Color), and to adjust the widths of the columns based on the banner installed.

In TypePad, we changed the banner, color scheme, and column widths within the Theme Builder.

In WordPress we ended up just installing a new banner after realizing that changing the background color did not work with the chosen zBench template. Keep in mind that when modifying a WordPress design, options available for customization depend on the chosen theme.

As I keep saying, I hope you continue experimenting with your blog's settings to find the look that exactly suits your taste and blog purpose. In the next chapter we'll discuss how to set up a custom domain, so you see your own name (or whatever you prefer) rather than "Blogspot," "Typepad," or "WordPress" in the blog's address.

CHAPTER 6

■ ■ ■

Setting Up a Custom Domain

At this point I hope you have been using one or more of the blogging platforms we've been exploring; Blogger, TypePad, and WordPress. In writing this book, I've created one blog for each of these platforms: creativebloggingbyapress.blogspot.com, creativeblogging.typepad.com, and creativebloggingwithwordpress.wordpress.com. However, I want the name of my example blog for this book not to be tied to a particular platform, and instead to simply reflect the association with Apress, my publisher, so I will register a custom domain called www.creativebloggingwithapress.com. Chances are, at some point you're going to want a custom domain for your blog!

If you don't already have a domain name registered, you can purchase one through domain registrars like GoDaddy, Network Solutions, or Yahoo! Small Business (and there are many more). In this chapter, we purchase one through GoDaddy, and then go through the steps showing how to use this new domain with Blogger, TypePad, and WordPress. If you already have a domain through another registrar, I would be happy to help you map that domain to your blog, and you may contact me via e-mail (heather@blogsbyheather.com). However, the instructions will be similar to those described in this chapter in that you need to modify a CNAME record in a domain manager or zone file manager if you're using a Blogger or Typepad blog; or modify a nameserver if you're using a WordPress blog.

Don't worry! We'll be reviewing what these terms mean—domain name, domain registrar, CNAME, and nameserver—below and in the upcoming exercises.

Terminology

You don't have to be a technically savvy person to be able to set up and map your domain name to your existing blog. However, it helps to understand the terms used in the following exercises.

- Domain name: This is the name you would like for your blog. In my example, the domain name is CreativeBloggingWithApress.com (note that capitalization makes no difference in a domain name).

- Domain: This refers to the last section of your domain name. The most common one is ".com," which is derived from the word "commercial". The ".net" domain suffix is likely second in popularity and derived for "network." The ".org," ".gov," and ".edu" suffixes are also common domains; ".org" is typically used for nonprofit organizations; ".gov" for government offices; and ".edu" for educational facilities, universities, or programs. Another popular domain type uses the country code suffix, such as co.uk for a site from the United Kingdom, or .fr for a French site.

- Domain registrars: These are companies (like Go Daddy and many others) that sell, host, and manage domain names for you for an annual fee. Basically, you purchase the domain name to use for your web site or blog for a specific period of time, such as 1 year, 2-5 years, or more.

To apply these terms to my example, in the upcoming exercises I'll document how to set up an account with GoDaddy, a domain registrar company, and purchase a domain. The domain I'll purchase is a .com domain with the name CreativeBloggingWithApress.com.

I will then modify the settings in the CreativeBloggingWithApress.com domain manager (which some registrars refer to as a zone file manager) to demonstrate how you use it with your Blogger, TypePad, or WordPress blog. At that time I will discuss the CNAME and nameserver terms.

Purchasing a Domain

In the exercise below we'll go through the process of setting up a GoDaddy account and purchasing our domain name. Then we'll review the steps involved in making this domain work with your blog, a process known as mapping. What is "mapping" in this case? It is configuring blog and domain settings so your blog uses the name of your new domain instead of the default Blogspot, TypePad, or WordPress address.

My blog originally had the address heatherporto.typepad.com. I then purchased the domain name www.BlogsByHeather.com and mapped it to that TypePad blog. Now when you click on any post or page on my site, it will be in the form of http://www.blogsbyheather.com/2010/12/happy-holidays.html instead of http://heatherporto.typepad.com/2010/12/happy-holidays.html.

EXERCISE – PURCHASE A DOMAIN THROUGH GODADDY

Using a domain name is not a requirement of owning and operating a blog, but it is something bloggers often want. Not only do they not like the blogspot, typepad, or wordpress in their blog address, they feel it's more professional to use a custom domain that appears as if it truly belongs to them, especially if they plan to create business cards or advertising for their blog. So let's see how to do this.

1. Begin at GoDaddy's site, www.GoDaddy.com as shown in Figure 6–1.

Figure 6–1. GoDaddy's home page

2. In the middle of the screen you'll see a search box where you can begin typing in the name you'd like to use for your blog. If the name is not available (and a lot of names have already been taken, so don't be surprised if you can't get your first choice), GoDaddy will suggest alternatives (see Figure 6–2), or you can continue typing in and searching for other names until you find one that suits your blog (or the business, fundraiser, event, or other purpose it showcases).

Figure 6–2. As you can see, the `CreativeBlogging.com` *domain is already taken.*

3. Under the message that says `CreativeBlogging.com` is already taken, I next typed in `CreativeBloggingWithApress.com` and click Search. That domain is available (see Figure 6–3).

145

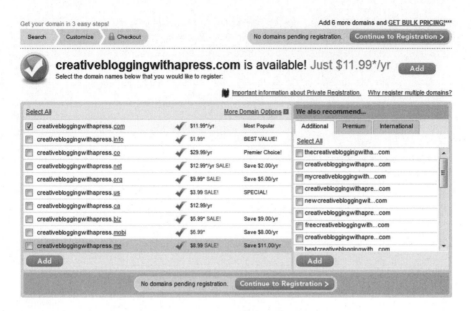

Figure 6–3. CreativeBloggingWithApress.com is available

4. Click Add.

5. Another window will open, letting you know the domain is pending registration and that you can continue to add 5 more to get bulk pricing. (We will not add other domains in this example.)

6. Click Continue to Registration.

7. You will see another GoDaddy ad about savings if you purchase additional domains. At the bottom, check "Don't show this again."

8. Click on No Thanks.

9. On the next screen, complete the registration form (shown in Figure 6–4) and click Next.

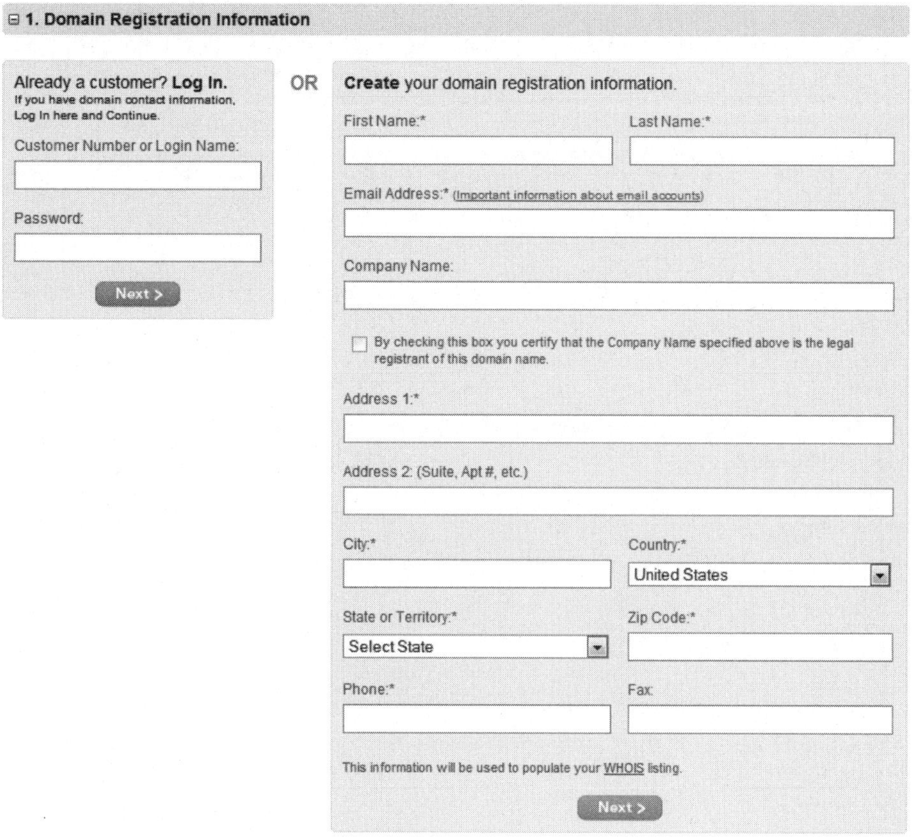

Figure 6–4. *The domain registration form*

10. On the next screen, Your Domain Settings (Figure 6–5), you can view or edit your domain name(s), select a Registration Length, verify or edit your Registration Contact, and choose to certify your domain (which allows you to show a Certified Website Seal on your site to let visitors know you are who you say your are). You can just leave it as Uncertified.

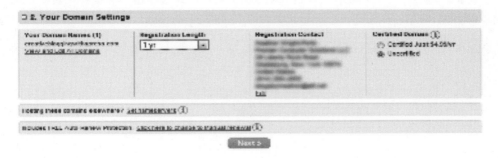

Figure 6–5. Entering your domain settings

11. Click Next.

12. Decide if you want protection or not (Figure 6–6). In my example, I left the standard option and clicked Next.

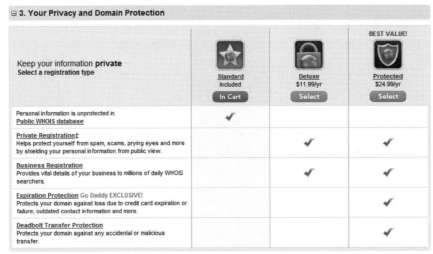

Figure 6–6. Privacy and Domain Protection

13. On the screen shown in Figure 6–7, you don't have to choose anything more if you are just purchasing this domain to be used with your blog. Note that the domain includes one free e-mail address (such as Heather@CreativeBloggingWithApress.com). Click Next.

Figure 6–7. Activate Your Domain

14. Review your shopping cart (see the example in Figure 6–8).

15. Click Continue to Checkout.

Figure 6–8. Reviewing your shopping cart

16. Next, enter your account and login information; choose whether to answer the survey; and, in the section numbered four (not shown in Figure 6–9), whether you want to receive e-mail updates from GoDaddy.

Figure 6–9. Entering account information

17. Click Continue to Checkout and then enter your billing information in the next screen (see Figure 6–10). In this example, I chose PayPal but you can enter credit card information instead.

Figure 6–10. *Entering billing information*

18. When you're finished, click Place Order Now.

19. You will receive a "thank you for your order" type of message.

Congratulations! You have now purchased a domain name to use with your new blog!

The steps in purchasing a domain name with GoDaddy are the same regardless of which blog platform you are using; Blogger, TypePad or WordPress. Alternatively, in Blogger and WordPress, you can purchase a domain directly from them. In Blogger, from the Dashboard, go to Settings ➤ Publishing and you can Buy a Domain. In WordPress, from the Dashboard, go to Upgrades ➤ Add a Domain. If the domain name you want is available, you can continue with its registration. However, I recommend using GoDaddy or other registrant, as it is easier to modify the nameservers or DNS Manager if you happen to change your blog's location; such as if you move from Blogger to Typepad, or simply want to point to another blog, web site or other online group.

In the following exercises, we'll go through the steps necessary to map your blog to your new domain.

Domain Mapping with Blogger

In order to perform the mapping, that is to setup your new domain to work with a Blogger blog, you need to modify the CNAME record in the Domain Manager in GoDaddy and then also modify the Publish settings within Blogger. It is important that you change the settings in GoDaddy first, and then modify those in Blogger.

■ **Note** CNAME record stands for Canonical Name record; that is, it is a record that informs the Domain Name System (DNS) that the domain name is an alias and what the alias is (in our case a blog).

EXERCISE – DOMAIN MAPPING WITH BLOGGER AND GODADDY

This exercise includes both sets of steps needed to complete the domain mapping: the settings you'll need to first enter in GoDaddy, and then those required to complete the mapping in Blogger.

At this point, you have registered a domain name with GoDaddy as instructed in the previous exercise. We will continue here by logging into your new GoDaddy account. (If you already had an existing domain, the steps will be similar, but you'll use its domain manager or zone file manager or equivalent DNS manager.)

1. Go to www.GoDaddy.com.

2. At the top of the page, log in using your Log In ID# as shown Figure 6–9 (from when you entered your Account and Login Information) and your password.

3. Click the black arrowhead to login.

4. Within your account, under Domains you'll see your newly purchased domain (CreativeBloggingWithApress.com in my example), as shown in Figure 6–11.

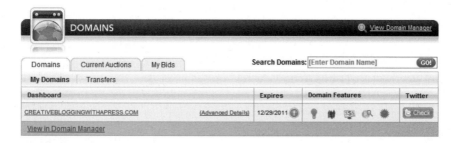

Figure 6–11. Your new domain

5. Click the View in Domain Manager link.

6. Click on your Domain Name (in my example, CreativeBloggingWithApress.com).

7. A Domain Details screen will appear. We need to go to the DNS Manager section (see Figure 6–12).

DNS Manager

DNS Manager: (Available)
A	@	68.178.232.100
CNAME	e	email.secureserver.net
CNAME	email	email.secureserver.net
CNAME	ftp	@
MX	@	mailstore1.secureserver.net
MX	@	smtp.secureserver.net

Launch

Figure 6–12. DNS Manager in Domain Details

8. Click on Launch.

9. Under the Zone File Editor, in the CNAME (Alias) area (see Figure 6–13), look at the bottom where you see "www" and click on the "@" symbol as highlighted in Figure 6–13.

Figure 6–13. *Zone File Editor*

10. Replace the "@" with "ghs.google.com" and then click on the Saved button at the top. With this step you are basically setting an alias so that if someone types www.<your domain name>.com it will point to "ghs.google.com."

11. The Saved button changes to Save Zone File. Click on that.

12. A message will pop up that your zone file was saved successfully. Click OK.

13. You can now log out of GoDaddy and log in to your Blogger account.

14. Within Blogger, go to Settings ➤ Publishing.

15. Click on Custom Domain.

16. Since you've already purchased your domain, simply click on Switch to Advanced Settings (as shown in the upper right area of Figure 6–14).

Publish on a custom domain

Switch to: • blogspot.com (Blogger's free hosting service)

Buy a domain for your blog

Already own a domain? <u>Switch to advanced settings</u>
Use our <u>Getting Started Guide</u>!

**What address would you
like your blog to have?**

http://www. [   ] .com [▼]   **CHECK AVAILABILITY**

Google Checkout 🛒
VISA MasterCard AMEX DISCOVER

Domains are registered through a Google partner and cost $10 (USD) for
one year. As part of registration, you will also get a <u>Google Apps</u> account
for your new domain.

We won't leave your readers behind!
http://creativebloggingbyapress.blogspot.com will redirect to
your custom domain.

Word Verification

makijsv

[   ] ♿

Type the characters you see in the picture.

***Figure 6–14.** Publish on a custom domain*

17. Enter your new domain name, including the leading "www," such as
    "www.CreativeBloggingWithApress.com." Then type in the Word Verification.

18. Click on Save Settings as shown in Figure 6–15.

19. Refresh the page and then click on the check box next to "Redirect
    creativebloggingwithapress.com to
    www.creativebloggingwithapress.com."

20. Enter the Word Verification again and then Save Settings again.

21. Click on View Blog— and your domain is working!

Advanced Settings

Need a domain? **Buy one now**

Your Domain   http:// `www.creativebloggingwithapress.com`   (Ex: `blog.example.com`)

Your domain must be properly registered first. (setup instructions)

We won't leave your readers behind!
`http://creativebloggingbyapress.blogspot.com` will redirect to
your custom domain.

Use a missing files host?   ○ Yes ● No

If you specify a missing files host, Blogger will look there if it cannot find a
specified file on your regular domain. Learn more

Word Verification

imakijsv

`imakijsv`   ♿

Type the characters you see in the picture.

SAVE SETTINGS

Figure 6–15. Advanced Settings

Visitors can now get to your blog using either the original Blogspot address or the new domain (so you will not lose any followers)!

Domain Mapping with TypePad

In TypePad, in order to map your new domain to your blog, you need to change both TypePad and GoDaddy settings as we did in Blogger. However, this time you start this process in TypePad and then go to GoDaddy and modify the CNAME record. So, let's log in to TypePad first and make the necessary changes to our account settings, then log in to GoDaddy and modify the CNAME record in the Domain Manager or Zone File Editor.

EXERCISE – DOMAIN MAPPING WITH TYPEPAD AND GODADDY

This exercise includes the instructions to update your account settings and map your new domain in both TypePad and GoDaddy.

1. Sign in to TypePad.

2. Click on Account (on the top right of your screen).

3. From the available options on the left, click on Domain Mapping.

4. Click the button labeled "Begin Here: Map a Domain Name."

5. In the Domain Mapping area, shown in Figure 6–16, enter your custom domain name where indicated (I've entered `www.creativebloggingwithapress.com`) and then select your blog in the "Map this custom domain name to:" area. If you have more than one blog, be sure to use the drop-down box to select the correct blog to map it to.

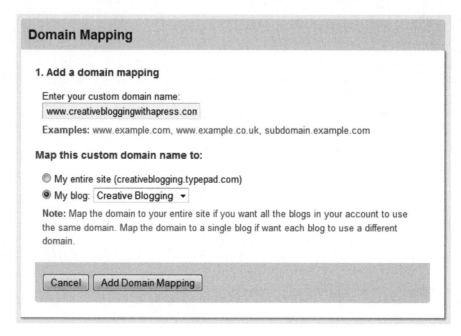

Figure 6–16. *Mapping your custom domain*

6. Click Add Domain Mapping.

7. Next configure your domain's DNS record as shown in Figure 6–17. Here you'll see the TypePad address you'll need when you modify the CNAME record in GoDaddy, in the "Points to:" line (creativeblogging.typepad.com, in this example). TypePad automatically creates the record under Domain Mappings (see Figure 6–17). You don't have to modify this at all. Later you will simply Activate it.

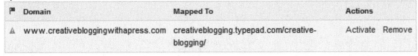

Domain Mapping

2. Configure your domain's DNS record

The next step is to configure the DNS record for your domain with the recommended DNS settings below. We've provided shortcuts to some common domain registrars below (you will have to sign in at their site if you haven't already).

CNAME Record
Domain: **www.creativebloggingwithapress.com**
Points to: **creativeblogging.typepad.com**

Here is a list of several popular registrars you may have registered with:
- pairNIC
- GoDaddy
- Network Solutions
- Dotster

Once you have configured the DNS record for your domain and your custom domain points to your site, blog, or album, return to this page and activate your domain mapping from the table below.

[Map Another Domain Name]

Domain Mappings

Note: Do not activate your domain until you are sure that the domain's DNS record has been updated.

⚑ Domain	Mapped To	Actions
⚠ www.creativebloggingwithapress.com	creativeblogging.typepad.com/creative-blogging/	Activate Remove

Figure 6–17. Domain Mapping and Domain Mappings

8. Log in to GoDaddy.

9. Follow the same steps (and look at the screenshots) in the Exercise–Domain Mapping with Blogger and GoDaddy: steps 1-9, Figures 6–11 through 6–13.

10. When modifying the CNAME record in the Zone File Editor, replace the "@" with whatever TypePad had in the Points To line shown in Figure 6–17 (in the CNAME Record). In my example, this was creativeblogging.typepad.com.

11. Click on the Saved button at the top.

12. Click on Save Zone File.

13. You'll see a message that your zone file has been saved.

14. Click OK.

15. Now, look at the bottom half of Figure 6–17 under Domain Mappings. You will see the new mapping you created. You should wait at least 24 hours before coming back here and clicking Activate.

16. You can then View Blog and see that your domain is active.

Caution: If you View Blog and your blog does not look normal, or looks unformatted, it means GoDaddy has not finished updating the CNAME change and you should go back to the Domain Mappings screen shown in Figure 6–17 and click Deactivate, then retry on another day. For most of my customers, 24 hours is sufficient, but I've had a few who have had to wait days and one who had to wait a week. This was due to GoDaddy and not something that was done "wrong." I just wanted to let you know in case you encounter a delay.

Domain Mapping with WordPress

Blogger and TypePad had very similar processes for mapping a domain using GoDaddy, in that they both involved modifying the CNAME record in the DNS Manager area. However, WordPress requires that you modify the nameservers (the name of the servers where your domain is hosted). So, in the next exercise, we will first modify the nameservers at GoDaddy and then make changes in WordPress.

Please note that updating the nameservers with GoDaddy may take 24-72 hours, and that to map your domain in WordPress, you need to go to Upgrades and pay $12.00.

EXERCISE – DOMAIN MAPPING WITH WORDPRESS AND GODADDY

This exercise contains two sets of instructions; those needed in GoDaddy and those needed in WordPress to complete the domain mapping. Due to the difference in instruction, I used the domain name CreativeBloggingByApress.com in this example.

1. Log in to GoDaddy and follow the same steps (and look at the screenshots) in the Exercise–Domain Mapping with Blogger and GoDaddy: steps 1-9, Figures 6–11 through 6–13.

2. From within the Zone File Editor, click on Set Nameservers (see Figure 6–18).

Nameservers

Nameservers: (Last Update 12/29/2010)
NS01.DOMAINCONTROL.COM
NS02.DOMAINCONTROL.COM

Set Nameservers

Figure 6–18. The Nameservers section of the Zone Editor

3. Select "I have specific nameservers for my domains" and then modify Nameserver 1 and Nameserver 2 as shown in Figure 6–19 (NS1.WORDPRESS.COM and NS2.WORDPRESS.COM respectively).

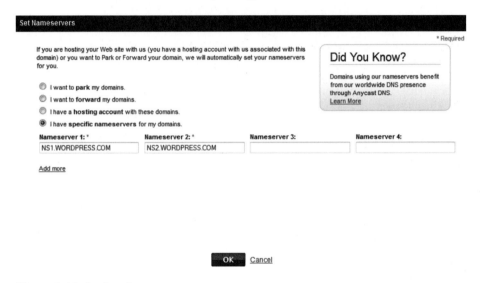

Figure 6–19. Setting the nameservers

4. Click OK and you'll receive a message about allowing a few minutes for the changes to take effect. Click OK again.

5. Log out of GoDaddy.

6. After allowing 24-72 hours for GoDaddy to process the change, log in to WordPress. Yes, I know it says a few minutes when you make the change in GoDaddy, but you will get an e-mail from GoDaddy that says they received the request to change the nameservers and to wait 24-72 hours.

7. From My Blog at the top of WordPress.com, click on Dashboard.

8. Then click on Upgrades and, under Add a Domain, pay the $12.00 needed to map the domain.

Figure 6–20. Add a Domain

9. Click Buy Now and the Domains screen shown in Figure 6–21 appears. We do not need to do the Registration, as we did not purchase it through WordPress and simply need to pay the $12 to map the domain.

Figure 6–21. Domains

10. Enter your new domain (for me, `creativebloggingbyapress.com`) in the Add a Domain area.

11. Click Add Domain to Blog button.

12. On the next screen, it lets you know you can add the domain for $12.00 per year.

13. Click Map Domain.

Figure 6–22. Mapping a domain in WordPress

14. In the next screen, choose a payment method. In this example, I again used my PayPal account, but you can use a credit card if you prefer (see Figure 6–23). If so, you will be prompted to enter your credit card and billing information.

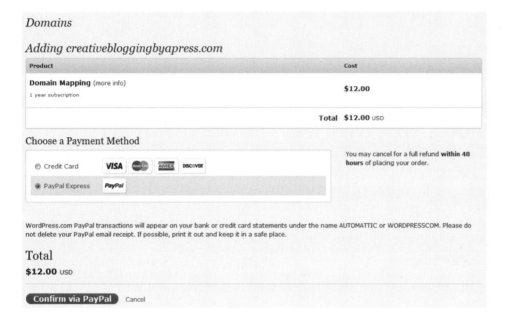

Figure 6–23. Paying to map your domain

15. I clicked on Confirm via PayPal. If using a credit card, you'd click "Purchase Domain Mapping."

16. Once you've purchased the domain, the Domains area of WordPress is updated, as shown in Figure 6–24, where you can now select your new domain and set it as the Primary Domain.

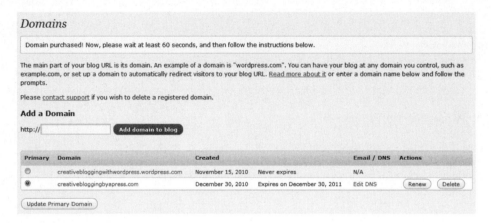

Figure 6–24. *Updating the primary domain*

17. Click on Update Primary Domain.

18. Click on the My Blog menu and then Read Blog to view your blog using your new domain name, or just open a new browser window and type in the domain. In my example, it's `http://creativebloggingbyapress.com`.

Summary

Do you need a custom domain? No. It is not required. However, many people want their own domain, especially for marketing purposes. They don't want the "Blogspot," "TypePad," or "WordPress" to be part of their blog address when publicizing their site, creating advertisements, or preparing marketing materials. In the exercises in this chapter, we used GoDaddy. However, there are many domain registrars you can purchase a domain name from. The steps in mapping a domain will be very similar and the steps on the Typepad, Blogger, or WordPress side will remain the same as those described.

Alternatively, you can purchase a domain directly from Blogger and WordPress. However, I recommend using GoDaddy or other registrant as it is easier to move your blog from one location to another or point to another blog.

Moreover, when using Typepad and Blogger, if you want to map the "non-www" versions of your domain (such as `CreativeBloggingWithApress.com`), then while in the Zone File Editor, under Domain Information, click Forwarding. Then simply enter your domain name with the "www" prefix, save changes, and you're all set. Now you can either use `www.CreativeBloggingWithApress.com` or `CreativeBloggingWithApress.com` (without the leading "www").

Now that you've created your blog, uploaded images and videos, played with the blog's layout and design, and know how to use a custom domain with your blog, in the next chapter, we'll discuss how to drive traffic to your site and how to improve your online visibility!

CHAPTER 7

■ ■ ■

Increasing Traffic & Visitor Tracking

This chapter is a hot one! Whether you are creating your blog for personal use or to help promote and build your business, you want to keep readers coming back. Moreover, you want your blog to be found in the first place! In this chapter we'll review tools, applications, gadgets, and tips to use to get your blog noticed, and to let you keep track of what's going on.

How are blogs found? Like web sites, they are generally found by someone searching for something, using a search engine like Google or Bing. There are techniques for making it more likely your blog will be found in such a search; this process is known as search engine optimization (SEO). And it is a kind of process where the more people visit and the more pages they visit, the more popular your blog becomes because search engine algorithms use visitor counts and page views (which we'll discuss in more detail) to help rank your site.In this chapter we look at some methods to help drive more traffic to your site and to build your online visibility. We'll see how to use keywords and meta tags; install feed subscriptions, share buttons, and gadgets, and take advantage of many Google applications to help increase your blog's online presence.

In addition, you will see how to track visitor activity and use that information to better focus your marketing efforts or to find out what most interests your readers. Let's get started!

Search Engine Optimization

Search Engine Optimization (SEO) is one of the best ways to boost your blog's online presence. SEO is the process of improving the chances that not only will your blog show up in a search, it'll show high up in a search—if not in the first five results, then at least on the first page. This involves many techniques, the installation of various tools and applications, and does not happen overnight. In short, there is no waving of a magic wand, unfortunately. However, here are a bunch of tips to get us started and to brainstorm about ways to help improve your ranking:

- Be patient and realistic. To increase your online presence and popularity takes time and more importantly, takes effort! You'll want to keep working on it, day after day, following the advice and tips you will find throughout this chapter.

- Be consistent and realistic. Don't make it a chore that you have to do every day if that's too much for you. Instead, make it a "task" and one that you can achieve— daily, weekly, twice a week—whatever schedule is realistic and attainable. You have to make it fit your lifestyle, but you do have to make the time to blog!

- Keep these tips in mind when posting:

    - Post consistently and regularly.

    - Post about relevant content and be sure to include keywords in your post.

    - Write about what interests your readers, something they'll enjoy and want to share with others.

    - Label each post with keywords (labels in Blogger, categories in TypePad and WordPress).

    - Place keywords in the post title. Try not to use "fluff" words like The, Great, Good.

    - Keep the title short, less than 40 characters.

    - Be sure to have share buttons on your blog, under your posts.

- Use titles and alternate text for images. As you're creating a post and inserting images, go to the HTML view (Edit HTML, or HTML in WordPress) and insert a Title for the image and Alt (alternate) properties, such as `<img src="http://heatherporto.typepad.com/blogsbyheathersignature.gif" title="Blogs By Heather" alt="Blogs By Heather Signature">`.

- Visit and post on other sites or online groups and communities. Join online groups, such as Yahoo groups in your specialty. Comment regularly on those sites and use your blog's address in your signature. Ask to be a guest author or featured blogger on another's site. It may be worth doing this free of charge in exchange for a link back to your blog. Increasing the number of links back to your blog helps improve your visibility on the Web.

- Socialize! Use Facebook and Twitter to help build your presence, and reach even more people who would not have found you otherwise. Use Facebook's "Find Friends" capabilities to help you reach out to new, potential followers. Have your blog posts automatically post to your Facebook page or Twitter account (to be covered in the next chapter).

- Take advantage of Google's search and tracking Tools—Google AdWords, Google Webmaster Tools, Google Site Submission, and Google Analytics (all to be discussed in this chapter). You can also use (and pay) other sites to submit your blog to search engines monthly. I've used `www.EnterURL.com`, but there are many others out there as well. And there are some where you download the software and submit your site to search engines yourself. One of these I can highly recommend is Dynamic Submission (`www.apexpromotion.com/ad/dynamic_submission.htm`).

- Consider purchasing online or print advertisements to help promote your company and site, such as Facebook Ads, ad space (such as a banner ad) on other related or popular sites, or print ads in magazines or local newspapers. Yes, this is costly but may help increase your blog and company exposure.

- Make sure to use your blog's URL (address) in your e-mail signature. This way everyone you e-mail has a link to your site!

- Use a newsletter to direct traffic to your site. Simply create articles and include a "Click here to learn more" link that goes to a post or page on your blog.

- Post often. Posting to your blog consistently and on a regular basis (a few times a week) has proven to increase popularity and traffic to your blog. This is because your subscribers get your posts and may forward them to friends who then may subscribe to or visit your blog; visitors may comment on your blog posts or link to them from their site; or they may use the social networking share buttons to share your information with their Facebook fans, Twitter followers, or MySpace friends. So, as you can see, a post may travel far and be seen by many!

Keywords

Keywords are the important words that best describe your blog or blog post. For example, my business and blog is about blogging and providing help on Blogger, TypePad, WordPress, Constant Contact Newsletter design, and more. If I were creating a post on where to add meta tags and a description to a TypePad blog, the keywords I'd use in the post and note at the bottom of the post editor would be "TypePad Meta Tags, Meta Tags, Meta Description, SEO, SEO for TypePad."

The reason for using keywords in the actual post, as well as in the Keyword area in TypePad's post editor, for example, is to improve my ranking when someone searches for "SEO for TypePad" in Google. I want my blog and my tutorial to appear towards the top of the search results so people will find me.

It is also a good idea to include keywords in the post title if possible. That will help potential customers who are searching for those keywords find you on the Internet. The ultimate goal in using keywords is to have a search engine, like Google, rank your site on the first or second page of search engine results.

Although it's important to use keywords, it is just as important not to overuse them. If you do, your site will be flagged as "spam" and won't show up at all on result pages. My recommendation is to keep your keyword usage to 4-8 percent. So out of 100 words, you should only use a keyword 4 to 8 times.

Meta Tags

A meta tag is a line of HTML code that describes your site. It used to be the case that you placed meta tags at the top of every web page; one meta tag for keywords, another for a description. Although they would not be seen by viewers of your web page, search engines used them. Here's what they look like (using Creative Blogging as an example):

```
<HEAD>
<TITLE>Creative Blogging</TITLE>
<META name ="description" content="Use your creativity to create and design a new blog,
find tips on how to organize your blog, set up a custom domain, learn how to use images
and videos, setup a blog store, integrate with Twitter and Facebook, learn basic HTML and
CSS, and how to be found on the Web!">
<META name ="keywords" content="Creative Blogging, Blogging, Blog Help, Create a Blog,
Blog Store, Blog images, Blog video">
</HEAD>
```

As we just noted, keywords are words that best describe your business's or blog's purpose. The description contains keywords but in a sentence-like format. So if someone used Google to search for one of your keywords and you were listed on the search results page, the meta description would appear under your listing, giving the user a brief summary of your business.

However, because so many people abused meta keywords, many search engines don't use the meta tags in their algorithms anymore. Still, it doesn't hurt to put them on your blog!

- The free version of WordPress.com doesn't allow you to add meta tags.

- In Blogger, you can copy and paste the META tags (lines of code such as those shown above) into the Edit HTML screen (Dashboard➤Design➤Edit HTML), in the <HEAD> area, below the Title as shown above.

- In TypePad, go to Dashboard ➤ Settings ➤ SEO and enter your Meta Keywords and Meta Description.

Next we'll see how some Google applications can help improve your site's ranking. These are Google Site Submission, Google Webmaster Tools, Google Places, and Google AdWords. Most of Google's tools are free, but you do have to pay for Google AdWords and we'll look at that shortly.

Google Site Submission

This is a quick and easy step to get your site listed in Google's index (although Google states that "…we cannot make any predictions or guarantees about when or if they will appear"). However, I recommend it as one of the first steps in getting your blog known in cyberspace. It's free and takes just a few seconds.

EXERCISE – ADD YOUR SITE TO GOOGLE

One of the first steps in getting your site listed on the web is to submit it to Google to be included in their index.

1. Go to `www.google.com/addurl` as shown in Figure 7–1.

Figure 7–1. *Adding your site to Google*

2. Enter your blog's address in the URL field, including the `http://` prefix, such as `http://creativebloggingwithwordpress.wordpress.com` (or I could use the new domain, `http://www.creativebloggingbyapress.com`).

3. In the Comments field, enter a short description of your site and some keywords. In this example I entered "Creative Blogging, Apress, Heather Wright-Porto, blogging, create a blog, blog help."

4. Enter in the CAPTCHA (Completely Automated Public Turing test to tell Computers and Humans Apart) characters, such as the distorted "deurshle" in my example, shown in Figure 7–1.

5. Click Add URL to complete your submission.

6. You're done. You will not receive a message that you have successfully completed the submission, but you have.

■ **Note** CAPTCHA is a program used to generate distorted and twisted characters to be typed in to make sure the visitor is a human. A human can pass this type of test (although I have difficulty at times), but a computer can't. Its primary purpose is to prevent or reduce spam or false or fraudulent entries.

Google Webmaster Tools

Google Webmaster Tools is another great free tool whose purpose is to help you improve your site's ranking in search results. It also offers detailed reports on your blog page's visibility on Google. I discuss the various types of reports after the exercise, such as the number of search queries that returned your site in search results over the last 30 days and how many clicks it received, or a list of external sites linking to yours, or a list of the most significant keywords found on your site.

EXERCISE – SETTING UP GOOGLE WEBMASTER TOOLS

The next step in increasing your visibility is to see where you are currently and then review and use the detailed reports provided by Google to improve your site. But first, you need to set up Google Webmaster.

1. Go to www.google.com/webmasters/tools.

2. Log in to Google if you are not currently signed in (see Figure 7–2).

    a. If you created a Blogger blog back in Chapter 3, this would be your Blogger login (as Blogger is owned by Google and you needed a Google account to complete that exercise).

    b. If you do not have a Google account, simply click on Create An Account Now. Then enter your e-mail address, set a password, choose a location (country), enter your birthday, enter the Word Verification and click the "I accept, create my account" button.

Figure 7–2. Signing in to your Google account

3. After entering your Google Account login information and clicking Sign In, you then enter Google Webmaster Central (see Figure 7–3), where you verify any sites associated with your Google Account.

   a. Notice in my example that when I logged into the Google account I used for this book, it appears verified (under Verification). This is because in Chapter 6 I set up a custom domain (www.creativebloggingwithapress.com) to use with my Blogger blog and in doing so verified that I was the owner of the blog.

Figure 7–3. Google WebMaster Tools

   b. You, however, may instead see the Verify This Site button shown in Figure 7–4, so we will walk through the steps of verifying your site— that is, to verify you are the owner of your blog.

Figure 7–4. An unverified site

c. Click on Verify This Site and the Verification screen appears. You have a few different ways of verifying ownership of your blog. We discuss two different methods (one for Blogger and WordPress, and then a different method for TypePad).

Using Blogger

Select the second option, highlighted in Figure 7–5. In Blogger, click on Design from the Dashboard, and then Edit HTML. Then copy and paste the HTML code provided, as shown in the example in Figure 7–5. Find the <head> tag and paste the code beneath it. Click Save Changes.

Figure 7–5. Verify Ownership By Adding Meta Tag

Using WordPress

Using the same method (Add a meta tag…), from the Dashboard, click on Tools. Then under Webmaster Tools Verification, in the textbox for Google Webmaster Tools, enter only the large key (the group of characters following the `content=` and surrounded by single quotes, as shown in Figure 7–6). Click Save Changes.

Tools
Tools
Import
Export
Delete Site
Settings
Webmaster Tools Verification (?)
Enter your meta key "content" value to verify your blog with Google Webmaster Tools, Yahoo! Site Explorer, and Bing Webmaster Center
Google Webmaster Tools
Example:
Yahoo! Site Explorer
Example:
Bing Webmaster Center
Example:
Save Changes

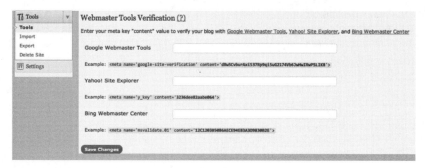

Figure 7–6. Verifying ownership in WordPress

Using TypePad

Select the third option about uploading an HTML file to the server and follow the instructions detailed in Figure 7–7.

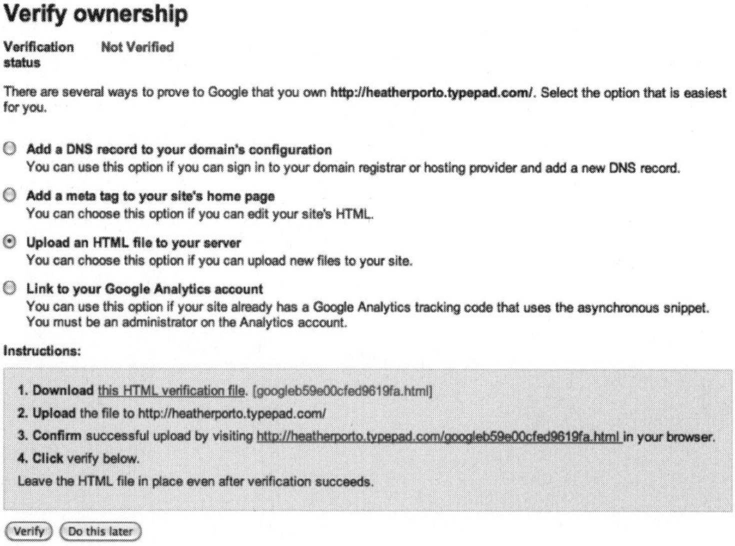

Verify ownership
Verification status
Not Verified
There are several ways to prove to Google that you own http://heatherporto.typepad.com/. Select the option that is easiest for you.
Add a DNS record to your domain's configuration
You can use this option if you can sign in to your domain registrar or hosting provider and add a new DNS record.
Add a meta tag to your site's home page
You can choose this option if you can edit your site's HTML.
Upload an HTML file to your server
You can choose this option if you can upload new files to your site.
Link to your Google Analytics account
You can use this option if your site already has a Google Analytics tracking code that uses the asynchronous snippet.
You must be an administrator on the Analytics account.
Instructions:
1. Download this HTML verification file. [googleb59e00cfed9619fa.html]
2. Upload the file to http://heatherporto.typepad.com/
3. Confirm successful upload by visiting http://heatherporto.typepad.com/googleb59e00cfed9619fa.html in your browser.
4. Click verify below.
Leave the HTML file in place even after verification succeeds.
Verify
Do this later

Figure 7–7. Verifying ownership by uploading an HTML file

d. No matter which platform you use, when you're finished using the recommended method, click the Verify button in Google Webmaster Tools. You will then be brought to the Dashboard shown in Figure 7–8.

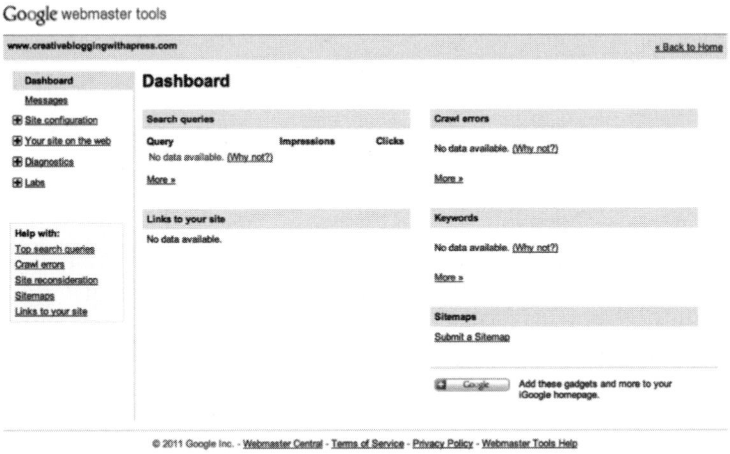

Figure 7–8. Webmaster Tools Dashboard

Yes, it is normal that there are no results! Don't worry. We just set up Google Webmaster tools and verified your site. There hasn't yet been any time to accumulate and tally statistics. Give it about a week and then check back to view new statistics as you begin blogging, writing posts, using keywords, and so forth. Just go to `www.google.com/webmasters/tools` and log in with your Google account. Then click on your verified site and the Dashboard will appear.

We will now continue with what each section means and what you can expect from Google Webmaster Tools and the results displaying in the Dashboard.

Now that you have set up Google Webmaster Tools, let's review the areas it tracks, queries, and reports. As you can see in the left sidebar in Figure 7–8, the main areas of the Dashboard are: Search queries, Crawl errors, Links to your site, Keywords, and Sitemaps. We'll briefly discuss Internal Links and Subscriber Status (which is inside the Your site on the web area) and HTML suggestions in Diagnostics, and Site Performance (in Labs).

Search Queries

This reports the number of search queries that returned pages from your site over the specified period (the default is 30 days), as well as how many impressions (the number of times pages from your site were viewed from the search results), and clicks (the number of times your blog's listing(s) were clicked in search results for a specific query) your site received. This section also provides your click-through rate (CTR) and average position. The CTR is a percentage—the number of impressions that resulted in a click to your site. The average position is where your site appears in the search results for a given query.

Crawl Errors

This area reports which URLs could not be reached. The most common errors are the HTTP Status Code 404 (page not found/doesn't exist) and a URL or page timeout (where the page takes too long to load and the server times out). The Crawl Errors page lists all the different type of errors and codes.

Links to Your Site

This lists the top external sites that link to yours and reports which sites link to which pages on your blog.

Keywords

Google lists the most significant terms it finds on your site. If you are expecting different terms, this gives you some insight on what keywords are currently determined, which can help you work on modifying your content in the future to try and bring new terms to this list.

Sitemaps

This area allows you to submit a sitemap of your site, which Google will analyze to see if there are any errors or potential errors in the pages listed on your sitemap. In short, a sitemap is an index of pages on your site. You can create your own sitemap to make sure Google knows about all of your pages.

Internal Links

This shows a list of pages that have links to other links (pages) on your site. Interlinking is the term used when you create links to other pages or posts on your own blog. For example, at the bottom of a post you may create a list of related posts or topics.

Subscriber Stats

Subscriber stats show those subscribed to your site. This may differ from the number you have in FeedBurner (feedburner.google.com, a popular subscription service), for example, because Google Webmaster Tools is based on a specific domain/site (it reads www.CreativeBloggingWithApress.com separately from creativebloggingbyapress.blogspot.com). So if you use both, you need to add both to your Google Webmaster Tools account. If you use the http://CreativeBloggingWithApress.com as well as www.CreativeBloggingWithApress.com, you need to add both sites.

HTML Suggestions

Google detects any problems with your pages, such as duplicate, missing, or problematic title or meta tags. These will not prevent your site from being listed, but correcting these problems may improve your results.

Site Performance

Site Performance is an experimental feature of Google Webmaster Tools labs. It shows you the average page load time for pages in your site, and offers some suggestions on how to make the pages load faster. The load time is determined from the point the user clicks on a link on your site until the entire page is loaded. It is collected from users who have installed the Google Toolbar and have enabled the optional PageRank feature. You can click on Install PageSpeed (on Mozilla FireFox only) to gain more insight on the speed of your pages and how to improve it.

Additional Notes

We have just touched the surface of using the Webmaster tools. They are a great help in analyzing your site, and by viewing the statistics and records, you can figure out how to make improvements to your blog. As noted in the Subscriber Stats area, it is very important that you add all the necessary sites to your Google Webmaster Tools account. Whether you use the "www" prefix or not when using a domain makes a difference! You should list the original non-domain site address as well (such as your BlogSpot, TypePad, or WordPress URL address).

You can find more information here:

- Understanding This Data:
  www.google.com/support/webmasters/bin/answer.py?answer=96568&hl=en

- Webmaster Tools Help: www.google.com/support/webmasters/

- Webmaster Help Forum: www.google.com/support/forum/p/Webmasters

- Webmaster Blog: http://googlewebmastercentral.blogspot.com

Google Places

You can use Google Places to claim your business listing on Google. It's free and very easy to set up. Once registered and verified with Google Places, your listing can appear on Google search results. The ranking process is the same with Google Places and any Google search and is based on the relevance of search terms entered and the geographic location of your business, as well as other factors. So, when completing the information for your listing, be sure it is accurate because Google pulls information from the web site listed.

When creating your listing, you'll be asked for your business name and physical mailing address (a must). You can also upload a business logo or up to 10 additional photos. In my examples for Blogs By Heather, shown in Figure 7–9, notice my business badge as well as samples of blog work I've done. You'll also see a map of my business (Google Places is integrated with Google Maps), as well as my business and personal site address listed below More About This Place. And be sure you add categories for your business (you must enter at least one); Blog Design and Setup is one of mine (shown in Figure 7–9). Go to places.google.com/business and log in to your Google account.

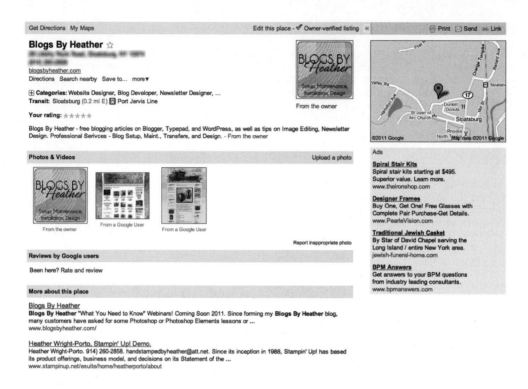

Figure 7–9. Blogs By Heather Listing using Google Places

EXERCISE – SETTING UP GOOGLE PLACES

After logging into your Google account, you'll be listed in Google Places in just a few minutes!

1. Click the List Your Business button.

2. Enter your country and phone number.

3. On the next screen, add your Basic Information as shown in Figure 7–10; the asterisked fields are required. You can also enter other sets of information (Service Areas and Location Settings, Hours of Operation, Payment Options, Photos, Videos, and Additional Details).

▼ **Basic Information**

Please note that changing your address or business name will require additional verification via mail or phone.

* Required Fields

Country: *	United States ⬍
Company/Organization: *	
Street Address: *	
City/Town: *	
State: *	Select state ⬍
ZIP: * [?]	
Main phone: *	

Example: (201) 234-5678 **Add more phone numbers**

Email address:

Example: myname@example.com

Website:

Example: http://www.example.com
☐ I don't have a website.

Description:

200 characters max, 200 characters left.

Category: *

Which categories (up to 5) best describe your business?
Ex: Dentist, Wedding Photographer, Thai Restaurant
Add another category

Figure 7–10. Basic Information for Google Places

4. Click Submit.

5. On the next screen you'll be asked to validate your listing; you'll be sent a postcard (in the mail, not e-mail).

6. Click Finish.

7. You're done with the registration. However, your site will not be listed until it is verified (until you prove you are the site owner). Google will send you a post card with your PIN code and tell you where to enter your PIN for verification on Google Places. This is a required process and can't be avoided or skipped.

Soon you will be able to find your listing in the Google Places business directory, as well as in Google search results.

Google AdWords

This is the only "paid" Google service we will be discussing in this section. So, what is Google AdWords? It is a service that lets you create an ad with Google and pay for it only if and when a visitor clicks on that ad. You actually create the ad within the Google AdWords setup process. You don't have to pay a designer or use another application to create an ad to upload later. It is all done in Google AdWords, and you can use images as well as text. We'll go through the setup process together in the next exercise.

You also manage your own budget and cost (so you won't be overcharged unexpectedly). You can set a daily monetary limit (such as $10) or you can set a price per click (such as 10 cents). I suggest beginning with a daily limit until you can analyze your results and see how many clicks you are receiving so you can calculate a weekly or monthly "pay per click" budget. You can also set up the duration of your ad; you may choose to run it for a week, a month, or without end.

What's the benefit of using Google AdWords? I'm sure you've notice when you search on Google that some results show at the top in a shaded area. Ever wonder why? Those are the results of using Google AdWords. They help build your visibility and improve your ranking in search results; that's what you're paying for.

Figure 7–11 shows the separation of Google AdWords search results and those results that are "organic" in that they occurred without the use of Google AdWords. However, that doesn't mean some other paid service isn't being used to improve placement in search engine results. As I mentioned, I've used www.EnterURL.com to submit my site to search engines monthly.

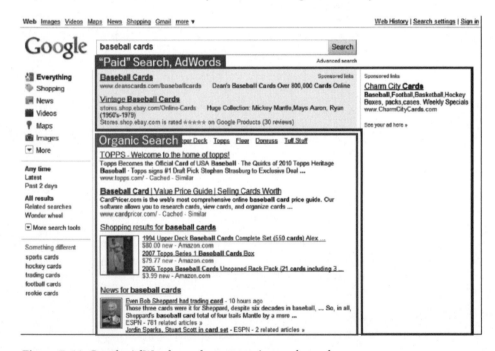

Figure 7–11. Google AdWords results vs.organic search results

EXERCISE – SET UP GOOGLE ADWORDS

1. Go to `adwords.google.com` and log in to your Google account if necessary.

2. Enter the time zone and currency for your account. Important: the time zone and currency can't be changed once set up.

3. Click Continue.

4. Your AdWords account is created. No ad will run until billing information is entered.

5. Click Sign In into your AdWords Account to see the AdWords Dashboard, shown in Figure 7–12.

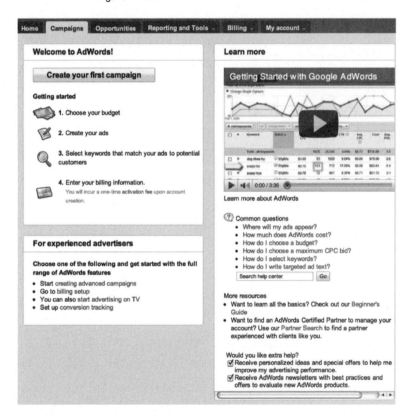

Figure 7–12. Welcome to AdWords

6. Click the Create your first campaign button.

7. You will see Select campaign settings (partially shown in Figure 7–13) with your information filled in.

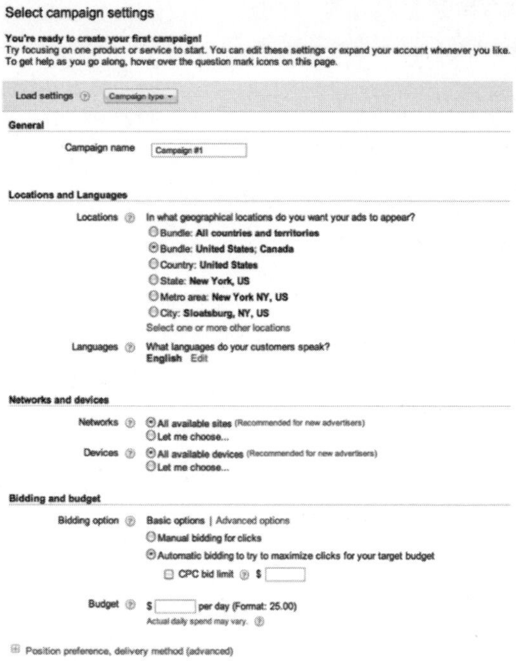

Select campaign settings

You're ready to create your first campaign!
Try focusing on one product or service to start. You can edit these settings or expand your account whenever you like.
To get help as you go along, hover over the question mark icons on this page.

Load settings ⑦ [Campaign type ▾]

General

Campaign name   [Campaign #1]

Locations and Languages

Locations ⑦ In what geographical locations do you want your ads to appear?
○ Bundle: All countries and territories
◉ Bundle: United States; Canada
○ Country: United States
○ State: New York, US
○ Metro area: New York NY, US
○ City: Sloatsburg, NY, US
Select one or more other locations

Languages ⑦ What languages do your customers speak?
English Edit

Networks and devices

Networks ⑦ ◉ All available sites (Recommended for new advertisers)
○ Let me choose...

Devices ⑦ ◉ All available devices (Recommended for new advertisers)
○ Let me choose...

Bidding and budget

Bidding option ⑦ Basic options | Advanced options
○ Manual bidding for clicks
◉ Automatic bidding to try to maximize clicks for your target budget
☐ CPC bid limit ⑦ $ [   ]

Budget ⑦ $ [   ] per day (Format: 25.00)
Actual daily spend may vary. ⑦

⊞ Position preference, delivery method (advanced)

Figure 7–13. Select Campaign Settings

8. Click Save and Continue.

9. Next, you'll create your ad and set keywords (see Figure 7–14). We'll just create a text ad here, but you can create an image ad as well and use Google's ad creator. You don't have to have another company or designer create an ad for you—you can do it yourself within Google AdWords!

Figure 7–14. Create your ad and set the keywords.

10. Fill in all the requested information, then click Save and continue to billing.

11. Choose your Country and click Continue.

12. Set up your billing profile (see Figure 7–15).

Figure 7–15. Billing profile

13. Click Continue.

14. Enter your desired payment options and settings (see Figure 7–16), such as setting up automatic payments. Although Google recommends automatic

payments, you may want to keep them manual until you know for sure the ad is working and the charge is what you expected.

Figure 7–16. Payment settings

15. Click to agree to the terms and conditions.

16. Finish by clicking Submit & Activate My Account. You'll see a note that you'll be charged an extra $5 activation fee in your first payment.

17. Your setup is complete and your ad is live. You are now at the Account Snapshot screen shown in Figure 7–17.

18. To view your online ad, look under Active Campaigns in the right pane. In my example in Figure 7–17, you'll see a "1;" click on the Online link.

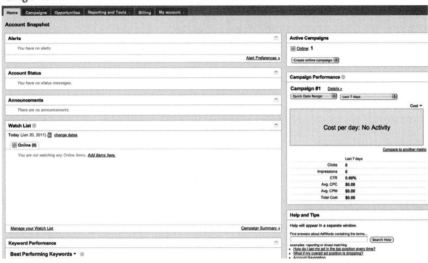

Figure 7–17. *Account Snapshot (partial)*

From the Account Snapshot you can see all the activity on your ad—its performance, best-performing keywords, access to help, and more. Notice the tabs at the top, where you can go to modify your campaigns and billing information, as well as run reports and use other tools.

Feeds and Subscriptions

FeedBurner is a very popular free feed management service that Google provides. A feed is simply a data format for your posts that's used to keep readers updated with your most recent activity. In the following exercise we'll see how to set up your blog for e-mail subscriptions as well as to enable users to subscribe in a reader (such as Google Reader). This gives visitors two ways to follow you and stay up-to-date with your blog posts. You want to give your readers every opportunity to subscribe to your blog and to keep updated with its content.

How does it work? If visitors come to your blog and chooses to subscribe, they will be notified whenever your blog has been updated, and will see the posts published on a given day. So if you post daily, your subscribers are updated daily. If you post weekly, they receive weekly updates. If they subscribe to your blog via an e-mail subscription, they will receive an e-mail message whenever you post content (on a given day). Figure 7–18 shows a sample of an e-mail subscription I received from Monica Weaver (www.MonicaWeaver.com). I subscribe to her blog because she creates beautiful projects with metal sheets (she's a paper crafter like me). When I helped Monica set up her feed, we added a logo (in this case her holiday caricature) and modified the color of the links (to red) to coordinate with the rest of her blog's theme.

Others prefer to use a "reader" to view all of their subscriptions. For example, if I subscribe to 10 blogs, I might receive 10 different e-mails a day. Instead, I could use a reader, like Google Reader, which allows me to view all my subscriptions in one place without having to go through a bunch of e-mail, as shown in Figure 7–19. I used Monica's example again so you can see the same post in two layouts to help you decide which subscription method you prefer, e-mail or reader. You get the same information either way; it's just a personal preference.

Add a Little Dazzle News

[+ Google]

Lots of Love Class Planner....

Posted: 19 Jan 2011 02:03 PM PST

Good Afternoon Stampers,

I am so excited to share with you the release of **"Lots of Love Class Planner"**. This planner features the amazing **"Lots of Love Letterpress Plate"** using a very unique technique I came up with. The combination of metal sheets, this new technique, and amazing stamps will be loved by all. You MUST use the technique I came up with in order for this to work. This ensemble is dazzling, elegant, and perfect for a Valentine's Day gift.

Have you been struggling trying to come up with a design that has a masculine, adult-like feel to it for Valentine's Day? Look no further; this is the planner for you. In this planner, you will learn how to create these amazingly beautiful projects just in time for Valentine's Day or any other occasion using the amazing **"Lots of Love Letterpress Plate"**. You will be amazed at how beautiful this looks in person as you learn this new technique.

Figure 7–18. *Feedburner e-mail subscription sample*

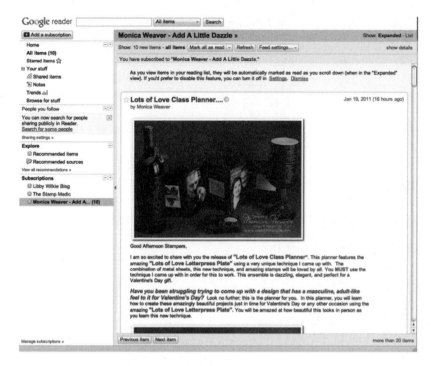

Figure 7–19. *Google Reader sample*

Why use FeedBurner (or any subscription service)? Because you want to make sure your visitors know about your new content. If they like what they read and are excited about a promotion you're running, for example, they'll forward the message to a friend or tell friends and family to "check out this blog!" and drive traffic and new visitors to your site. In the next chapter we discuss how to integrate your feeds with social networking sites such as Facebook and Twitter to spread your posts and expand visibility even further.

■ **Note** To learn about Google Reader, go to `http://reader.google.com` and take a tour.

Although we go through all the steps for setting up your feed and adding the FeedBurner gadget to the sidebar of your Blogger or TypePad blog in the following exercise, we won't be able to cover all aspects, tools, or functionality of FeedBurner. Also, note that FeedBurner e-mail subscriptions don't work with WordPress.com (the JavaScript code is not accepted), but the "subscribe in a reader" feature does work. Don't worry, though. WordPress.com has a built-in e-mail subscription service for your blog readers who prefer to receive e-mail updates. We'll review that in a separate exercise following the FeedBurner example.

EXERCISE – SETUP FEEDBURNER AND BLOG SUBSCRIPTIONS

In this exercise you will install an e-mail subscription service using FeedBurner (for Blogger and TypePad only). WordPress has its own e-mail subscriptions widget called Blog Subscriptions (as the FeedBurner code will not work properly). In addition, you will add the "subscribe in a reader" component (for all three platforms) using FeedBurner.

You will be going back and forth between FeedBurner and your blog, so I recommend having two browser windows open, one for your blog, one for FeedBurner.

1. Let's begin at FeedBurner. Go to `feedburner.google.com`. You may have to reenter your Google Account username and password (if you are using Blogger, this is the same login information).

2. In the next screen, you are creating a feed for your blog (see Figure 7–20). Copy and paste your blog's address (including the `http://` prefix) into the text box "Burn a feed right this instant." Then click Next.

Figure 7–20. Burning a feed

3. In the next screen, Identify Feed Source, choose either format (see Figure 7–21). In this example I left the default, which is Atom. You really don't need to worry about the difference between Atom and RSS; both are widely used and accepted. In short, the formatting in the Atom feed is better and more robust.

Figure 7–21. Identify Feed Source

4.   Click Next and you'll see a screen with the Feed Title and Feed Address that have been generated for you (see Figure 7–22).

Figure 7–22. Feed Title and Address

5.   You can modify the Feed Title if necessary, but don't play around with the Feed Address. Click Next.

6.   Your feed has now been set up (see Figure 7–23). Click Next to set up and review FeedBurner Stats or click "Skip directly to feed management."

Figure 7–23. Your Feedburner feed is live

7. Let's continue setting up the Feed Stats (it's only one additional step), as shown in Figure 7–24. By tracking your readers' actions, you will learn more about what they like. Note that if you chose "I am a podcaster" on the screen shown in Figure 7–20, you'll see a different screen from the one in Figure 7–24. This is where you'd set up options for your podcasting, such as iTunes podcasting elements, as well as add your podcast to Yahoo! Search.

8. As you can see in Figure 7–24, using my Creative Blogging example, I checked Clickthroughs as well as "I want more! Have FeedBurner Stats also track…."

   • Clickthroughs track how often people click back to your site.

   • Feedburner Stats also tracks the popularity of items and how many people viewed the feed and click content on your feed.

Figure 7–24. *Configuring Feedburner Stats*

9. Click Next to complete the FeedBurner setup (see Figure 7–25).

Figure 7–25. Successfully updating the feed

10. In the future when you want to review your FeedBurner statistics, go to the Analyze tab. But for now, to add the gadget to your blog to allow e-mail subscriptions, click on Publicize.

11. Click on Email Subscriptions (see Figure 7–26).

Figure 7–26. *Setting up e-mail subscriptions*

12. Click on Activate. You only have to do this once, when you first set up the Email Subscriptions.

13. Within a few seconds, you should get a message about successfully activating the service. If you get an error, log out. Then log back in, go to your feed, click Publicize, Email Subscriptions, and try again.

14. In Figure 7–27, beneath the large text box where it states "Copy and paste the following code into any web page…" you will see the "Use as a widget in" drop-down and then a Go! Button. I have highlighted the code in Figure 7–27 so you can see which box I'm referring to.

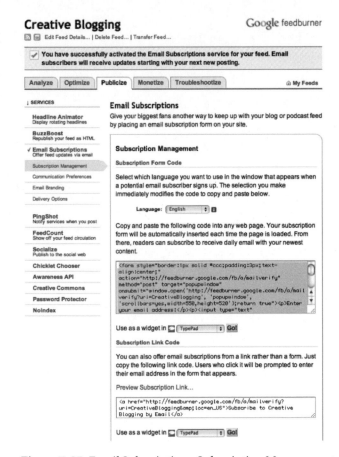

Figure 7–27. Email Subscriptions, Subscription Management

15. This is where you need to open another browser window and log in to your blog (Blogger, TypePad, or WordPress).

Using Blogger

16. Click on that "Use as a widget in" drop-down and choose Blogger.

17. Click Go! You'll see a screen like the one in Figure 7–28.

Figure 7–28. *The Add Page Element in Blogger*

18. For the Title, leave the default or change it to whatever you like (I modified it to "Receive Email Updates").

19. Click Add Widget and the element is then added to the top of the sidebar in your Blogger layout (the Page Elements area). Click Save. We'll come back to this in a few minutes.

20. Go back to FeedBurner, click on Chicklet Chooser from the left sidebar (see Figure 7–29).

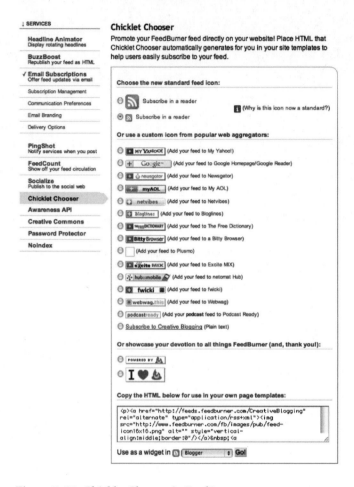

Figure 7–29. Chicklet Chooser in FeedBurner

21. Click the Subscribe in a Reader option shown, then scroll beneath the "Copy the HTML below for use in your page templates" and in the drop-down "Use as a widget in…" choose Blogger.

22. Click Go!

23. You'll see Blogger's Add Page Element box again.

24. Enter a Title if you wish. Since this widget says "Subscribe in a Reader," I left the Title blank.

25. Click Add Widget. It is then added to the Page Elements screen, at the top of the sidebar, with no title but as HTML/JavaScript.

26. You can leave it there or you can drag and drop it wherever you'd like in your blog's layout. If you change the layout, be sure to click Save Changes.

27. Click on View Blog.

Using TypePad

28. You are still at the Email Subscriptions area. Under the large text box (highlighted in Figure 7–27), you will see this area (shown in 7–30).

Figure 7–30. Email Subscriptions Widget for Typepad

29. Click on Go!

30. TypePad's Add a Sidebar Widget screen will appear. You need to check the name of the blog where you want the widget installed, and you can modify the Widget Name if desired (as I did in Figure 7–31). Please note, the name is to identify the widget in TypePad's design; it won't show on your blog.

Figure 7–31. Adding a sidebar widget for Typepad

31. Click Add Widget.

32. Click on Return To FeedBurner because we still need to add the Subscribe in a Reader.

33. In FeedBurner, go to Chicklet Chooser (left sidebar).

34. Select the small Subscribe in a Reader option at the top (shown previously in Figure 7–29).

35. Again, scroll to the bottom and find the "Use as widget in" drop-down shown in Figure 7–30. Since it already says TypePad, click Go!

36. In TypePad's Add a Sidebar Widget window, again check your blog (the one you want to add this widget to); change the Widget Name if desired (to Subscribe in Reader, for example).

37. Click Add Widget.

38. These new gadgets have been added to the bottom of your sidebar. If you wish to move them up to the top of your sidebar, click on Design Sidebar Content. Otherwise, click on View Blog.

   a. If you chose Design Sidebar Content, click and drag the widgets (one at a time) to a new location.

   b. Click Save Changes (at the bottom left) when finished.

Using WordPress

39. From within FeedBurner, go to the Chicklet Chooser (from the left sidebar). In WordPress, we'll only be adding the "Subscribe in a Reader" option through Feedburner. We'll be using WordPress's Email Subscriptions widget later in this exercise.

40. Click on the small Subscribe in a Reader button (as shown in 7–29), and then scroll to the bottom and copy the code.

41. Go to your WordPress blog, click on the Dashboard, then Appearance.

42. Click Widgets and drag a Text Widget to a sidebar. This opens it for editing, as shown in Figure 7–32.

Figure 7–32. Text widget in WordPress

43. Enter a Title (such as Keep Updated), and in the large text box paste in the code.

44. Click Save.

45. Click Close on the Text Widget.

46. Adding the e-mail subscriptions is done not through FeedBurner but within a widget in WordPress.

47. From the Widgets area in WordPress, drag the Blog Subscriptions widget to your sidebar and it will open for editing as shown in Figure 7–33.

Figure 7–33. Setting up the Blog Subscriptions widget in WordPress

48. Edit the Title if you'd like (as I did, to "Receive Email Updates").

49. Click Save on the widget.

50. Click Close on the Text widget.

51. View your blog (from the My Blog Menu, Read Blog).

That was a long exercise—but well worth it! Now your viewers can subscribe to your Blogger, TypePad, or WordPress blog via email subscriptions or in a reader.

Note: While in the Email Subscriptions area of FeedBurner, in the left sidebar under Email Subscriptions you'll see Delivery Options. This is where you can schedule when your subscribers will receive your updates. You can also click on Email Branding to add your logo and customize the color of text and links in the feeds.

Share Buttons

What are "share" buttons? They are the small buttons you see at the bottom of each of your blog posts that allow you to quickly share a post! Popular share buttons include those for social networking sites like Facebook, Twitter, Digg, Delicious, Buzz, MySpace, Email, and more. And here's some great news—there's no code to copy and paste to add them! Blogger, TypePad, and WordPress have now made it very easy to add these popular links to your posts! Below are three separate exercises, one each for Blogger, TypePad, and WordPress respectively.

EXERCISE – SHARE BUTTONS IN BLOGGER

1. Log in to Blogger and from the Dashboard, click on Design.

2. In Page Elements, click on the Edit link at the bottom right of the Blog Posts element. The Configure Blog Post window appears as shown in Figure 7–34.

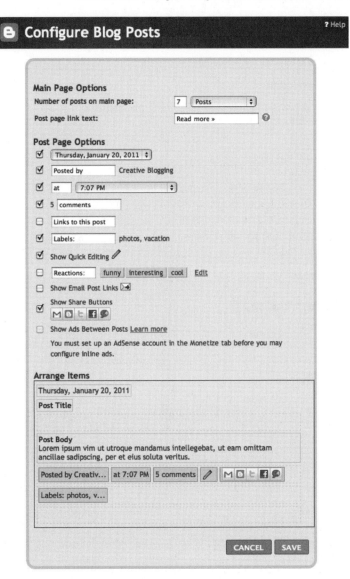

Figure 7–34. Configure Blog Posts in Blogger

3. Click the check box next to "Show Share Buttons."

4. Click the Save button.

That's it! You're done and have now enabled the feature that allows readers to quickly and easily share your blog posts.

EXERCISE – SHARE BUTTONS IN TYPEPAD

1. Login to TypePad and, from the Dashboard, click Design.

2. Click Content to access your blog's layout.

3. In the Post Footer element, click the Pencil icon to the right, which will open the element for editing (see Figure 7–35).

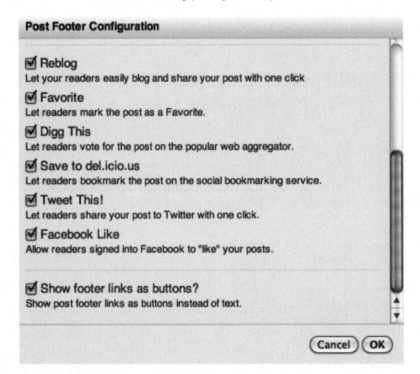

Figure 7–35. Post Footer Configuration in TypePad

4. Check the share buttons you want to have in the Post Footer, such as Tweet This! and Facebook Like.

5. Click OK.

6. Click Save Changes in the Content layout screen.

That's it! You're done and have now enabled the feature that allows readers to quickly and easily share your blog posts.

EXERCISE – SHARE BUTTONS IN WORDPRESS

1. Log in to WordPress, click on the My Blog menu and then on Dashboard.

2. Click on Settings, then on Sharing, and you'll see the Sharing Settings screen as shown in Figure 7–36.

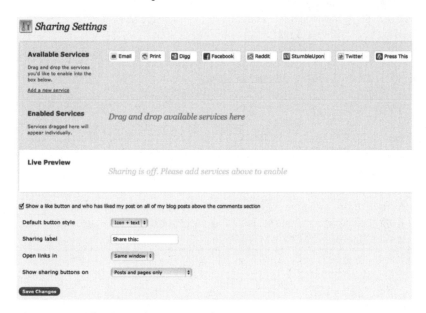

Figure 7–36. *Sharing Settings in WordPress*

3. Notice all the different share buttons at the top of Available Services. Click and drag those you want into the "Drag and drop available services here" area.

4. Note that they will not appear under each post unless you click on a specific post. Then the share buttons appear as shown in Figure 7–37.

Figure 7–37. *Share Buttons in a WordPress post*

> That's it! You're done. Although I wish the share buttons would appear under each post in the normal, main view of your blog (without having to click on a specific, individual post), you have now enabled the feature that allows readers to quickly and easily share your blog posts.

Visitor Tracking

Google Analytics is a very capable free solution for tracking visitor activity. It has an easy-to-use interface and a lot of powerful, customizable reports. In trying to find ways to improve your blog following, and therefore increase traffic to your site, it is important to know what pages, posts, categories, or sidebar items your visitors click on the most, as well as when are they visiting your site and how long they are staying. Those questions are probably the top three that business owners want to know about their blog or web site. With this information, you can make better marketing decisions, improve your site's design, or try to turn blog visitors into customers if you are using your blog for business purposes.

In the following exercises, we'll see how to install Google Analytics for Blogger and TypePad. Google Analytics does not work with WordPress.com blogs. It has instead, a comprehensive Site Stats area where you can see how many views you received when, which sites send you traffic (referrers), what the top ten posts and pages are, details on the number of clicks, top search engine terms, and more. In WordPress, from the Dashboard, click on Dashboard and then Site Stats to view this information.

EXERCISE – SETTING UP GOOGLE ANALYTICS

Although this book does not cover or review all the reporting and features of Google Analytics, in the exercise, you will set up an account and add the necessary HTML code to your blog to track visitor activity.

1. Go to the Google Analytics' home page, www.google.com/analytics/.

2. Click on Access Analytics.

3. Click on Sign Up.

4. Enter your blog's address, account name, country, and time zone on the New Account Signup screen, as shown in Figure 7–38.

Google Analytics   creativebloggin

Getting Started

Analytics: New Account Signup

General Information > Contact Information > Accept User Agreement > Add Tracking

Please enter the URL of the site you wish to track, and assign a name as it should appear in your Google Analytics reports. If you'd like to track more than one website, you can add more sites once your account has been set up. Learn more.

Website's URL: http://   creativebloggingbyapress.blogspot.com
                             (e.g. www.mywebsite.com)

Account Name: creativebloggingbyapress.blogspot.cor

Time zone country or territory: United States

Time zone: (GMT–05:00) Eastern Time

Cancel   Continue »

Figure 7–38. Sign up for Google Analytics

5. Click on Continue.

6. Enter your name and country and click Continue.

7. Click the check box to accept the Terms of Service.

8. Click Create New Account.

9. Leave the defaults and select and copy the HTML code shown in Figure 7–39, as we are tracking just one blog (a single domain).

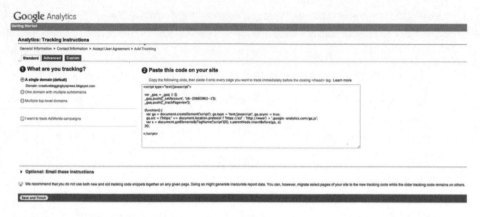

Figure 7–39. *Setting up tracking in Google Analytics*

Using Blogger

10. As instructed by Google in step 2, you will be adding this code before the `</body>` tag on your blog.

11. From the Dashboard, go to Layout, then Edit HTML.

12. Scroll down to the bottom of your page (or press Ctrl+F to use Find) to locate `</body>`. Immediately above that line, paste in the code provided for you in Google's step 2. (The code below is just an example for this book).

```
<script type="text/javascript">
var gaJsHost = (("https:" == document.location.protocol) ? "https://ssl." :
"http://www.");
document.write(unescape("%3Cscript src='" + gaJsHost + "google-analytics.com/ga.js'
type='text/javascript'%3E%3C/script%3E"));
</script>
<script type="text/javascript">
try {
var pageTracker = _gat._getTracker("UA-15101154-1");
pageTracker._trackPageview();
} catch(err) {}</script>

</body>
```

13. Click on Save.

In Google Analytics, when you click Save and Finish, you will be directed to the Analytics Settings Overview Screen as shown in Figure 7–40. It will take a couple of minutes for the Status to change as it is newly installed and needs to collect information.

Figure 7–40. Overview of Google Analytics account

Using TypePad

14. You will not copy any code but instead click Save and Finish immediately as you need the UA number.

15. Copy your UA Number and go to TypePad.

16. From the Dashboard go to Settings ➤ Add-Ons (see Figure 7–41).

17. Copy and paste the UA number in the UA Number box under Google Analytics.

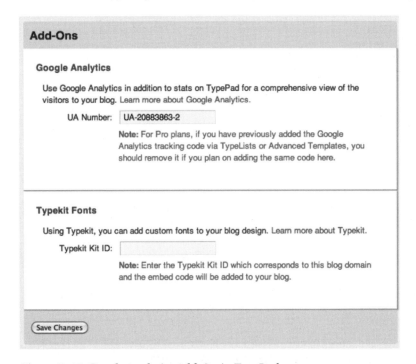

Figure 7–41. Google Analytics Add-On in TypePad

If Using Eiher TypePad or Blogger

Although you should wait a little while before really tracking your blog since you are still in the process of developing it, you can always come back to the page shown in Figure 7–42 to view your reports.

a. Click on the View Report text link.

b. You will see Site Usage categories like Visits and Page Views, as well as a pie chart showing where your traffic is coming from, and more (see Figure 7–42).

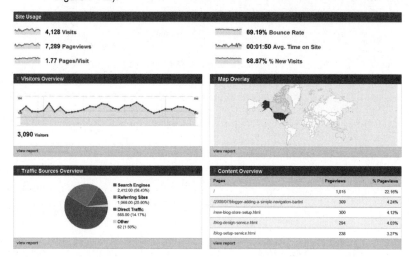

Figure 7–42. Google Analytics reports

If you are experiencing a problem, visit the Common Questions area in the upper left corner.

To use Google Analytics in the future, go to www.google.com/analytics and log in using your Google Account username and password.

In Google Analytics, notice the screenshot of a live sample where it shows the number of visits, page views, average times on site, and more! You can click on Visits, then Custom Reports, and then build your own detail reports!

Here are a few notes on how Google Analytics tracks clicks, visits, and pages views:

Visits vs. Visitors: Analytics measures both visits and visitors on your site. Visits represent the number of individual sessions initiated by all the visitors to your site. When someone visits your site during a given session, it is counted as a visit and increases the visitor counter by 1. If during the same session, the same visitor revisits your site, the visits count will increase but not the visitors.

Clicks vs. Visits: The clicks column in your reports indicates how many times your advertisements were clicked (if you are using Google AdWords), while visits indicate the number of unique sessions initiated by your visitors. There are several reasons why these two numbers may not match.

- If within the same session (such as a 30-minute period) a visitor clicks the same AdWords ad multiple times, AdWords records it as several clicks while Google Analytics only records it as one visit.

- However, if the same visitor clicks on the same ad in a different session (say after leaving the computer idle for a while), this is reported as multiple visits.

- If a visitor clicks on your ad and the page does not load all the way, AdWords records it but Google Analytics won't.

Pageviews vs. Unique Pageviews: A pageview is defined as a view of a page on your site. However, if someone visits the same page multiple times during the same session, it is counted each time as a page view but only once as a unique pageview.

Summary

Wow! This was a loaded chapter! It contains lots of information you can use to help build your ranking and improve your blog's visibility, as well as track visitor activity. Google provides many free tools, and in this chapter we discussed the SEO and visitor-tracking tools—Google Site Submission, Google Webmaster Tools, Google Analytics—as well as Google FeedBurner to allow visitors to subscribe to your blog. We reviewed Google AdWords, which is not free but is very valuable to help drive traffic to your site and, most importantly, on your budget!

We added share buttons to your blog posts, which let your readers quickly share posts on many sites (including Facebook and Twitter). In the next chapter, we'll take this topic one step further as we discuss Twitter and Facebook and how to use them to grow your audience, reach potential customers, and build your list of blog followers.

CHAPTER 8

■ ■ ■

Social Network Integration

In the last chapter you learned how to add share buttons to the bottom of your blog posts to let your blog readers quickly and easily share your content with others, and by doing so, hopefully bring new visitors to your blog. Now we'll expand on this topic. Twitter and Facebook are the most popular social networking sites, so let's use them to help drive traffic to your site. We'll create Twitter and Facebook accounts, in case you don't already have them, and add Facebook and Twitter widgets to your blog. And we'll configure Facebook and Twitter settings so when you post to your blog, your Facebook and Twitter accounts will automatically update without you having to do a thing! This saves you valuable time and effort in managing your blog, Facebook, and Twitter. Post once and all three accounts are updated.

To make all three work together, the first step is to go back and edit the FeedBurner account you created in the last chapter. Under Socializing, we'll set it up to post automatic updates to your Twitter account. People following you on Twitter who don't already know about your blog will then get your blog posts, thus increasing your blog's exposure. Similarly, we'll use Facebook's NetworkedBlogs application to link your blog posts to your Facebook account. Your Facebook friends will then know immediately that you have a blog that may interest them!

Using Twitter

Twitter is a popular networking tool in which you post small, frequent messages (called tweets) of at most 140 characters. They are simple text messages—no images or videos allowed—and they are becoming an increasingly important way of communicating with friends, family, and potential customers, known as Followers in Twitter. Followers are those who want to be updated when you tweet, so they choose to "follow" you. In the next exercise, when you set up your Twitter account (if you don't already have one), you will also choose people to follow. This means you will then see their tweets on your Twitter page every time they tweet.

It may turn out that your Twitter followers are an entirely different set of people than your Facebook friends or your blog followers. Some people prefer Facebook, others may just use Twitter. Therefore, it's worth making sure that your Twitter followers know when your blog's been updated (by publishing your posts automatically to Twitter); and that your blog readers know what you're tweeting about (by adding the Twitter Updates widget to your blog). You will add a widget to display your last four Twitter messages in your blog's sidebar, giving your blog readers the option to follow you on Twitter as well.

EXERCISE – CREATE A TWITTER ACCOUNT

In this exercise, you'll create a Twitter account. If you already have one, just skip this exercise and continue reading.

1. Go to www.twitter.com.

2. Click Sign Up and enter your information in the form displayed in Figure 8–1.

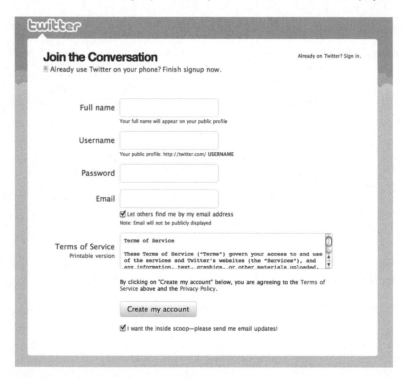

Figure 8–1. *Create a Twitter Account*

3. Enter your Full Name, Username, Password, and Email (check to allow others to find you by email). If you want, check to have Twitter send you email updates. When entering a Username (maximum of 15 characters), Twitter checks to be sure it's not already in use. The password must be at least six characters.

4. Click Create my account. When you do, you are agreeing to Twitter's Terms of Service and Privacy Policy.

5. Complete the "Are You Human?" CAPTCHA test (see the example in Figure 8–2) and click Finish.

Figure 8–2: Are you human?

6. Click Finish. Now you can search to find topics that interest you (see Figure 8–3).

Figure 8–3. Finding topics of Interest

7. Choose to follow any that you find of interest.

8. Click Next Step: Friends to bring up the screen in Figure 8–4.

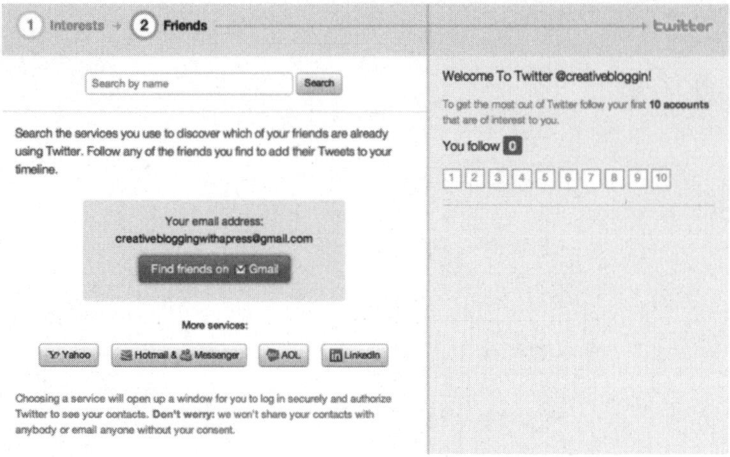

Figure 8–4. Finding friends on Twitter

9. You can choose to skip this step, or you can use your e-mail and other services to locate friends. You can also search by name. If you choose to search your e-mail contacts, another dialog box will appear, prompting you to log in and grant access to your account. You can then choose friends to follow.

10. Click Finish if you chose to import contacts or click Skip Import.

11. You have now created a Twitter account and will receive a confirmation e-mail.

In the next exercise, you'll use this account to add a Twitter Updates widget to your blog's sidebar. This will display recent tweets in your blog. Then we'll modify your blog feed to update Twitter.

The next step is to enter your contact information, bio, and so forth. To do this, under your account name at the top, click the drop-down, then Settings. Here you can change your password, enter profile information, or click on Design to choose a look for your Twitter account.

Finally (and most importantly), click on Home and begin tweeting, that is, posting messages. Under What's Happening, you can use up to 140 characters to post a short message. These can be links to your blog or announcements of upcoming events, for example. In the next exercise, we'll add a widget that displays the most recent tweets in your blog's sidebar.

EXERCISE – ADDING THE TWITTER UPDATES WIDGET

In this exercise, you'll add a widget to your blog that shows your readers your last four tweets.

1. While logged into Twitter go to `http://twitter.com/goodies/widgets`.

2. Click on My Website.

3. Click on Profile Widget and you'll see a preview of the widget on the right (see Figure 8–5). Don't worry; we'll be modifying the Appearance and Dimensions to coordinate with the color scheme of your blog and to adjust the width to fit in your blog's sidebar.

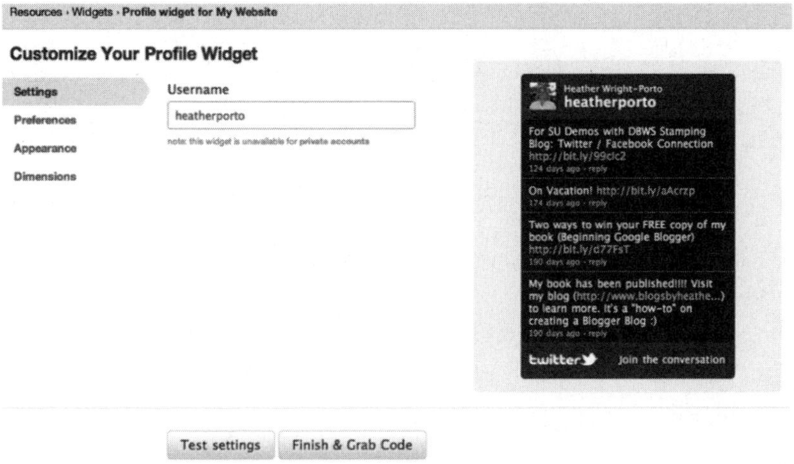

Figure 8–5. You can customize your Twitter Profile Widget.

4. Click on Appearance (see Figure 8–6) and you can customize the color of your widget shell and shell text, links, tweets, and background. As you can see, I used blues and grays to match the overall theme of the Creative Blogging blogs used throughout this book.

Figure 8–6. You can customize the appearance of your Twitter Profile widget

5. Click on Dimensions and change the width to 180 to be sure it fits in your blog's sidebar, or you can try the Auto Width setting.

6. Click Finish & Grab Code (see Figure 8–7).

Figure 8–7. Grabbing the Twitter Profile Widget code

Using Blogger

7. Click on the Add to Blogger button under the code.

8. You will be prompted to log in if you aren't already.

9. The Add Page Element screen will appear and you can edit the Title, as I have, to "Follow Me on Twitter" or whatever you prefer (see Figure 8–8).

Figure 8–8. Adding the widget to Blogger

10. Click Add Widget. The Twitter widget is added to the top of your sidebar in the Page Elements section.

11. Click and drag it wherever you like. Then click Save Changes.

12. Click View Blog.

Using TypePad

13. Select the code in Twitter and copy it.

14. Go to TypePad and log in.

15. Go to Design ➤Content.

16. From the middle box, under Modules, click Embed Your Own HTML, then click Add This Module (from the box to right).

17. In the Custom HTML box that appears (see Figure 8–9), enter Twitter Updates as the Title (it will not show on your blog), and then paste in the code in the large text box.

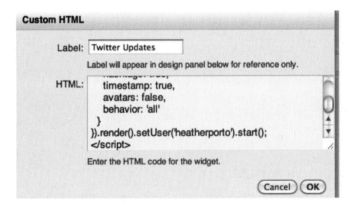

Figure 8–9. Custom HTML in TypePad

18. Click OK and the widget is added to the top of the sidebar.

19. Drag and drop it to where you'd like it to be.

20. Click Save Changes.

21. Use View Blog if desired to see the new widget.

Using WordPress

22. Due to the JavaScript limitations in WordPress, we can't paste this code into a Text Widget in WordPress.com. However, WordPress has its own Twitter widget.

23. Log in to WordPress.

24. Select Dashboard from the My Blog drop-down menu and then click on Appearance in the left sidebar area.

25. Click on Widgets.

26. Drag the Twitter widget to your sidebar (see Figure 8–10).

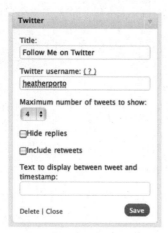

Figure 8–10. The Twitter widget in WordPress

27. Enter a Title and your Twitter username.

28. Select the number of tweets to show.

29. Click Save.

30. Click Close.

31. Go to My Blog and then Read Blog to view the widget.

Next, you'll edit your FeedBurner feed to automatically post to your Twitter account. How cool is that? This will eliminate the need to post the same information in both sites. However, in addition to your blog posts, you'll want send other tweets to your Twitter followers. That's just a suggestion but it's a good business practice.

EXERCISE – ADDING A TWITTER ACCOUNT TO A FEEDBURNER FEED

In the last chapter you set up a Google FeedBurner account. Now you'll set up your blog's feed to post to your Twitter account.

1. Go to `http://feedburner.google.com`. You may have to reenter your Google password.

2. Click on your existing blog feed or, if you already have it open from the earlier exercise, click on the Publicize tab.

3. Click on Socialize.

4. Click the Add a Twitter Account button.

5. Enter your Twitter account information (see Figure 8–11).

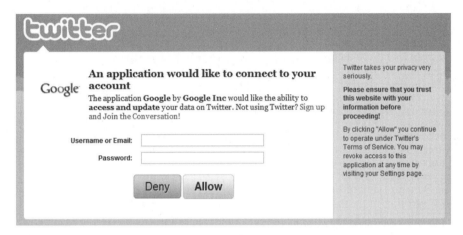

Figure 8–11: Add your Twitter account to Feedburner

6. Click Allow.

7. Now you'll see your Twitter account name, as in the example in Figure 8–12.

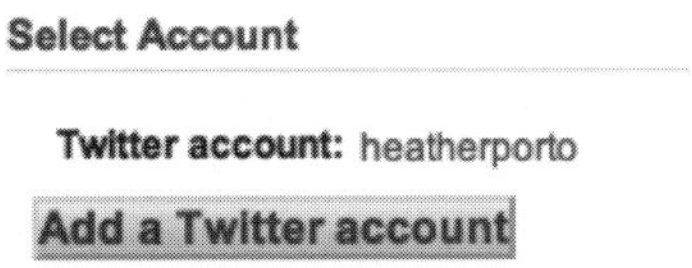

Select Account

Twitter account: heatherporto

Add a Twitter account

Figure 8–12: Twitter account added

8. Click the Activate button at the bottom of the screen.

9. In a few seconds you'll see a message that says you have successfully updated your feed.

10. That's all there is to it. Now your blog posts will be published to your Twitter account automatically.

Using Facebook

Facebook is probably the most popular social networking site right now. It's similar to blogging in that you can post messages to share with "friends." The messages can include text, links, images, and video, (but you are limited to the number of characters you can post). Facebook has built-in technology to help you find friends, which can be old high school friends, colleagues at work, members of a co-ed softball team, or business associates, among many others. Facebook has an amazing ability to connect you with people you know and those you don't but may be interested in following as they may share similar interests and you may have mutual friends.

You can use Facebook personally and professionally. However, if you are using it for business purposes, you must use what is called a "Page." For example, I have a Facebook account and I post often about my family, what the kids are up to, what we may be doing today, or maybe that I have a migraine and am looking for miracle solutions! But I also use the same Facebook account for both my stamping business and my blogging business, and of course I wouldn't post this type of personal information to these. Instead, on those pages I post about stamping kits and tutorials I may be selling, or about an upcoming crafting event, or a tip on blogging, or about my book *Beginning Google Blogger*.

Although I could post about an upcoming event or free blogging tip on my "Wall" (the main posting area in Facebook), Facebook policy prohibits posting things for sale or promoting business services. If don't plan to use your blog or Facebook for business, you don't need to create a business page. As we go through the upcoming exercises, I will note where the instructions differ. We could write a book on Facebook alone, but in this chapter we'll focus on getting your blog and Facebook to "talk."

By integrating your blog with Facebook and Twitter, you expand your blog's visibility in that by using them, people may find your blog who otherwise wouldn't. For example, suppose you put your Facebook badge on your blog's sidebar and, say, ten of your blog readers ask to be a Facebook friend. Their Facebook friends then read their Walls and find out about you and become your Facebook friends as well—and find out about your blog. This type of growth and exposure can continue exponentially through Facebook networking.

EXERCISE – CREATE A FACEBOOK ACCOUNT

In this exercise you will quickly set up a Facebook account. If you already have a Facebook account, skip this exercise and continue reading.

1. Go to www.Facebook.com.

2. You can create a Facebook account right on the opening page (see Figure 8–13). Whether you plan to use Facebook for business or personal reasons, we'll first create an account this way and then later create a page for business.

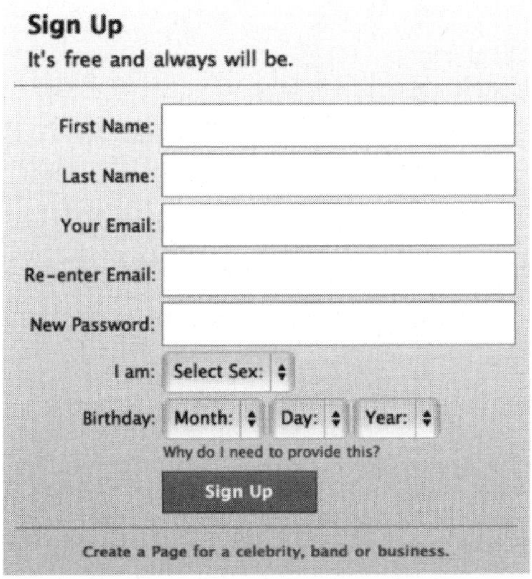

Figure 8–13. Creating a Facebook account

3. Enter your First Name, Last Name, Email (twice), Password, Sex, and Birthday.

4. Click Sign Up.

5. Enter the words in the Security Check (see the sample in Figure 8–14).

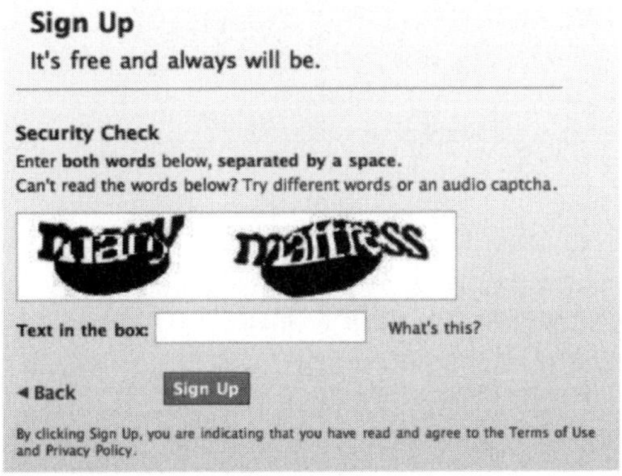

Figure 8–14. The Security Check during Facebook Setup

6. Click Sign Up again (which means you accept the Terms of Use and the Privacy Policy).

7. You have the option to use your e-mail contacts to find Facebook friends (see Figure 8–15). For the purpose of this book, we'll click Skip this step (bottom right).

Figure 8–15. *Find friends on Facebook*

8.   Enter your Profile Information (see Figure 8–16). Once you're in Facebook, you can click on Profile and enter a lot more information about yourself. This is just to get you started.

Figure 8–16. *Enter profile information*

9.   Click Save & Continue.

10. You will then be shown potential "friends" based on the information you entered.

11. For this example, I chose to move straight past this step and click Skip.

12. Enter your Profile Picture by uploading a photo from your computer or by taking a live photo (if you have a webcam). Or you can choose to Skip.

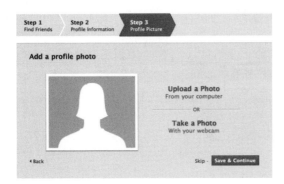

Figure 8–17. *Upload a profile picture if you like*

13. Click Save & Continue.

14. You are now in your new Facebook account. Notice, however, that you must go to your e-mail to complete the process (see Figure 8–18).

Figure 8–18. *Inside Facebook*

15. Be sure to check your e-mail for a message from Facebook like the one in Figure 8–19.

Figure 8–19. E-mail from Facebook

16. You have now completed your Facebook account setup!

There is so much to learn about Facebook . I recommend reviewing the account and security settings (from the main Account menu at the top) so you can keep private what you want and share other information with the public. However, it's relatively easy to begin posting. Click on Home and then type a message in "What's on your mind?" This is writing on your Wall. Don't forget—you can post personal or informational messages, but you can't sell or promote products or services.

Now that the Facebook account is created and you have begun posting messages, you'll want to know how to put a Facebook Badge in your blog's sidebar. This lets blog visitors easily get to your Facebook page.

EXERCISE – CREATING A FACEBOOK BADGE FOR PERSONAL USE

In this example, you'll add a Facebook Badge to your blog's sidebar. This set of instructions includes those for Blogger, TypePad, and WordPress, for those using Facebook for personal use.

1. Once you log in to Facebook, click on Profile, and at the bottom of the left side, click on "Add a Badge to your Site."

2. If you are using this Facebook account for personal use, you can stay on Profile Badges (Figure 8–20).

Figure 8–20. Profile badges for Facebook

Using Blogger

a.   If you use Blogger, click on the Blogger button to bring up the Add Page Element box (see Figure 8–21). Click Add Widget and it's added to your blog's sidebar (the top). Drag and drop where desired and Save changes.

Figure 8–21. Adding a widget in Blogger

Using TypePad

b.   In TypePad, click the TypePad button to bring up the Add a Sidebar Widget window (Figure 8–22). Mark the check box next to your blog's name and click Add Widget. It is added to your sidebar (the bottom). To move it, click on Design Sidebar Content and drag and drop the widget to where you like. Save changes.

Figure 8–22. Adding a sidebar widget in TypePad

Using Wordpress

c. To add a widget in WordPress, click on Other, then select and copy the code. From My Blog, click on Dashboard ➤ Appearance. Click on Widgets and drag a Text Widget to the sidebar (Figure 8–23). Leave the Title blank and paste in the code in the larger text box. Click Save, then click Close.

Figure 8–23. *Adding a text widget in WordPress*

Now your blog visitors can also follow you on Facebook!

EXERCISE – CREATING FACEBOOK BADGES FOR BUSINESS USE

In this exercise, you will add a Facebook Badge to your blog's sidebar. This set of instructions is for those using Facebook for business use, and includes instruction for setting up a Facebook business page.

1. Log in to Facebook, click on Profile, and at the bottom of the left side, click on "Add a Badge to your Site."

Creating a Facebook Page for Business

2. Click on Page Badges. If this is a brand new Facebook account, you don't have any pages set up yet, so click on the word "Page" in the text as shown in Figure 8–24. It's a link to the Create a Page area in Facebook.

Figure 8–24. *Creating a Page Badge*

3. Select the type of business, cause, or topic that best describes the use of the page you are creating (Figure 8–25).

Figure 8–25. *Creating a Facebook Page*

4. In this example, I chose Company, Organization, or Institution, as shown in Figure 8–26.

Figure 8–26. *Enter the category and name and agree to the terms*

5. Click Get Started.

6. Complete the Security Check and click Submit.

7. Click to upload an image. This can be a picture of you or your company's logo, for example.

8. Notice the Internet address bar. And note your Facebook Page address. In my example, it is `http://www.facebook.com/pages/Creative-Blogging/199397096742386?created`. This is the part you will need to copy, and then use in the next step: `http://www.facebook.com/pages/Creative-Blogging/199397096742386` (the part before the question mark).

Creating a Like Box for your Facebook Business Page

9. In Step 5 (Promote This Page on your Website), click Add Like Box (shown in Figure 8–27). This is what you will use as your Facebook badge. If you prefer the traditional Facebook badge, you can skip these steps and continue at the section titled "Adding a Traditional Facebook Badge for Personal or Business Use."

Figure 8–27. *Configure Facebook Like Box*

10. Paste the Facebook URL you noted in step 8 into the Facebook Page URL box.

11. Adjust the Width to 180 so the Like Box will fit in your blog's sidebar.

12. Click Get Code (Figure 8–28).

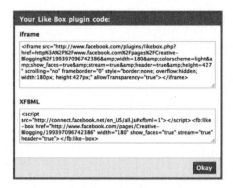

Figure 8–28. Plugin Code for Facebook Like Box

13. Copy the code in the top box (iframe).

Using Blogger

a. In Blogger, go to Design➤Page Elements and click Add a Gadget. Choose HTML/JavaScript. No Title is necessary. Paste in the code in the large text box and click Save (see Figure 8–29). Drag and drop the gadget where you want it in the sidebar and click Save.

Figure 8–29. Adding a gadget in Blogger

Using TypePad

b. In TypePad, go to Design➤Content and, from the middle box (Modules), choose "Embed your own HTML." Then click Add This Module from the right under Details. In the box that appears, leave the Title blank and paste in the code in the larger text box (see Figure 8–30). Save changes.

Drag and drop the gadget where you would like it in the sidebar and again save changes.

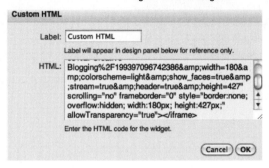

Figure 8–30. *Using custom HTML in TypePad*

Using WordPress

c. In WordPress, you can't add this gadget. Instead you'll add the traditional Facebook badge.

Adding a Traditional Facebook Badge for Personal or Business Use

14. To add a traditional Facebook Badge (shown in Figure 8–31), go back to the Facebook home page, www.facebook.com.

Figure 8–31. *A tradtitional Facebook page badge*

15. Click on Profile and at the bottom left click on "Add a Badge to Your Site."

16. Click on Page Badges (Figure 8–32).

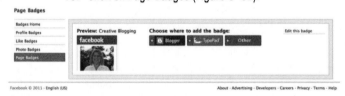

Figure 8–32. *Creating a page badge*

Using Blogger

a. If using Blogger, click on the Blogger button and the Add Page Element box appears (see Figure 8–33). Click Add Widget and it's added to your blog's sidebar (the top). Drag and drop where desired. Save changes.

Figure 8–33. Add Page Element

Using TypePad

b. In TypePad, click the TypePad button and the Add a Sidebar Widget window appears. Click the check box next to your blog's name and click Add Widget. The widget is added to your sidebar (the bottom). If you wish to move it, click on Design Sidebar Content. Then drag and drop the widget to where you'd like it to be. Save changes.

Figure 8–34. Add a Sidebar Widget

Using WordpPress

c. To add the widget in WordPress, click on "Other." Select and copy the code. From My Blog, click on Dashboards ➤ Appearance. Click on Widgets and drag a Text Widget to the sidebar. Leave the Title blank and paste in the code in the larger text box (see Figure 8–35). Click Save and then Close.

Figure 8–35. Adding a Text Widget

Now your badge allows your blog visitors to also follow you on Facebook!

We have one more step to go through to complete the integration with Facebook. The badge is a great widget to have in the sidebar as it lets visitors know you're on Facebook. However, to save time and to keep your Facebook fans up-to-date with your blog posts. We will now use the NetworkedBlogs application in Facebook to configure your blog posts to automatically publish to your Facebook page (or to your Wall if you're not a business user).

Using NetworkedBlogs

NetworkedBlogs is a community of connected bloggers who read and write about similar topics. The application has a feature that allows you to connect your blog to your Facebook account. First, you have to install the NetworkedBlogs application to your blog and then register your blog with NetworkedBlogs (adding your blog to its directory of blogs). Lastly, you use a process called syndication to link your blog and Facebook.

EXERCISE – SETTING UP NETWORKEDBLOGS IN FACEBOOK

We're still in Facebook, so let's now go through the process to get your blog posts to begin feeding into your Facebook Page or Wall using the Facebook application called NetworkedBlogs.

1. Go back to the main page in Facebook, www.Facebook.com.

2. In another browser window, go to www.facebook.com/networkedblogs (see Figure 8–36). We have to add this application to your Facebook account.

Figure 8–36. NetworkedBlogs main page

3. Click Go To App.

4. On the next screen, click Allow to allow NetworkedBlogs to access your basic information.

5. Choose at least one blog to follow—ProBlogger is a good one! See Figure 8–37.

Figure 8–37. Selecting blogs to follow

6. Click Next.

7. Choose friends' blogs to follow if you'd like (see Figure 8–38).

Figure 8–38. Choosing friends' blogs to follow

8.   Click to go to the NetworkedBlogs home page (see Figure 8–39).

Figure 8–39. *The NetworkedBlogs home page*

9.   Click Register a Blog.

10.   Enter your blog's information (see Figure 8–40).

Figure 8–40. *Registering a blog with NetworkedBlogs*

11.   Click Next.

12.   Are you the author? If so, click Yes. (See Figure 8–41.)

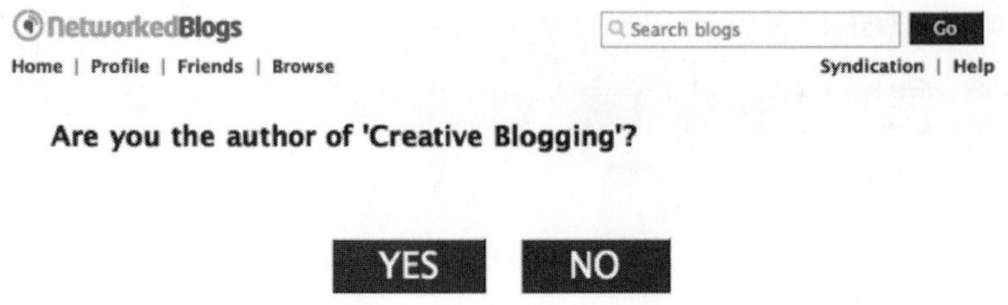

NetworkedBlogs
Search blogs
Go
Home | Profile | Friends | Browse
Syndication | Help
Are you the author of 'Creative Blogging'?
YES
NO

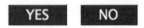

Figure 8–41. Are you the author

13. Now you have to verify that you own the blog (Figure 8–42).

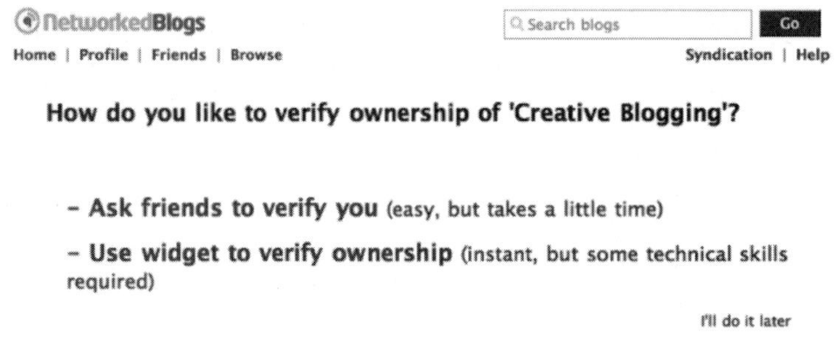
NetworkedBlogs
Search blogs
Go
Home | Profile | Friends | Browse
Syndication | Help
How do you like to verify ownership of 'Creative Blogging'?
- Ask friends to verify you (easy, but takes a little time)
- Use widget to verify ownership (instant, but some technical skills required)
I'll do it later

Figure 8–42. Choosing how to verify ownership of the blog

14. Click Use widget to verify ownership and you'll see the screen shown in Figure 8–43.

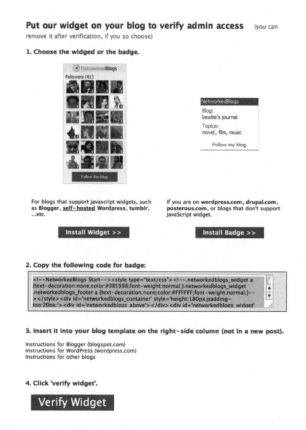

Put our widget on your blog to verify admin access (you can remove it after verification, if you so choose)

1. Choose the widged or the badge.

For blogs that support javascript widgets, such as Blogger, <u>self-hosted</u> Wordpress, tumblr, ...etc.

If you are on **wordpress.com, drupal.com, posterous.com,** or blogs that don't support JavaScript widget.

Install Widget >>

Install Badge >>

2. Copy the following code for badge:

```
<!--NetworkedBlogs Start--><style type="text/css"><!--.networkedblogs_widget a
{text-decoration:none;color:#385998;font-weight:normal;}.networkedblogs_widget
.networkedblogs_footer a {text-decoration:none;color:#FFFFFF;font-weight:normal;}--
></style> <div id='networkedblogs_container' style='height:180px;padding-
top:20px;'> <div id='networkedblogs_above'> </div> <div id='networkedblogs_widget'
```

3. Insert it into your blog template on the right-side column (not in a new post).

Instructions for Blogger (blogspot.com)
Instructions for WordPress (wordpress.com)
Instructions for other blogs

4. Click 'verify widget'.

Verify Widget

Figure 8–43. *Choosing the widget*

15. We'll quickly go over how to install the Verify widget on Blogger, TypePad, and WordPress. If you don't feel like doing it now, you can click "I'll do it later" and go to step 18.

Using Blogger

a. If using Blogger, click on Install Widget and copy the code provided. Go to Design➤Page Elements and click Add a Gadget. Select the HTML/JavaScript gadget and paste the code into the large text box. Click Save.

Using TypePad

b. If using TypePad, click on Install Widget. Select and copy the code and go to Design➤Content. From the Modules box, choose Embed Your Own HTML and click Add This Module. Paste the code into the large text box. Save.

Using WordPrss

c. If using WordPress, click Install Badge. Select and copy the code provided. From My Blog, click Dashboard➤Appearance➤Widgets. Drag a Text Widget to the sidebar and paste in the code. Click Save. Click Close.

16. No matter which platform you used, now click on Verify Widget (Figure 8–44). Once the verification succeeds, you can either leave the widget on your blog or remove it. We needed it simply needed to show ownership of the blog.

    a. I actually recommend removing it, as blog visitors may get a bit overwhelmed and confused with following you on your blog, then Twitter, then Facebook, and now NetworkedBlogs. Furthermore, they may not know what NetworkedBlogs is. So remove the widget, which you can easily do by editing the gadget or widget and clicking Remove (Blogger) or Delete (WordPress). In TypePad, go to Design➤Content and click the "x" in the widget your just added.

Figure 8–44: *Verification Successful*

17. Click Next to begin syndication. Just a few more steps left to complete the integration process!

18. Click Set Up Syndication (shown in Figure 8–45).

Figure 8–45: *Setting up syndication*

19. On the next screen click Grant Permissions.

20. Click Allow to permit access.

21. Now select a target to publish new posts to as shown in Figure 8–46.

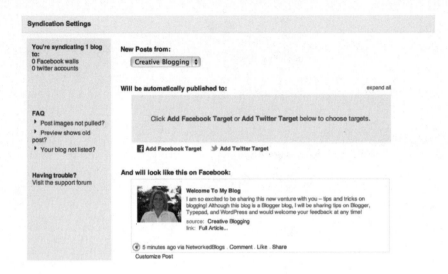

Figure 8–46. The Syndication Settings page

22. Click Add Facebook Target to go to the screen in Figure 8–47.

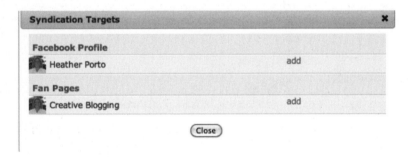

Figure 8–47. Syndication Targets

23. Click "add" to the right of your Fan Page (business users) or to the right of your Facebook Profile if this is for personal use.

24. Click Close to complete syndication.

Figure 8–48. Syndication is complete.

25. Notice in my example, Creative Blogging (Fan Pages) is now added under the "Will be automatically published to" target area.

26. You're done!

Now your blog posts will be automatically published to your Facebook Page!

This will save you lots of time as you won't have to post the same updates to your blog, Facebook, and Twitter. But of course you should post additional messages besides your blog posts. But that's for another book!

Summary

You have now successfully integrated your blog with Facebook and Twitter. By adding the gadgets to your sidebar, you allow blog visitors to see that you're on Twitter and Facebook and you give them an opportunity to follow you as well. More importantly, by having Facebook and Twitter accounts, you use the strength of social networking to expand your following and online visibility, and increase your potential to find new customers.

And speaking of customers, in the next chapter you will learn how to build an online blog store! Yes, we create pages in your blog, list services or items for sale, and find out how to use PayPal to add payment buttons to yiour blog. With a store right in your blog, there's no need to manage a second, external web site. You can do it all from your blog!

CHAPTER 9

■ ■ ■

Setting Up Shop

In addition to using your blog to share information with your readers and keep them informed about what's going on in your life or your business, you can also use your blog to sell the products or services you offer. Of course, you'll want to post immediately about any new product or service you'll be offering so people who subscribe to your blog will find out about them as soon as possible. But you should also create a page to list all of your products and services. A page lets your readers quickly and easily access everything you want to promote without having to search your blog. In this chapter you will learn how to create pages and setup an online store.

 So what's the difference between a post and a page? In most ways, there is no difference. Both can contain text, images, video, and so on, and in terms of creation and layout, they're almost identical. But you can think of a post as being more dynamic—the idea of a post is that it's fresh and new and it tends to supplant the previous one. Each time you publish a new post, your subscribers are updated automatically.

In contrast, a page is more static. Moreover, blog subscribers are not informed when a page is published. Blogger has a Pages gadget that you can add to your blog, in the sidebar or the header area, preferably under your banner. If you put it in the header area, it serves as a navigation or menu bar! Many WordPress themes include a built-in menu that automatically adds your pages as they are created. TypePad allows you to create pages, but you have to manually add them to the built-in navigation bar feature (we'll do this during the upcoming exercises).

The Pages gadget gives your visitors access to your pages. In the upcoming exercises you will create two pages—About Me and Services—and in doing so you will gain a better understanding of the use and purpose of pages.

In addition to these pages, you may also want to experiment and create a page for Contact Me or for Testimonials, or for any sort of information you want to include on your site that isn't likely to change very often. A little homework!

Furthermore, creating pages is the first step in setting up shop—your online blog store! In creating the Services page, you will learn how to use PayPal to accept payments online, as shown in Figure 9–1. (Google Checkout can't be used in WordPress.com blogs, so PayPal will be our preferred method in this book).

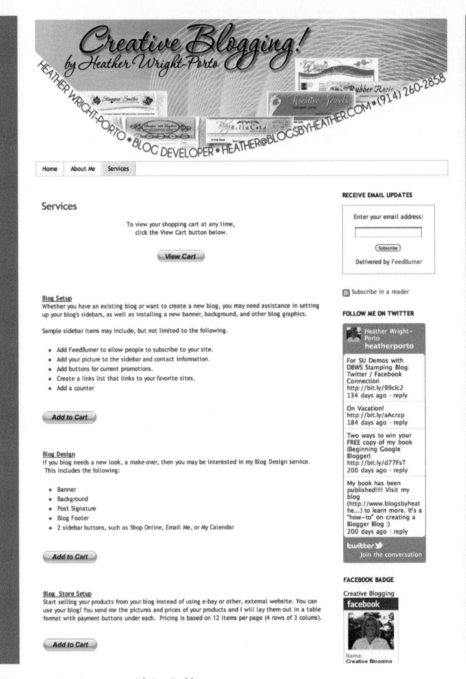

***Figure 9–1.** Services page with PayPal buttons*

This chapter also touches on the use of HTML in the WordPress example when we create a hyperlink and custom PayPal button image. It's a loaded chapter in which you'll be switching back and forth between your blog and PayPal, as well as editing HTML code; so you may want to go get a cup of coffee before we start!

Creating Pages

You can create pages in Blogger, TypePad, and WordPress. In the exercises throughout this chapter, we'll see how to create pages, and a blog store, using all three platforms.

Of the three, WordPress is the only platform that actually has a separate Pages option or area on the Dashboard. In Blogger and TypePad, the Pages feature is somewhat hidden in that you first have to go to Posts to access Pages. Hopefully a direct link to Pages will be a feature TypePad and Blogger add in the future. For now, do the following:

- In Blogger, click Edit Posts from the Dashboard, then Edit Pages. Then click on the New Page button.

- In TypePad, click on Posts from the Dashboard, then click on Pages on the left.

Share Your Story

Let's begin by creating an About Me page. This is a page that focuses on you or your business. It should include a brief biography or business history (how and when the business was started, its mission and purpose or benefits), as well as a picture of you. An About Me page makes it personal and allows your readers and customers to learn more about you. Let your personality shine and show off your skills and experiences!

EXERCISE – CREATING A PAGE AND ADDING THE PAGES GADGET

In the next exercise you will create an About Me page. You will then add the page to a menu bar so visitors can quickly find and access it.

Using Blogger

1. From your Dashboard, click on Edit Posts.

2. Click on Edit Pages.

3. Click on New Page, which brings up the Pages Editor shown in Figure 9–2. The Pages Editor looks similar to the Post Editor you used earlier in this book to compose and publish posts.

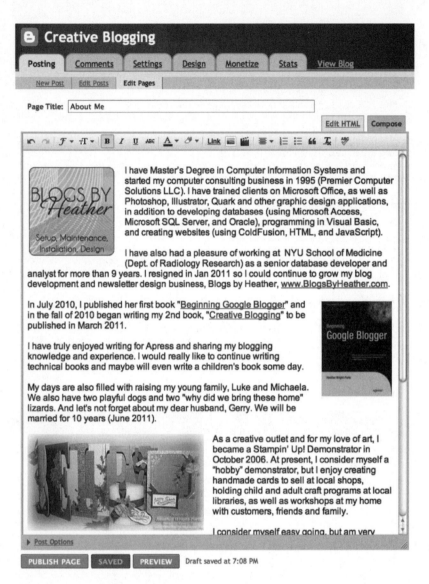

Figure 9–2. The Blogger page editor

4. In my example, I used "About Me" as the Page Title, but "About Us" or simply "About" are also popular.

5. Write your content just as you would if you were creating a new post. The toolbar is the same and you can still format your text, insert images, and so on. Whatever you can do with a post, you can do here when creating a page.

6. When you're finished, click on Publish Page. As shown in Figure 9–3, Blogger now asks "How would you like the Pages Gadget to appear?".

    a. If you want to add a quick navigational bar (or menu) to your blog, choose Blog Tabs (Figure 9–3).

    b. If you prefer to have the links to your pages appear as a list in the sidebar, click Blog Sidebar.

    c. At this point, I don't recommend the No Gadget option, as this gives your blog visitors no way to access your page.

7. In this example, choose Blog Tabs.

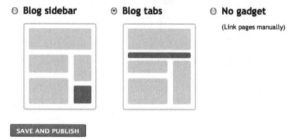

Figure 9–3. Adding the Pages Gadget

8. Click Save and Publish.

9. You should get a message that the page was published successfully.

10. Click on View Page to view your new page. In Figure 9–4, note the new menu bar (under the banner), which includes Home and About Me. Figure 9–4 shows the About Me page I created. Notice that it's very similar to a post but without the Date Header. Other than that, it has the same formatting, the same look and feel as a post.

Figure 9–4. *The new menu bar containing View Blog and Menu*

11. Click Design (on the top right) and you're back at Page Elements, where you see a visual layout of all the gadgets added to your blog, in the header, sidebars, and footer areas. The newly added Pages gadget has been added beneath the header (banner) area.

Using TypePad

12. From your Dashboard, click on Posts.

13. Click on Pages (on the left).

14. Click on the New Page link to bring up the Pages Editor shown in Figure 9–5. Now begin entering your content (your mini bio). Use the toolbar to format text, just as you would in writing a post.

Figure 9–5. Creating a new page in TypePad

15. Click on Publish.

16. Click on View Page. Select and copy the URL in the address bar (or be sure to note it in a temporary document or on a piece of paper).

17. In Figure 9–6, notice the built-in Navigational Bar consisting of Home, Archives, Profile, and Subscribe items. You will now add About Me in place of Profile.

Figure 9–6. *Viewing the About Me page*

18. Close the window that popped up.

19. To add a Navigational Bar (menu) to your blog, click on Design.

20. Click on Content and you will see a visual layout of your blog as shown in Figure 9–7.

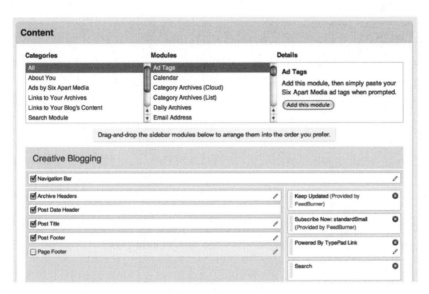

Figure 9–7. The Content View of your blog

21. Click on the pencil icon all the way to the right of Navigation Bar. Notice the table of titles and links (URLs) as shown in Figure 9–8.

Figure 9–8. Navigation Bar Configuration

22. Click on the word Profile to select it. Type "About Me" to replace Profile, then paste in the URL you copied in step 16.

23. Click OK to save the change to the Navigation Bar.

24. Click Save Changes at the bottom (a requirement or your menu will not update).

25. Click on View Blog to view the updated menu.

Using WordPress

26. From your Dashboard, click on Pages.

27. Notice there is already an About page (added by default when you created the blog).

28. Click on Trash under the About to delete that page since we'll create our own. Yes, you could have clicked on Edit to edit the existing About page, but I want you to learn how to create a new page.

29. Click on the Add New button.

30. Enter About Me as the Title and your "about me" content in the post body area (see my sample in Figure 9–9).

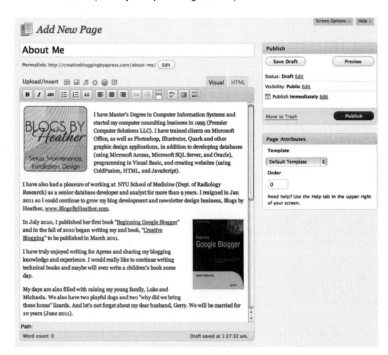

Figure 9–9. Adding a new page in WordPress

31. Click Publish.

32. Click on View Page to see the new page and navigation bar. Unlike Blogger and TypePad, in WordPress you don't have to make any additional changes, such as adding a Pages Gadget or updating the Navigation Bar; WordPress automatically adds new pages to its page element, which is called the Menu Bar. Note that the placement of this Menu Bar may differ depending on the WordPress Theme chosen. In the zBench theme I've been using throughout this book, the menu bar is in the top of the banner area, on the left side. Other themes may put it on the right.

Figure 9–10. *Viewing the page*

You have now successfully added a new page to your blog! Congratulations! But we are not finished, in fact, we are just getting started. Next we'll create a Services page.

Share Your Services

Now we'll create a page that lists the different services you offer and we'll also add a payment button for each service as shown back in Figure 9–1. Please keep in mind that we'll be going back and forth between your blog (on all three platforms) and PayPal while adding payment buttons to your pages. You should have at least two browser windows open to quickly and easily go back and forth.

The exercises are long because we review how to insert the buttons in Blogger, TypePad, and WordPress. If your coffee cup is empty, now would be a good time for a refill!

EXERCISE – CREATING A SERVICES PAGE

To begin, go back to your blog's Dashboard. In this exercise you'll create a new page to list services you offer. In our example, we'll use a few blog setup and development services with the Creative Blogging sample.

1. Whether using Blogger, TypePad or WordPress, following the steps from the previous exercise to create a new page, this time with the Title "Services."

2. In the page body area, create a list of services. See my example in Figure 9–11. This is a Blogger view, but it will look very similar regardless of which platform you are using.

3. When you're finished, click Publish (or Publish Page) to save your work.

4. You can view the page if you'd like, but let's go on to add payment buttons for using PayPal in the next exercise.

Figure 9–11. My sample Services page in Blogger

Using PayPal

PayPal is a very popular service that allows you to receive (and make) online payments. Purchasers can pay using their PayPal account or a credit card, which is why many merchants like it. Basically you can use PayPal as your online merchant account (credit card processor). However, like a traditional merchant account, PayPal charges you a fee for every online transaction (that is, every payment received). The rate can vary from 1.9 percent to 2.9 percent, depending on the previous month's sales volume.

Add to Cart Buttons

In the next exercise, you'll add Add to Cart payment buttons to the Services page you just created (similar to my Services page in Figure 9–1). The Add to Cart buttons allow your customers to purchase more than one service before checking out and paying via PayPal, so they don't have to do separate payment transactions for each item, as they would with Buy Now buttons.

EXERCISE – CREATE A PAYPAL ACCOUNT AND ADD PAYPAL BUTTONS

Since we'll be going back and forth between PayPal and your blog, be sure to have another browser window open. Now go back to Edit Posts and click Edit to edit your Services page (or click Back in your browser to get back to the Services page in the compose/rich text/visual view).

1. Go to `www.PayPal.com`.

2. Click the Sign Up link on the top to go to the screen shown in Figure 9–12.

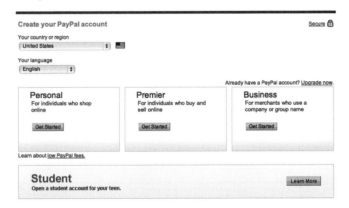

Figure 9–12. Creating a PayPal account

3. Click Get Started under Premier since you need "selling" capabilities.

4. On the next screen enter the information requested, as shown in Figure 9–13.

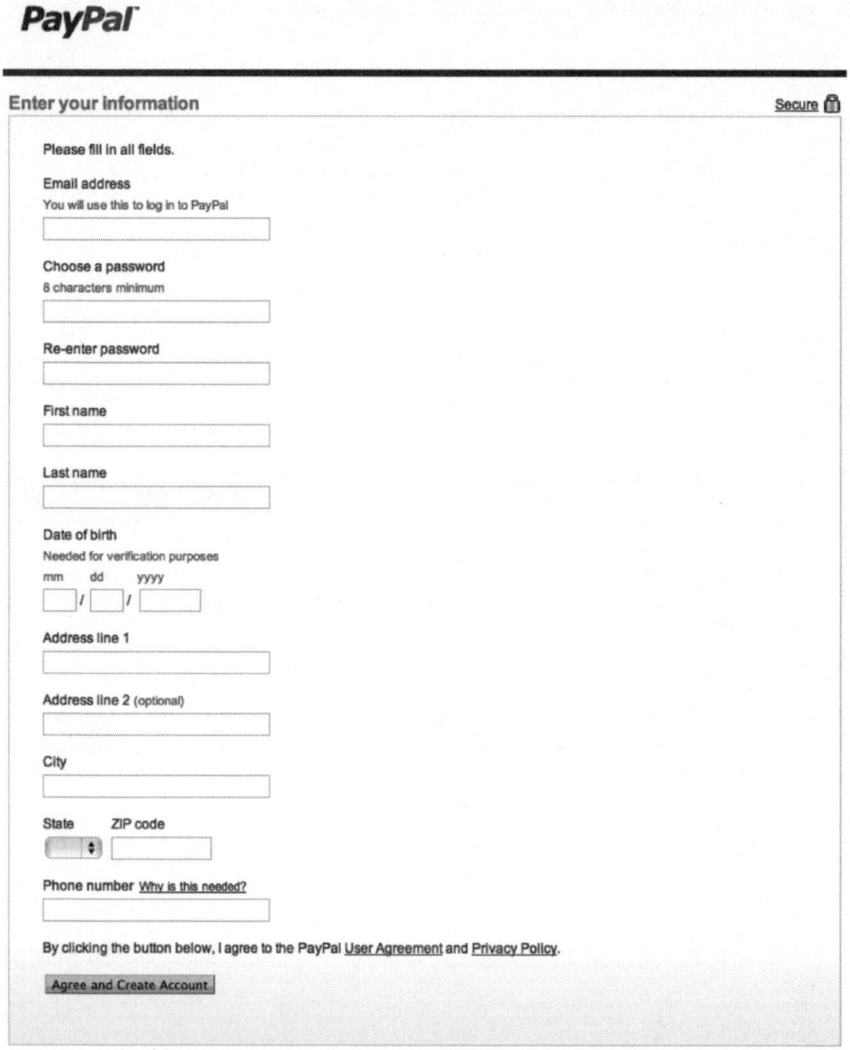

PayPal

Enter your information   Secure 🔒

Please fill in all fields.

Email address
You will use this to log in to PayPal

Choose a password
8 characters minimum

Re-enter password

First name

Last name

Date of birth
Needed for verification purposes
mm   dd   yyyy

Address line 1

Address line 2 (optional)

City

State   ZIP code

Phone number Why is this needed?

By clicking the button below, I agree to the PayPal User Agreement and Privacy Policy.

Agree and Create Account

Figure 9–13. Enter your information

5. Click Agree and Create Account to continue.

6. On the next screen (Figure 9–14), choose how to pay for purchases—bank account or credit card. You can enter this information later if you prefer. For now we'll continue to set up the buttons.

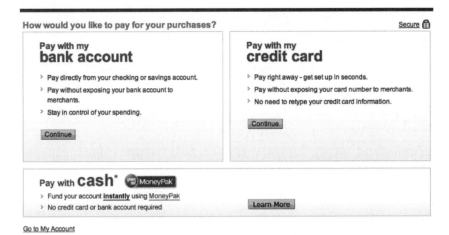

Figure 9–14. Choosing how to pay

7. Click on Go to My Account at the bottom left. We will address entering bank or credit card information at the end of the exercise. For now, we simply want to proceed with creating payment buttons.

8. Next, to create a button, go to the Merchant Services tab (see Figure 9–15).

Figure 9–15. Merchant Services

9. Click the Add to Cart button; the form shown in Figure 9–16 appears.

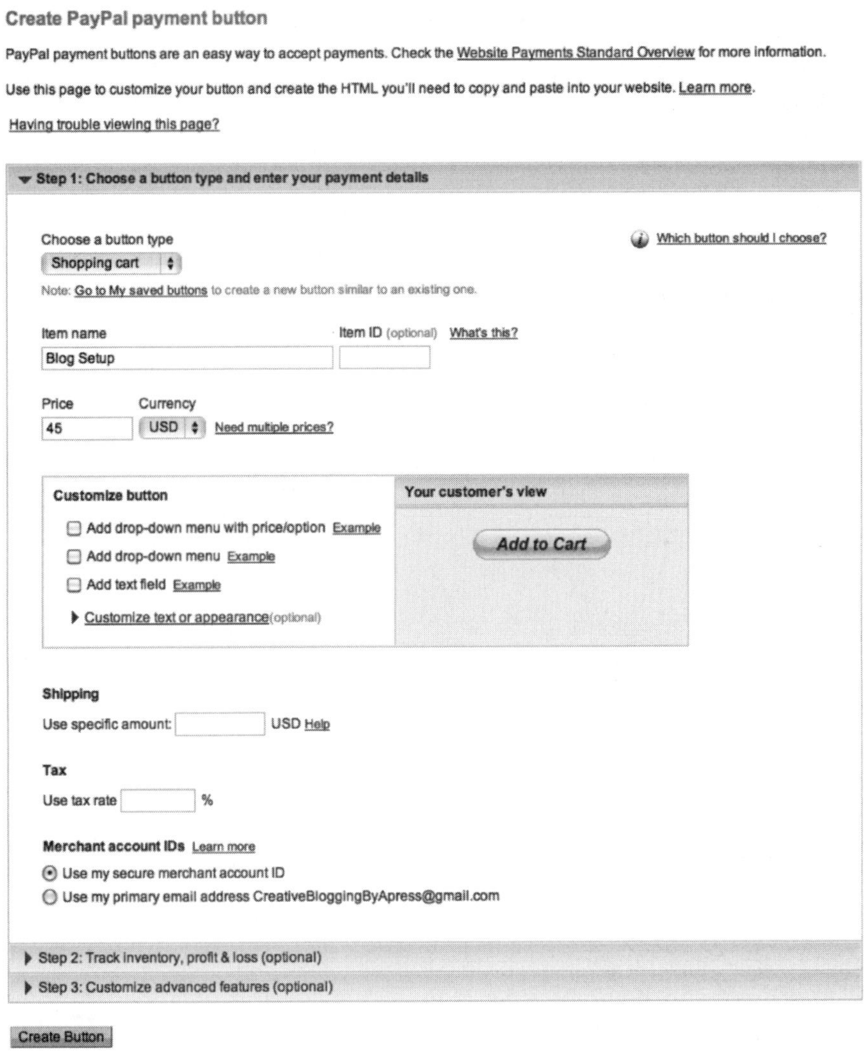

Create PayPal payment button

PayPal payment buttons are an easy way to accept payments. Check the Website Payments Standard Overview for more information.

Use this page to customize your button and create the HTML you'll need to copy and paste into your website. Learn more.

Having trouble viewing this page?

▼ Step 1: Choose a button type and enter your payment details

Choose a button type   ⓘ Which button should I choose?

[Shopping cart ⬍]

Note: Go to My saved buttons to create a new button similar to an existing one.

Item name   Item ID (optional) What's this?

[Blog Setup]   [   ]

Price   Currency

[45]   [USD ⬍] Need multiple prices?

Customize button   **Your customer's view**

☐ Add drop-down menu with price/option Example

☐ Add drop-down menu Example   (Add to Cart)

☐ Add text field Example

▶ Customize text or appearance (optional)

Shipping

Use specific amount: [   ]   USD Help

Tax

Use tax rate [   ] %

Merchant account IDs Learn more

◉ Use my secure merchant account ID

○ Use my primary email address CreativeBloggingByApress@gmail.com

▶ Step 2: Track inventory, profit & loss (optional)

▶ Step 3: Customize advanced features (optional)

[Create Button]

Figure 9–16. Configuring the Add to Cart button

10. Enter the Item Name (Blog Setup in my example).

11. You do not need to enter an Item ID. However, if you use an ID of some type with your services or products, or an associated account number in Quickbooks or other financial package, for example, you can enter it here. If you will be using PayPal's inventory tracking, (Step 2: Track inventory, profit & loss (optional) at the bottom of Figure 9–16), you would use this Item ID. This is outside the scope of this exercise, though.

12. Continue to enter the Price and currency ($45 in USD in my example).

13. Enter Shipping amount (if applicable).

14. Enter Tax (if applicable).

15. Click Create Button; the page shown in Figure 9–17 appears.

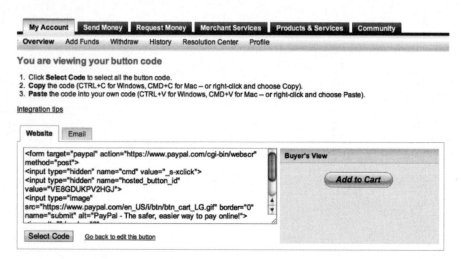

Figure 9–17. *Viewing the button code*

Using Blogger and TypePad

16. Click Select Code, then copy the code. That code should look something like this:

```
<form target="paypal" action="https://www.paypal.com/cgi-bin/webscr" method="post">
<input type="hidden" name="cmd" value="_s-xclick">
<input type="hidden" name="hosted_button_id" value="FEGJ2RE6ALQUN">
<input type="image" src="https://www.paypal.com/en_US/i/btn/btn_cart_LG.gif" border="0"
name="submit" alt="PayPal - The safer, easier way to pay online!">
<img alt="" border="0" src="https://www.paypal.com/en_US/i/scr/pixel.gif" width="1"
height="1">
</form>
```

Switch to your blog.

17. Go to your Services page.

18. Click on Edit HTML (in Blogger) or HTML (in TypePad).

19. Scroll to where you want to insert the first button.

20. Paste in the code (see Figure 9–18).

Page Title: Services

Edit HTML   Compose

B *I* ABC **Link** ✉ ❝

well as installing a new banner, background, and other blog graphics.

Sample sidebar items may include, but not limited to the following.

```
<ul>
<li>Add FeedBurner to allow people to subscribe to your site.</li>
<li>Add your picture to the sidebar and contact information.</li>
<li>Add buttons for current promotions.</li>
<li>Create a links list that links to your favorite sites.</li>
<li>Add a counter</li>
</ul>

<form target="paypal" action="https://www.paypal.com/cgi-bin/webscr" method="post">
<input type="hidden" name="cmd" value="_s-xclick">
<input type="hidden" name="hosted_button_id" value="VE8GDUKPV2HGJ">
<input type="image" src="https://www.paypal.com/en_US/i/btn/btn_cart_LG.gif" border="0" name="submit" alt="PayPal - The
safer, easier way to pay online!">
<img alt="" border="0" src="https://www.paypal.com/en_US/i/scr/pixel.gif" width="1" height="1">
</form>
```

▶ Post Options

PUBLISH PAGE   SAVE AS DRAFT   PREVIEW

Back to list of Pages

Figure 9–18. Copying the button code to your page

21. Click on Compose (Blogger) or Rich Text (TypePad) to see the newly added PayPal button.

Switch to PayPal.

22. Click on Create Similar Button to create a button for your next item.

23. Repeat steps 9–20 (switching between your blog and PayPl) until you have created Add to Cart buttons for all of your services (Figure 9–19).

Services

Blog Setup

Whether you have an existing blog or want to create a new blog, you may need assistance in setting up your blog's sidebars, as well as installing a new banner, background, and other blog graphics.

Sample sidebar items may include, but not limited to the following.

- Add FeedBurner to allow people to subscribe to your site.
- Add your picture to the sidebar and contact information.
- Add buttons for current promotions.
- Create a links list that links to your favorite sites.
- Add a counter

Blog Design

if you blog needs a new look, a make-over, then you may be interested in my Blog Design service. This includes the following:

- Banner
- Background
- Post Signature
- Blog Footer
- 2 sidebar buttons, such as Shop Online, Email Me, or My Calendar

Blog Store Setup

Start selling your products from your blog instead of using e-bay or other, external website. You can use your blog! You send me the pictures and prices of your products and I will lay them out in a table format with payment buttons under each. Pricing is based on 12 items per page (4 rows of 3 colums).

Figure 9–19. An Add to Cart Button for each service

After selecting, copying, and pasting the code for the last item, switch back to PayPal and click on Create a View Cart Button. This button lets customers see their shopping carts in PayPal at any time. Click Create

Button and then select and copy the code (as you did for the Add to Cart buttons) and add this PayPal button at the top or the bottom of your page. You'll see it at the top of the page in my example in Figure 9–1.

Using WordPress

23. You are still at the screen shown in Figure 9–17 where you've completed the Add to Cart form and clicked Create Button. By default the Website tab is selected and the code is shown (as in Figure 9–17), but with WordPress you need to create the button differently, so click the Email tab. You'll see the screen shown in Figure 9–20.

Figure 9–20. Email Button Code

24. Click Select Code.

25. Copy the link shown on your screen (as in Figure 9–20).

26. Go to your Services page in your WordPress blog and scroll to where you want to insert the button.

27. WordPress handles this very differently from Blogger and TypePad. You have to use your own image to serve as a link to PayPal, using the code you just copied (Figure 9–20).

28. You need to replace only the bolded link section of code with the Email code/link you copied in PayPal. We go over this in more detail in the Chapter 10; however, the HTML code you see below is for an anchor tag to create a hyperlink with an image tag that references an image stored in my Photobucket account. Feel free to use this so you don't have to worry about creating your own PayPal button image.

What does this code mean? It just links the Add to Cart button image to the PayPal page for this item. Don't worry about it for now; we will be looking at HTML in much more detail in the next chapter, which is specifically about using HTML and CSS code in your blog.

```
<a href="https://www.paypal.com/cgi-bin/webscr?cmd=_s-
xclick&hosted_button_id=N7XFM9RMDQUZJ" target=paypal>
<img src="http://i493.photobucket.com/albums/rr300/blogsbyheather/AddToCart.png">
</a>
```

29. Publish the page or click Visual to view the newly added button.

Switch to PayPal.

30. Click on Create Similar Button to create a button for your next item.

31. Repeat steps 9–14, then steps 23-29 (switching between your blog and PayPal) until you've created all the Add to Cart buttons needed for your services.

32. After adding all the Add to Cart buttons, click a Create a View Cart button.

33. Click the Email tab again and use this code, replacing the bolded link with yours.

```
<a href="https://www.paypal.com/cgi-bin/webscr?cmd=_s-
xclick&hosted_button_id=N7XFM9RMDQUZJ" target=paypal>
<img src="http://i493.photobucket.com/albums/rr300/blogsbyheather/ViewCart.png">
</a>
```

You can also set up shipping and tax (if applicable) so you don't have to enter them manually each time. To do that, go to the Merchant Services tab, then Shipping Calculator and Shipping Preferences. For tax, go to the Tax Calculator.

Lastly, to be able to transfer the money you receive from PayPal to your bank account, you can set up your bank information. Click on Profile and then under Financial Information, click on Bank Accounts, then Add Bank, and enter checking or savings account information.

Buy Now Button

You're doing great! There is just one more thing I'd like to cover in this chapter, and that's adding a Buy Now button. Why? To show you the difference between the Buy Now button and the Add to Cart buttons we've been using thus far. The Buy Now button allows you to link a PDF or other file (containing perhaps a special coupon or a tutorial or e-book you may be selling) to the button, so that after a successful payment, a customer can download the file rather than you to having to e-mail it to them.

EXERCISE – ADDING A PAYPAL BUY NOW BUTTON

In this exercise, you will be adding the e-book item at the very bottom of the Services page, under the list of services. Wherever you are now, go back to your Services page and open it for editing.

1. First, insert the image of your e-book (you can use any image for this example). You insert this image as you would any other image in your page (as you would for a post), by clicking the Insert Image button on the toolbar.

2. Underneath, enter the e-book name, price, publish date, or any other information (see the example in Figure 9–21).

Beginning Google Blogger
Published July 2010
$17.49

Figure 9–21. Sample image and information for an ebook

3. Let's add the Buy Now button. Again, we'll have two sets of instructions; one for Blogger and TypePad users and the second for WordPress bloggers.

Switch to PayPal.

4. If some time has elapsed, you may have to log back in to PayPal. Note that this may happen at any time as you're building your store pages if PayPal has been idle for too long.

5. Go to Merchant Services.

6. This time click on the Buy Now button; the form shown in Figure 9–22 appears.

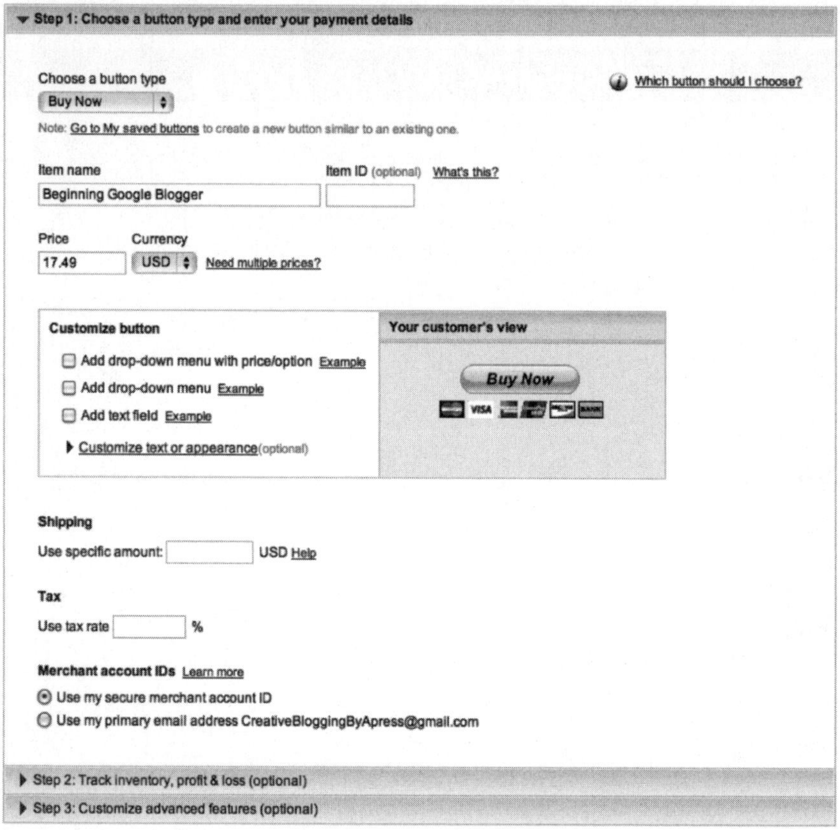

Figure 9–22. Choosing and configuring a Buy Now button

7. Enter the Item Name and Price. If you need to create a list of different item options and pricing, you can use the Customize Button section and check "Add drop-down menu with price option," and simply enter as many Item Names and Prices as needed.

8. Do not enter shipping for this example since it is a digital download.

9. Enter tax (if applicable).

10. You'll skip Step 2 on this form; you don't need to track your inventory. Click on Step 3: Customize Advanced Features (Optional). The page shown in Figure 9–23 appears.

▶ Step 1: Choose a button type and enter your payment details

▶ Step 2: Track inventory, profit & loss (optional)

▼ **Step 3: Customize advanced features (optional)**

Customize checkout pages

If you are an advanced user, you can customize checkout pages for your customers, streamline checkout, and more in this section.

Do you want to let your customer change order quantities?

○ Yes
◉ No

Can your customer add special instructions in a message to you?

◉ Yes
    Name of message box (40-character limit)
    | Add special instructions to the seller |
○ No

Do you need your customer's shipping address?

○ Yes
◉ No

☐ Take customers to this URL when they cancel their checkout

    | |
    Example: https://www.mystore.com/cancel

☑ Take customers to this URL when they finish checkout

    | http://www.blogsbyheather.com/GoogleBlogger.pdf |
    Example: https://www.mystore.com/success

Advanced variables What's this?

Use a line break between each variable. The variables will appear in your button's HTML code. Learn more

☐ Add advanced variables

    | | **Example**
    | | address_override=1
    | | notify_url=https://www.mywebsite.com/PayPal_IPN
    | | business_cs_email=frank.zweitek@elomenopee.com

Figure 9–23. Customizing advanced features

11. Click on No for "Do you need your customer's mailing address" and check "Take customers to this URL when they have finished checkout."

12. Paste in the URL where your e-book or tutorial (or whatever) is stored.

   - You can link to any online document. Google Docs is a popular free service. If you'd like to learn more, visit `docs.google.com`. If you're using TypePad or WordPress, you can upload a document to the built-in file manager.

13. Click the Create Button.

Using Blogger and TypePad

14. Select and copy the code that PayPal provides in the Web text box (the default code shown).

15. Go back to your Services page, click on Edit HTML (Blogger) or HTML (TypePad) and go all the way to the bottom of the page and paste in the code (under the price of the e-book for example).

16. Publish Page.

17. View Page.

Using WordPress

18. Click on the Email tab.

19. Select and copy the link that PayPal provides.

20. Go back to your Services page. Click on HTML and go all the way to the bottom of the page and paste this code, replacing the bolded URL with yours.

```
<a href="https://www.paypal.com/cgi-bin/webscr?cmd=_s-
xclick&hosted_button_id=PP2CAQLH7CKVE" target=paypal>
<img src="http://i493.photobucket.com/albums/rr300/blogsbyheather/BuyNow.png">
</a>
```

21. Publish Page.

22. View Page (see Figure 9–24).

Beginning Google Blogger
Published July 2010
$17.49

Figure 9–24. The Buy Now button has been added.

You are done! Congratulations!

Before concluding this chapter, I want to note an important difference between the Add to Cart and Buy Now buttons. With Add to Cart buttons, although you can add a link that customers would be directed to after payment, I don't recommend it. If a customer clicks more than one Add to Cart button, PayPal won't know which link to go to. It can only go to one location, not many, when the purchase is complete. That's why in our example I used the Buy Now button with the link option (which again is not required although I have mentioned it a few times), for it is a one-to-one relationship and it works.

■ **Note** With Buy Now buttons and links—there's a catch! PayPal changed its functionality so users now have to click on "Return to `<your PayPal email address>`" after the successful transaction, and only when they do will they be directed to the online document you linked the PayPal button to.

Due to the potential problem of users not taking that final step, some blog owners add a note to their store page if they are using Buy Now buttons to deliver digital content. For example, you can add some text to your store page, near the Buy Now button, like this: "Upon completion of your PayPal payment, you must click the Return to `<this is where your email address associated with PayPal will be shown>` to download the PDF." On my page, for example, it might say "Upon completion of your PayPal payment, you must click the Return to blogsbyheather@att.net to download my e-book." There is no "click here to download" button or link. PayPal has complicated this type of digital download process, but at least there is still an option that lets customers download PDFs (or other document type) as soon as they complete the purchase so they don't have to wait for an email attachment.

Summary

We began this chapter by looking at why you would use pages, in addition to regular postings. With pages, you can quickly and easily create a navigational bar or menu that allows visitors to easily find information about you and your services. To enhance your blog, we created an About Me page and a Services page.

We then took that concept to the next level, by adding payment options to your Services page using PayPal. However, we're not quite done! In the next chapter, we'll expand the discussion of HTML and see how to use it to enhance your blog store pages using a table format like what's shown in Figure 9–25. We will also discuss how and where to add custom CSS code to your blog. You'll want to become familiar with HTML and CSS so you can customize your blog when you can't use a menu or template to do so!

Figure 9–25. Snippet of the blog store at www.sandimaciver.com/sandi_maciver/sandis-blog-store.html

CHAPTER 10

HTML/CSS Basics

In the last chapter you learned how to create a page, and then to turn a page into a blog store. First, we created a Services page to hold a list of services (or, for that matter, products) for sale, then we set up a PayPal account so we could process payments. To complete the process, we added PayPal's Add to Cart and Buy Now buttons to the Services page so you could receive payments online from your customers. This is an efficient, real-time solution. It allows your customers to pay promptly, and it means that you, as a business owner, don't have to use other e-commerce web sites or stores, like eBay or Etsy, to sell your products. You can keep it all in one place within your blog!

Now we're going to take your blog store one step further and see how to organize your products in a table format (rows and columns). Tables let you fit more items on a page in a neat and organized manner. As you can see in the page shown in Figure 10–1, there is an opening paragraph about the products, and then the products are presented in a table with a PayPal button under each item. This is where we will start our discussion on how to use HTML to enhance your blog's look and functionality.

In addition to HTML tables, we'll take a look at other useful HTML tags for links, images, and paragraphs; and then begin our CSS lesson by seeing how to add CSS code to your HTML tags to format your text and images. Lastly, we'll take writing CSS code up one more level by using it to modify your blog's layout.

- In Blogger, you do this in the new Template Designer ➤Advanced area, or by clicking Design ➤ Edit HTML.

- In TypePad, you do this in the Custom CSS area by clicking Design from the Dashboard; however, you can do this only if you have the Unlimited TypePad version or higher.

- In WordPress, you click on Appearance from the Dashboard, then click Edit CSS to access its CSS customization features.

You generally use custom CSS coding to format in ways that aren't available on standard menus or formatting bars, although you can also customize any element of your blog's design using CSS code. For example, you can use CSS code to add a background image to your blog, to set or remove margins and borders in your sidebars, or to change the font size and background color of your sidebar titles.

In the last chapter I suggested you start with a fresh cup of coffee, then when we were mid-way through, I proposed you get a refill. Well, since this chapter is a little more advanced, now I'm recommending an espresso!

Products

We highly recommend the following products and use them in business and for our personal landscaping needs. You may purchase these products from us at cost but will have to pay for shipping which will be calculated at checkout based on weight (U.S. Sales only).

Figure 10–1. HTML table example of a store page

HTML Tables

An HTML table is code that organizes content in columns and rows. It is a handy way to display your products using text, images, or both. Figure 10–1 showed one way to use a table to display items for sale and their prices; Figure 10–2 shows another.

Product Name	Price
Scott's Turf Builder	$10.00
Miracle Gro Plant Food	$8.00
Miracle Gro Shake 'n Feed	$8.00
Scott's Liquid Turf Builder	$8.00
Red Mulch	$2.00
Garden Soil	$2.00

Figure 10–2. HTML table using text

We're going to jump right in and look at the HTML code needed to build a table like the one in Figure 10–1. We will do this in steps, first creating the code, then adding the pictures and descriptions of products and prices, and finishing with the PayPal buttons. Don't worry; we won't be typing this straight in now. We'll explain it a bit first, and then step through the writing of it so you understand exactly what's going on. Listing 10–1 shows the code for creating an HTML table.

Listing 10–1. Creating an HTML Table

```
<table align=center cellpadding=10>
<tr>

<td valign=bottom align=center>
Image Here<BR/>
Description Here<BR/>
Price Here<BR/>
PAYPAL Button
</td>

<td valign=bottom align=center>
Image Here<BR/>
Description Here<BR/>
Price Here<BR/>
PAYPAL Button
</td>

<td valign=bottom align=center>
Image Here<BR/>
Description Here<BR/>
Price Here<BR/>
PAYPAL Button
</td>

</tr>

<tr>

<td valign=bottom align=center>
```

```
Image Here<BR/>
Description Here<BR/>
Price Here<BR/>
PAYPAL Button
</td>

<td valign=bottom align=center>
Image Here<BR/>
Description Here<BR/>
Price Here<BR/>
PAYPAL Button
</td>

<td valign=bottom align=center>
Image Here<BR/>
Description Here<BR/>
Price Here<BR/>
PAYPAL Button
</td>

</tr>
</table>
```

In this example, I specifically added spacing in the code to make it more readable. You don't have to include blank lines when writing HTML code for your blog. Figure 10–3 shows how the table this code creates would appear in your blog at this moment if you're using Blogger or WordPress. With TypePad, in contrast, there would be no padding or space between the Image Here, Description Here, Price Here and PAYPAL button. We'll address formatting the table as we go through the examples.

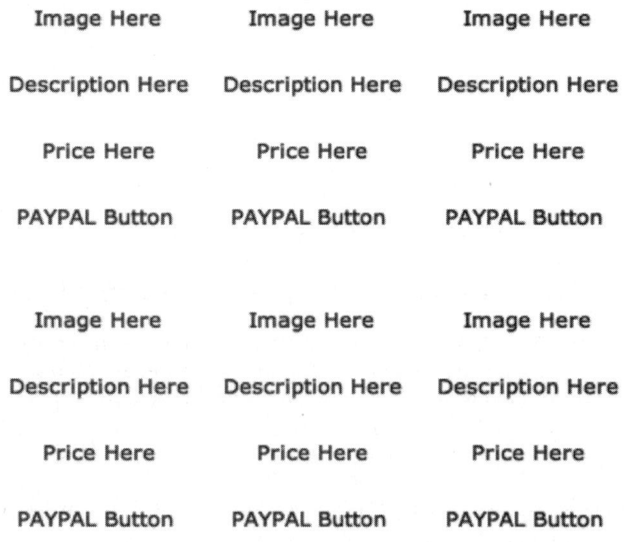

Image Here	Image Here	Image Here
Description Here	Description Here	Description Here
Price Here	Price Here	Price Here
PAYPAL Button	PAYPAL Button	PAYPAL Button
Image Here	Image Here	Image Here
Description Here	Description Here	Description Here
Price Here	Price Here	Price Here
PAYPAL Button	PAYPAL Button	PAYPAL Button

Figure 10–3. HTML table created from the code in Listing 10–1

Before you create this page in your blog, let's take a look at the tags and at how HTML works. When you write HTML, you use tags that are paired; i.e., there's an opening tag and a corresponding closing tag, each enclosed in angle brackets, < and >. Closing tags are denoted by the "/" (forward slash) mark. In Listing 10–1, all the sets of bracketed items you see are tags.

To create a table, you start with the `<table>` tag and close with `</table>`. As you see in Listing 10–1, lots of tags and data can come in between the opening and closing table tags. Rows are represented by the sets of `<tr>` and `</tr>` tags, while `<td>` and `</td>` represent columns. So, in Listing 10–1, there is one table composed of two rows and six columns—three columns per row.

Notice that the table tag `<table align=center cellpadding=10>` contains an alignment setting and one for cellpadding. These are called "attributes" and are used in formatting the table. In this example, the table is aligned to the center, so it will appear centered in your page, and each table cell (the area where one row and one column intersect) is padded with extra space (10 spaces between the contents of each cell and its border). Figure 10–4 shows examples of a table with and without cellpadding. I use cellpadding often so the table cells do not appear crowded or too close together.

For each column,`<td valign=bottom align=center>`, I aligned the items to the center, but also aligned them vertically to the bottom (so all the PayPal buttons will later line up later regardless of the different image heights). Do note that although these attributes—`valign` and `align`—work, they are not used in HTML5 and so should generally be avoided. However, since we haven't discussed using CSS to format tags, we'll use these tags so your table is nicely formatted.

Without cellpadding:

With cellpadding:

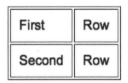

Figure 10–4. HTML table displaying the use of cellpadding

The `<BR/>` tags you see in the table code (Listing 10–1) are for hard returns (line breaks). They help organize and format the content in your table.

Let's continue, implementing what we've learned so far. In the next exercise we'll create a page and then copy and paste the code in Listing 10–1 if you have the e-book version of this book. If you have the print version, just type in the code. Or you can download all the code in the book at www.Apress.com.

■ **Note:** If you are reading a print copy of this book, you can type in the code for one row of the table, and then copy and paste it to quickly create as many rows needed.

EXERCISE – CREATING AN HTML TABLE PRODUCTS PAGE

In this exercise you'll create a Products page using an HTML table. We'll review the steps using Blogger, TypePad, and WordPress.

1. As in the previous chapter, create a new page in your blog and give it a title like Products.

2. Switch to the HTML layout of your page (in Blogger, click Edit HTML; in TypePad or WordPress, click HTML).

3. Add this code (the code is the same as in Listing 10–1 but without the extra line breaks).

```
<table align=center cellpadding=10>
<tr>
<td valign=bottom align=center>
Image Here<BR/>
Description Here<BR/>
Price Here<BR/>
PAYPAL Button
</td>
<td valign=bottom align=center>
Image Here<BR/>
Description Here<BR/>
Price Here<BR/>
PAYPAL Button
</td>
<td valign=bottom align=center>
Image Here<BR/>
Description Here<BR/>
Price Here<BR/>
PAYPAL Button
</td>
</tr>
<tr>
<td valign=bottom align=center>
Image Here<BR/>
Description Here<BR/>
Price Here<BR/>
PAYPAL Button
</td>
<td valign=bottom align=center>
Image Here<BR/>
Description Here<BR/>
Price Here<BR/>
PAYPAL Button
</td>
<td valign=bottom align=center>
Image Here<BR/>
Description Here<BR/>
Price Here<BR/>
PAYPAL Button
```

```
</td>
</tr>
</table>
```

4. Click Preview to see what your page looks like; it should look similar to Figure 10–3.

5. We're going to start loading up our products, so switch to Compose if using Blogger, Rich Text if using TypePad, or Visual if using WordPress. Now you are looking at a visual representation of your page and it should look very similar to the preview you just did (see Figure 10–5).

6. I have highlighted the first column in the first row of the table, which corresponds to the following code:

```
<td valign=bottom align=center>
Image Here<BR/>
Description Here<BR/>
Price Here<BR/>
PAYPAL Button
</td>
```

7. This is the section of the table we will modify first, but we don't have to modify the code to do so.

Figure 10–5. *Visual view in WordPress with row 1, column 1 highlighted*

8. Click on Image Here, then click the Delete key on the keyboard to delete the text.

9. Now click on the Insert Image button (in Blogger and TypePad; it's called "Add an Image" in WordPress).

10. Select an image from your computer to load into your blog page, just as you would any other image for your blog posts. Be sure to set the size to Small (or Thumbnail in WordPress), otherwise it will appear too large for the table space.

   a. Don't worry—you can set it to Small/Thumbnail afterwards if you forgot! Just double-click on the image to bring up its properties and then set the size.

11. Select the "Description Here" text and begin typing. The text will be replaced with your new product description.

12. Do the same for "Price Here" to enter the product's price.

13. The first cell in your table should now look something like the one in Figure 10–6 (my WordPress example). In Blogger, it will look the same without the border guides; and in TypePad the extra line space between the product description, price, and PAYPAL button is not present.

Figure 10–6. Edited table in WordPress

14. Next, you need to add the PayPal button, which is a little tricky.

15. Take a look back at the exercise in Chapter 9 called "Exercise – Create a PayPal Account and Add PayPal Buttons" for a reminder of how to create the Add To Cart button in WordPress, Blogger, or TypePad.

16. Copy the code for the PayPal button, which will look like this if you're using WordPress:

```
<a href="https://www.paypal.com/cgi-bin/webscr?cmd=_s-xclick&hosted_button_id=N7XFM9RMDQUZJ"
target="paypal">
<img src="http://i493.photobucket.com/albums/rr300/blogsbyheather/AddToCart.png"/>
</a>
```

   or this if you're using Blogger or TypePad:

```
<form target="paypal" action="https://www.paypal.com/cgi-bin/webscr" method="post">
```

```
<input type="hidden" name="cmd" value="_s-xclick">
<input type="hidden" name="hosted_button_id" value="FEGJ2RE6ALQUN">
<input type="image" src="https://www.paypal.com/en_US/i/btn/btn_cart_LG.gif" border="0"
name="submit" alt="PayPal - The safer, easier way to pay online!">
<img alt="" border="0" src="https://www.paypal.com/en_US/i/scr/pixel.gif" width="1"
height="1">
</form>
```

Then switch back to Edit HTML (Blogger) or HTML (TypePad or WordPress) in your post editor.

17. Find the first "PAYPAL Button" text in your code.

18. Select it and then Paste the PayPal button code right over it to replace it.

19. Switch back to Visual/Rich Text/Compose view and your page should resemble my sample in WordPress shown in Figure 10–7.

Figure 10–7. One PayPal button added to table

20. Repeat steps 8 – 19, carefully, until all the images, descriptions, prices, and PayPal buttons are added to the table.

21. You can remove extra line spaces using Edit HTML or Compose in Blogger, or HTML in WordPress. TypePad handles formatting the best and you probably won't have to adjust anything!

22. Now, as you did in the last chapter, add a View Cart button to the top or bottom of your page.

23. In the end your blog page should resemble the one in Figure 10–1.

If you need more rows, simply copy and paste more rows (the code between `<tr>` and `</tr>`) before the `</table>`.

You did it! You created your products page! Create as many pages as you need for your type of business. Perhaps you have different categories of products to sell. For example, many of my paper-crafting buddies create a page for tutorials they sell, another for card making kits, and another for handmade items. You can do the same if you need to categorize products, such as clothing; shirts, pants, accessories, shoes, and so forth.

HTML Links and Images

Now let's discuss HTML link and image tags, which are often combined, though of course they can be used separately as well. A link is what connects an image or text on your blog to an address—to another site or to someone's e-mail. It's what underlies a "Click here for more information" or "Contact Me" button on someone's sidebar. Let's see how to use these in your blog!

The two tags we'll be look at, together and individually, are the anchor tag, `<a>` and `</a>`, and the image tag, `<img>`. The attribute typically used in the anchor tag is `href`, which is the location of the site or e-mail address to be directed to when the link is clicked. The `target` attribute, which is also used frequently, opens a site in a new browser window so it doesn't overlay your blog. Take a look at the code in Listings 2 through 5.

Listing 10–2. HTML Anchor Code

```
<a href="http://www.blogsbyheather.com" target="_blank">Click here</a> to go visit my site,
Blogs By Heather.
```

Listing 10–3. HTML Anchor Tag with mailto:

```
<a href="mailto:heather@blogsbyheather.com" target="_blank">Contact me</a> for more
information.
```

Listing 10–4. HTML Image Tag

```
<img src="http://i493.photobucket.com/albums/rr300/blogsbyheather/bbhfanbadgeglitter.gif"
alt="Blogs By Heather" title="Blogs By Heather"/>
```

Listing 10–5. HTML Anchor and Image Tags

```
<a href="http://www.blogsbyheather.com" target="_blank">
<img src="http://i493.photobucket.com/albums/rr300/blogsbyheather/bbhfanbadgeglitter.gif"
alt="Blogs By Heather" title="Blogs By Heather"/>
</a>
```

The code in Listing 10–2 simply uses the anchor tag and links to my site, `www.BlogsByHeather.com`, when a visitor clicks the text "Click here." The text can be in a post, on a page, or even as a text or HTML/JavaScript widget on your blog's sidebar. The `target` attribute is set to `_blank`, which forces a new browser window to open with my site.

The code in Listing 10–3 is very similar, except it opens a new e-mail message with the To address set to `heather@blogsbyheather.com`. An important note is that the `mailto:` code does not always work; it depends on the visitor's e-mail client/system and its ability to launch a new e-mail. For example, it doesn't work if the visitor is using AOL. I just don't want you to be alarmed if customers mention that the button isn't working. In any case, it's a good idea to have your e-mail address listed on your site along with additional contact information to make sure customers can contact you.

The code in Listing 10–4 uses an image tag to display an image stored online, such as in Photobucket or your file manager. As it is now, it is not a link; the code simply displays the image, just as it would if you used the Insert Image button on your blog's toolbar.

Lastly, Listing 10–5 combines the anchor and image tags so that when you click the image, you are taken to www.BlogsByHeather.com, opened in a new browser window. This is something you see often when visiting a site and there is a "Grab My Button" sidebar widget. Typically you see the HTML code beneath the button (see Figure 10–8), which you can "grab." You would copy this code (or create it from scratch as in Listing 10–5) and do the following:

- In Blogger, from the Dashboard, click Design ➤ Add a Gadget. Then choose HTML/JavaScript and copy and paste (or create) the code. Be sure to save changes.

- In TypePad, from the Dashboard, click Design ➤ Content. From the Modules, middle box, choose Embed Your Own Code ➤ Add This Module. Copy and paste (or create) the code there. Be sure to save changes.

- In WordPress, click on Appearance from the Dashboard, then Widgets and drag a Text Widget to the sidebar. Copy and paste (or create) the code there. Be sure to save changes.

Figure 10–8. Grab My Button HTML example

As noted earlier, to use any of the code in Listings 10–1 through 10–5 in a post or page, you have to switch to Edit HTML (Blogger) or HTML (TypePad or WordPress) mode, copy and paste or create the HTML code, and then switch back to the visual mode if you'd like. Many people do like to switch back to Compose/Rich Text/Visual because they like to see what the post looks like while composing it and would rather not compose the post or page in HTML.

HTML Paragraphs

When you compose posts and pages in your blog, you naturally type and hit the Enter/Return key to add space between paragraphs or between images. And you can use the toolbar in the post or page editor to align text or paragraphs. However, sometimes, especially when using PayPal buttons, the toolbar options don't work. In such cases, you can switch to Edit HTML/HTML to modify the HTML code. In this view, you will see sets of paragraphs enclosed with `<p>` and `</p>`. When using the paragraph tag, there is space at the top and at the bottom of the text block contained within the open and close tag.

The code in Listing 10–6 centers a paragraph as shown in Figure 10–9 (third paragraph), and contains the "style" attribute we'll be discussing in more detail shortly. If you simply use `<p>` and `</p>` without any attributes, the paragraph is left-aligned by default and looks as if you hit the Enter key twice (notice the space between the paragraphs in Figure 10–9).

Listing 10–6. *HTML Paragraph Code*

```
<p style="text-align: center;">
```

First, let's talk briefly about Technorati.com. Technorati is a blog directory service (in short a search engine for blogs) so you definitely want to get your blog claimed there. And it's free! Go to www.technorati.com and click on JOIN, and you'll be on your way! This is a wonderful site and you should take a look around and find all the popular blogs posts on specific categories. Another site I like to visit is www.blogs.com (and then it's top ten blogs lists at www.Blogs.com/topten) which is site created by SixApart (owner of TypePad). I also had the pleasure of creating one of their top ten lists (Top 10 Blogs on Blogging) where I specifically chose blogs that were not pushing a book or product or service, but more on just plain helping you out.`</p>`

 I've had the pleasure of listening to recordings from the Blogging Success Summit 2011! It is wonderful and as promised, I will share my recap of each course here on my blog and recap of additional bonus materials with newsletter subscribers.

There are still weeks left and I still have many recordings to go through, but today's post is on the keynote from **Richard Jalichandra (CEO of Technorati)** on the state of the blogosphere.

First, let's talk briefly about Technorati.com. **Technorati** is a blog directory service (in short a search engine for blogs) so you definitely want to get your blog claimed there. **And it's free!** Go to www.technorati.com and click on JOIN, and you'll be on your way! This is a wonderful site and you should take a look around and find all the popular blogs posts on specific categories. Another site I like to visit is www.blogs.com (and then it's top ten blogs lists at www.Blogs.com/topten) which is site created by SixApart (owner of TypePad). I also had the pleasure of creating one of their top ten lists (Top 10 Blogs on Blogging) where I specifically chose blogs that were not pushing a book or product or service, but more on just plain helping you out.

Okay, so let's get back to Richard's wonderful presentation and keynote on the state of the blogosphere. You can find the report here, on the Technorati site, but he spoke a lot about the following topics:

- Blogging and social media
- Classes of bloggers
- Blogs and brands
- Consumer attitutude and trust
- Women bloggers and their role in the blogosphere

Figure 10–9. A centered paragraph

Using CSS with HTML Tags

Listing 10–6 introduced the style attribute, which centered the text (`text-align: center;`). Let's look at a little more CSS code. You can use the style attribute with almost any HTML tag, to align text, change the font size and color, or float images as in Figure 10–9. Though you can often use the toolbars to accomplish these tasks, sometimes you just need to manually edit the HTML code yourself. Let's go through a few quick examples of using CSS inside paragraph, span, and image tags.

You use the span tag `<span>` and `</span>` when you want to apply formatting to a section of text that is not necessarily an entire paragraph or any other text-like HTML tag. Look at the examples using the style attribute in Listings 10–7 through 10–9.

Listing 10–7. *Setting Font Size with the Style Attribute*

```
<p style="font-size: 10pt;">…</p>
```

Listing 10–8. *Setting Color with the Style Attribute*

```
<p style="color: #cc000;">…</p>
```

Listing 10–9. *Floating an Image and Adding Space with the Style Attribute*

```
<img style="float:left; padding:10px;" src=" http://www.socialmediaexaminer.com/images/bss11-
badge.gif"
alt="Blogging Success Summit" title="Blogging Success Summit"/>
```

In Listing 10–7, the text within the paragraph is set to a font size of 10 points(font size is measured in units of points; there are 72 points to the inch). In Listing 10–8, the text in the paragraph is set to red (hex code #cc0000).

■ **Note** Visit `www.colorschemer.com/online.html` for a color chart where you can select a color and get its hex code. Of course, if you use Photoshop, Photoshop Elements, Dreamweaver, or another graphics program, you can get hex codes for colors there as well.

Notice that the style element in Listing 10–9 includes more than one set of formatting CSS code, separated by semicolons. In this example, using the style attribute within the image tag forces the image to float to the left (which forces the text to wrap around it to the right), and then adds padding (space) of 10 pixels so the text isn't right up against the image. Look at the Blogging Success Summit 2011 image, floating to the left in Figure 10–9.

Using CSS to Modify Your Blog Layout

There may come a time when you need to alter your blog's layout and there just isn't any option to do so in the available menus or toolbars. At this point, you would use CSS, as follows:

- In Blogger you do this in the new Template Designer ➤ Advanced area or by clicking Design and then Edit HTML.

- In TypePad you do this in the Custom CSS area after clicking Design from the Dashboard, but only if you have the Unlimited version or higher.

- In WordPress, you click on Appearance from the Dashboard, then click Edit CSS to access its CSS customization feature.

In upcoming exercises, we'll use CSS code to install a static background or set a background color, and to change the formatting of the sidebar heading area. The instructions are similar in Blogger, TypePad, and WordPress. However, while you are reviewing the existing code in Blogger and WordPress, you may see where you can set margins, adjust column widths, add borders, or change the color of things (using hex code numbers). Using templates and themes the exercises would vary dramatically, so we'll stick with the background and sidebar title changes. Don't worry! In the next chapter I will provide information on where to get more CSS and HTML help. But for now, let's get to work on your blog!

EXERCISE – ADDING AND MODIFYING CSS IN BLOGGER

In this example, we'll see how to modify CSS code in Blogger to install a static background, and make a few minor adjustments. Results will vary depending on the template you've chosen. I have used the Simple, White template throughout most of this book.

1. From the Dashboard, click Design, then Edit HTML.

2. As good practice, you should always backup your template before making any CSS or HTML changes. Click Download Full Template.

3. Now we'll begin the CSS changes.

4. Let's start with the background. In this example, I am using a custom background I loaded online in my other TypePad account (see Figure 10–10). You can go to sites.google.com. Create a site, then go to More Actions ➤ Manage Site ➤ Attachments and upload your image there. The image has to be stored somewhere in order to use it in CSS code.

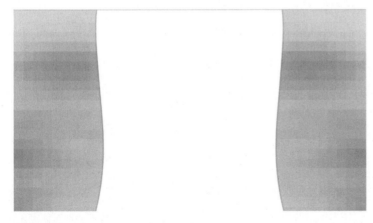

Figure 10–10. Sample background image

5. This code is placed below the <body> tag .

```
background-image: url("http://heatherporto.TypePad.com/portobg.jpg");
background-attachment: fixed;
background-position: top center;
background-repeat: no-repeat;
```

It replaces this line `background: $(body.background);` with the code below:

```
Body {
font: $(body.font);
color: $(body.text.color);
background-image: url("http://heatherporto.TypePad.com/portobg.jpg");
background-attachment: fixed;
background-position: top center;
background-repeat: no-repeat;
padding: 0 $(content.shadow.spread) $(content.shadow.spread) $(content.shadow.spread);
$(body.background.override)
}
```

6. This code sets the body's background image to the specified image, positions it to the top, center (fixed), and does not repeat. If instead of a single large image, you were using a small one you wanted to repeat, the code would say "repeat" instead of "no-repeat."

7. Although we have installed the new background image (see Figure 10–11), we still have work to do. We are using the Simple template chosen when we created the Blogger blog and modifying this template. We need to remove the blue at the top and reduce the column widths as you don't see the curve of the background yet.

Figure 10–11. Background installed

8. Scroll down and remove the bolded code, as that is what is keeping the blue header area showing over the background. Remember to click Save Template.

```
.body-fauxcolumn-outer .cap-top {
  position: absolute;
  z-index: 1;
  height: 400px;
  width: 100%;
  background: $(body.background);
  $(body.background.override)
}
```

9. Next, we'll change the column widths. Since we're using one of the templates in Blogger (Simple, White), save changes thus far. Then click on Template Designer ➤ Adjust Widths and set the Entire Blog width to 870px (in my example) and the background image now displays correctly.

10. Click Apply To Blog, then Back to Blogger.

11. Now let's revise the sidebar titles; we'll add borders and a background color. So add the code bolded below. Most sidebar titles have h2 formatting. If your template has a specific sidebar area in the code, then modify that specific h2 setting.

```
h2 {
margin: 0 0 1em 0;
font: $(widget.title.font);
color: $(widget.title.text.color);
text-transform: uppercase;
background: #f1eeee;
padding:10px;
border-top: 1px solid #333333;
border-bottom: 1px solid #333333;
border-left: 1px solid #333333;
border-right: 1px solid #333333;
}
```

12. Since the Date Header uses the same h2 formatting, we now have to modify it as it doesn't look quite right yet, as you can see in Figure 10–12.

Figure 10–12. *Sidebar titles modified*

13. To fix this, modify this code:

```
.date-header span {
  background-color: $(date.header.background.color);
  color: $(date.header.color);
  padding: $(date.header.padding);
  letter-spacing: $(date.header.letterspacing);
  margin: $(date.header.margin);
}
```

14. To the following, which removes the background color and changes the color of the font to a medium gray.

```
.date-header span {
  color: #333333;
  padding: $(date.header.padding);
  letter-spacing: $(date.header.letterspacing);
  margin: $(date.header.margin);
}
```

15. The end result looks like what you see in Figure 10–13.

Figure 10–13. *Date header with the formatting fixed*

Have fun experimenting with different colors and looks on your blog!

Blogger and WordPress let you view all the source code, which is actually very useful in helping you learn more CSS code (if you're interested). Next we'll look at the WordPress example. It is similar to that of Blogger in that you have access to all source code; but it's different in that it is difficult to find the areas you may want to change.

EXERCISE – ADDING AND MODIFYING CSS IN WORDPRESS

In WordPress you can preview your CSS changes. However, if you want to save them, you'll need to purchase the CSS Upgrade ($14.97 USD per year). In this example, we'll modify background settings as well as reformat the sidebar and post titles.

1. From the Dashboard, click Appearance, then Background.

2. Set the background to a color as we did in Chapter 5. However, depending on the template you're using (I used zBench), this may not have worked. Now we'll change the CSS code to get it to work.

3. Save the changes and then click Edit CSS (under Appearance).

4. Again, I am using zBench, so this code is for modifying that template. To figure out how to modify your template, click on View Original Stylesheet; this shows you all the current CSS code for your template. You have to search for and pick out the h2 and title settings and basically experiment as each template differs. Hopefully, following my example will help you customize your WordPress template.

5. Look at the code I copied and pasted from the Original Stylesheet into the CSS Editor area. I've added comments next to the code I modified (which differed from the original stylesheet). The comments are enclosed by /* and */.

```
#content {
width:100%;
max-width:960px;
min-width:300px;
border:0 solid #333333;    /*  set the border from 1 to 0 so the border wouldn't show */
background:#ffffff;        /* set main blog area to white and now just the background in
dark gray */
margin:0 auto;
}

h2.title {
font-size:18px;               /* set new font size to 18 */
text-shadow:1px 1px 1px #aaa;
background:#b2c6da;     /* set background of title area to a blue-gray */
border-top:1px solid #333333;    /* border, gray */
border-bottom:1px solid #333333;     /* border, gray */
border-left:1px solid #333333;          /* border, gray */
border-right:1px solid #333333;         /* border, gray */
margin:10px 0 0;
padding:5px;        /* adding spacing */
}

.sidebar h3 {
color:#445566;
font-size:18px;               /* set new font size to 18 */
line-height:30px;
text-shadow:1px 1px 1px #aaaaaa;
background:#b2c6da;       /* set background of title area to a blue-gray */
border-top:1px solid #333333;    /* border, gray */
border-bottom:1px solid #333333;     /* border, gray */
border-left:1px solid #333333;          /* border, gray */
border-right:1px solid #333333;         /* border, gray */
margin:0;
padding:5px;        /* added spacing */
}
```

6. As you can see in Figure 10–14, basically I added borders to the titles and changed the background area of the title (to blue-gray). I also changed the background color of the blog (to medium gray) and the main blog area (to white).

Figure 10–14. *WordPress Blog Reformatted*

Have fun experimenting with different colors and looks on your blog!

WordPress is generally easy to navigate and use, but some do have trouble with modifying CSS code as all the templates are different. So keep in mind that what works for me may not work for you (unless you are using zBench). With that said, I hope you gave it a shot! You learn in making mistakes and some mistakes turn out to be hidden treasures.

TypePad is the most difficult in the sense that there is no access to the original source code, so you have to search their knowledgebase (for CSS and Advanced Templates) to try and figure out what elements you want to change. In our example, we'll change the background and the sidebar titles.

EXERCISE – ADDING AND MODIFYING CSS IN TYPEPAD

As mentioned previously, in order to perform this exercise you need to have the TypePad Pro Unlimited version (or higher).

1. From the Dashboard, click Design, then Custom CSS.

2. Use the following code to get started and then change the colors to match your blog using the Color Schemer (`www.colorschemer.com/online.html`)

```
body {
background: url("http://heatherporto.TypePad.com/portobg.jpg");
background-position: top center;
background-attachment: fixed;
background-repeat: no-repeat;
}

.module-header {
background:# b2c6da;
border-top: 1px solid #333333;
border-bottom: 1px solid #333333;
border-right: 1px solid #333333;
border-left: 1px solid #333333;
}
```

3. The background is set to an image in my TypePad File Manager, and then positioned to the top, center (fixed), and set not to repeat.

4. The sidebar title in TypePad is not h2; it's called "module-header" and it's where I set the background to a blue-gray with a medium gray border to make the titles stand out a little.

5. Click Save Changes.

6. The result is shown in Figure 10–15.

Figure 10–15. TypePad Blog Reformatted

If you want to add formatting for the post title, use `h3.entry-header`. In the next chapter I'll note where you can find help with CSS code. Have fun experimenting with different colors and looks on your blog!

Summary

I'm hoping your blog now has a new look! Working with HTML and CSS can be frustrating at times, but it's rewarding in the end. Even if you're not ready to start coding now, you never know where your blogging will take you! In this chapter we started by seeing how adding an HTML table to a Products page can neatly align your products for sale. Then we saw how to use the popular HTML anchor and image tags to direct your visitors to another site or to e-mail when text or an image is clicked.

We then reviewed the HTML paragraph tag to lead into our CSS discussion. To add CSS to HTML tags, you use the style attribute. Sometimes you need to modify your blog's layout, and menus and toolbars may not be available to make those changes, so you learned how to use CSS code to add a custom static background and modify some of the titles in your blog.

In the next chapter I will be listing sites where you can find additional help and continue to enhance your blogging skills. We'll also go over some blogging dos and don'ts, see some useful tips, and review some common mistakes and their resolutions.

CHAPTER 11

■■■

Blogging Tips

Breathe. No coffee or espresso required this time! I'm so proud of you and hope you enjoyed creating your blog with me. Do you remember where we started? And look at where you are now! We began by brainstorming about what to name your blog, what it would look like, and what you would be posting about. Next we discussed organization and blog layout, as well as some creative writing tips. You then created a Blogger, TypePad, or WordPress blog—or maybe you created all three! We continued the journey by working with images and videos and learned how to get them from your camera or video recorder to your blog. We experimented with blog design, adding a banner and changing colors, setting up a custom domain, and learning how to integrate your blog with the very popular Facebook and Twitter. We then discussed SEO and how to track visitor activity, how to set up an online store, and in the last chapter how to use HTML and CSS to further customize your blog.

Although we discussed all these things, there's a lot more you can learn. I hope you will continue blogging and growing your skills and I want you know where you can look for additional help, as well as be aware of common mistakes and their resolutions. We'll go over some of that here in this chapter.

Where to Find Help

Throughout the book we've mentioned a few sites where you can find free blog templates or a color schemer, but don't worry; I will recap here and then some!

Recommended sites for finding beautiful blog templates:

- bTemplates (`http://.bTemplates.com`) organizes its free Blogger and WordPress templates by number of columns, style, color, width, most viewed, and in many other ways as well.

- Blogger Templates Free (`www.BloggerTemplatesFree.com`) offers beautiful free Blogger templates.

- The Cutest Blog on the Block (`www.TheCutestBlogOnTheBlock.com`) provides backgrounds for Blogger, WordPress, MySpace, and Twitter, as well as banners and accessories like animated buttons.

- This WordPress-oriented site (`www.wordpress2u.com`) delivers free and premium WordPress templates, compatible with WordPress 2.7 – 2.9 and widget-ready.

Recommended sites for finding blogging and SEO tips as well as cool gadgets for your site:

- Blogger Stop (`http://bloggerstop.net`) is great source for articles and tips relating to fonts and design, marketing, and writing, and it has a list of recommended Blogger widgets.

- Blogging Basics 101 (`www.bloggingbasics101.com`) features tips on content writing, HTML help, microblogging, tutorials, and more.

- Blogging Tips (`www.bloggingtips.com`) has helpful tips about keeping your blogging goals, search engine optimization (SEO) tips, using social media, and installing plug-ins.

- Blogger Tips and Tricks (`www.bloggertipsandtricks.com`) is full of helpful blogging tips in general as well as tips specific to Blogger, including search engine optimization, CSS customization, HTML help, favicons (the small picture appearing in the address bar), hacks, and more.

- Bloggussion (`www.blogussion.com`) focuses on tips to help you become a better blogger; it includes writing tips, blog design, SEO, blog marketing, and blog tools.

- Daily Blog Tips (`www.dailyblogtips.com`) presents a new blog tip every day on everything from ways to drive traffic to your blog and make money, to tips on creating a good post.

- SEOMozBlog (`www.seomoz.org/blog`) delves into search engine optimization and how to get your blog noticed.

- The Blog Herald (`www.blogherald.com`) is an online "newspaper" about blogging using many different platforms, social networking, wireless applications, and more.

- Three Column Blogger (`http://threecolumnblogger.com`) contains instructions on how to convert your Blogger templates to a three-column format.

- Tips for New Bloggers (`http://tips-for-new-bloggers.blogspot.com`) offers tutorials on how to add different types of sidebar items, including a search box, music lists, and chat boxes. It also has help on blog templates, HTML for customizing the look of your blog, and increasing traffic.

Recommended sites for getting HTML and CSS help:

- The w3 schools site (`www.w3schools.com`) is such a wonderful source for HTML, CSS, JavaScript, and many web programming and scripting languages. You literally could spend hours on this site! There are coding samples with explanations, as well as "Try It" areas where you can experiment and test the code you're building before loading it onto your site.

- HTML Goodies (http://`www.htmlgoodies.com`) is "the ultimate HTML resource" and very much like a blog with new articles, featured articles, "Web Developer Daily News," and so much more! This site also features lots of information on scripting languages and CSS that can help enhance the functionality of your site.

- Color Schemer Online (`www.colorschemer.com/online.html`) is the color chooser we used in this book. With HTML and CSS, you often have to know the hex value for a color you want to use. This site lets you select a color and then gives you the code, or you can enter a hex code and click Set and you'll get the corresponding color.

- Adobe's Kuler widget is another great source in experimenting with color combinations and themes. It's free and can be downloaded from Adobe here: www.adobe.com/products/kuler.

- CSS Zen Garden, www.csszengarden.com, is a site where you an view many different designs where all that changes is the CSS code. You may even view the CSS source file so you may experiment with it on your own and learn from the CSS Zen Garden's graphic artists.

HTML and CSS Problems

Even with step-by-step instruction, you can receive error messages or run into problems. We all do! And that old saying is true: You learn from your mistakes. In this section, we'll look at a few common mistakes and see how to fix them.

First and foremost, if you are planning on making changes to your layout using HTML or CSS code, back up your current template if possible. In Blogger you can do this by clicking the Download Full Template link in the Edit HTML section, which saves a copy of the template to your computer. If a problem occurs when you are editing the HTML, you can always revert back to the original by clicking Browse to upload the template previously saved and clicking the Upload button. TypePad and WordPress don't have the same option, as they work with CSS code and customization differently. For information on backing up your WordPress blog, visit http://codex.wordpress.org/WordPress_Backups. And for TypePad blogs, the TypePad Knowledgebase provides some information at http://tpsupport.mtcs.sixapart.com/tp/us-tp1/how_do_i_backup_my_content.html.

Case One: Right Column Disappears

You're working on your blog and realize that the right column (in a three-column layout) has disappeared (though really it has just dropped beneath all of your posts). It was fine when you looked at your blog yesterday. What happened?

The most common reason is incorrect HTML code either added in one of your recent posts or in a new HTML/JavaScript gadget. If you recently added a new gadget, remove the gadget and view your blog. If the blog appears normal and the third column is back in place, you know something is wrong with the way that gadget was added (maybe it is missing quotes around a URL or missing some brackets). If the problem persists when you view your blog after carefully adding the gadget back, contact the gadget's author, add a comment on the site where you got it, or check the Help section or user forums.

If you haven't recently added an HTML/JavaScript gadget or removing it hasn't solved the problem, the error most likely resides in a recent post. I recommend trying to remove the last post and then recreating it. If you are copying and pasting code in your post content or using code from an external source, it may not paste properly. In my experience, the most common HTML errors in a post are a missing </div> or </p>. These are the closing tags for the <div> (division or section) and <p> (paragraph) HTML tags. As you know from Chapter 10, HTML tags come in pairs with opening and closing tags, such as the <div>...</div> and <p>...</p>. These two tags are very similar in function and are used to format and style text in paragraph form. The Post Editor often automatically adds a pair of <div> or <p> codes when you press the Enter key while composing a post.

The problem is typically at the end of the post. While in the post editor, switch to Edit HTML (Blogger)/HTML (TypePad or WordPress) view, scroll through the post, and see if there is an opening <div> or <p> without a matching </div> or </p>. If so, add it. Click Publish Post and View Blog to see if the column is back on the right side. Hopefully your problem is now solved!

Case Two: Missing Code

You're working on you blog but when you save your changes, whatever it was you were editing has not changed as you expected. When we worked with CSS code in Chapter 10, you may not have noticed that the semicolon is used at the end of a line of CSS code or when separating many lines (as when using the style attribute of an HTML tag). It may be that when you modified your code, you forgot to add the ";" at the end of a line.

For example, you may have tried setting the sidebar color or background color to white (#FFFFFF in hexadecimal coding) and instead of entering #FFFFFF; you only entered #FFFFFF. Basically, every line of CSS code needs to end with a semicolon (;) unless it is a comment, which is enclosed within /* and */.

If that's not the problem, you may have forgotten another piece of code. For example, in Chapter 10 we added borders to the sidebar titles with a line of code similar to `border-left: 1px solid #000000;`. If you forgot the border width element (`1px`), no border would appear. It is very common for people to forget the pound/number sign (#) when setting color as well. If you need help with HTML or CSS, visit `w3schools.com/html` or `w3schools.com/css`.

Image Problems in Posts

At times, people have trouble inserting images into their posts. Either they're too large or too small, or they don't end up where you want them to be. Two of the most common mistakes people make when inserting images into a post or page are in trying to float an image (to the right or left) or using the wrong size image (forgetting to resize it or use the custom settings to set to Medium).

Case One: Floating an Image

Blogger, TypePad, and WordPress all have the ability to "float" images to the left or right. Notice the image of Michelle Laycock I floated to the left in a post I recently featured her in (see Figure 11–1). If I had used an image that was too large or too wide, the text might have run alongside the image just one or two letters at a time, which is undesirable and difficult for viewers to read. If you want to float images to the right or left, be sure they have a width of 300px or smaller (or use the Medium or Small setting). This image of Michelle is only 160px wide as my blog layout is narrower than most due to the curvy background.

Meet Michelle Laycock

As many of you already know, Michelle is my head designer for Blogs By Heather. I asked her to write up an article to share with you on Blog Design. Her 13+ years in professional graphic design allows her to create fantastic blog banners and graphics for you! To learn more about Michelle, please read her story here or you can visit her at www.LaycockDesigns.com.

Question: "How wide do you want my blog to be?"

Answer: I optimize customer blog graphics for a 1024x768 monitor resolution. The reason I do this is because I've done research and looked at statistics. About 92-99% of my customers are viewing my own blog at 1024x768 monitor resolution. Therefore, that is the current "popular" resolution which should be taken into consideration when designing graphics.

Question: What is monitor resolution?

Answer: Monitor Resolution is the display size of a computer monitor based on the number of pixels it can display in width and length. A resolution of 1024x768 means 1024 pixels wide by 768 pixels high.

Customers can decide if they want me to design for a lower or higher resolution and I gladly design to their requested size. However, I always let them know that if they go higher than 1024px wide (making sure to account for scroll bars and borders, etc.) their blog may not look good for the majority of their readers. It may look great on their own computer, but not on their neighbors'.

Figure 11–1. A floating image

Case Two: Image Size

When inserting images into your post and pages, keep in mind that the average width of the main posting area is between 400-500px, so your pictures should generally be no more than 400px wide. If you like floating images to the left or right, I recommend resizing your images to half the posting area space. If your main posting area is 400-500px, for images you want to float, resize them to approximately 200-250px. You can use Photoshop, Photoshop Elements, photo editing software that came with your camera, or online free photo resizing programs like ones we used in Chapter 4, such as FastStone's Photo Resizer (faststone.org/FSResizerDetail.htm).

Other Image Issues

In addition to problems with posting images, you may have difficulties adding images to your sidebar, banner, background, or other page elements. They may appear too large, too small, or simply just don't fit the way you'd like. To review the process of working with images, see Chapter 4. For convenience, Table 11–1 recaps the image sizes generally used for standard blog elements (note that this is a guide; it's not written in stone):

Table 11–1. Recommended Image Sizes for Blog Elements

Element	Size (pixels)	Notes
Sidebar	150 – 200	Images for sidebars should be about 180px wide for most blogs as sidebar width is usually 200px. Some templates have narrower sidebars, so you may need a smaller width of 125px.
Post	400	For Blogger, TypePad, and WordPress, the width of the main posting column varies, but an image width of 400px will fit most templates and themes.
Banner	700 – 960+	When you insert a custom banner into your blog's layout, the width will vary depending on the template you choose in Blogger, TypePad, or WordPress. In Blogger, if you use a custom 2-column layout, the banner image should be 700-720px wide; for a custom 3-column layout, it should be 900-920px. . If you use the Template Designer, the banners may be as wide as 950px. In WordPress, the theme you use will state the recommended banner size. In TypePad, if you're using Theme Builder, for a 3-column format, 870px is best, while 670px is best for a 2-column layout.
		The banner (TypePad) in Figure 4-1 is 950px wide; the banner in Figure 4-2 (Blogger) is 890px wide.
Background	Variable	For the background, if you are going to use a tiled or repeated image, it can really be any size. It depends on the image you're using or the look you are trying to achieve. There is no right or wrong size to use for this type of background image. Do keep in mind that larger images will, of course, cause your page to load slower.
Static Background	Variable	Take a look again at Figure 4-1 and Figure 4-2 and notice the background in each blog. You can see a white center with a design on either side. This large central image is referred to as a Static Background. An image used like this has to be large enough to let the sidebar(s) and main posting area fit in the center. Note that the white (center) of my background is actually part of the one large image that makes up the background. They are no separate images on the left or on the right.
		As noted, the size will vary depending on how wide your main posting area is and the width of your sidebar(s). You'll want it wide enough to serve as the center of the static background image, plus an additional 200-300 pixels on each side to allow for the actual background design (such as the blue waves in Figure 4-1 or the vintage scallop floral in Figure 4-2). Again, note that larger images take longer to download and may result in a slower page load time.

Professional Blog Assistance

You can find a lot of help on the Internet, especially on the sites listed earlier in this chapter. However, you may not have the time to search for or experiment with installing new gadgets or modifying HTML code on your own and prefer to hire someone to help. The following is a list of services for hire:

- Blogs by Heather (`www.blogsbyheather.com`): This is my personal blog and it contains many helpful articles on blogging in general, new tools and tips, HTML and image editing help, and many tutorials on Blogger, TypePad, WordPress, Constant Contact and more. In addition to the free tutorials, I provide paid services including setting up a blog, maintaining a blog, converting it to a three-column format, transferring blogs to a different platform, setting up a blog store, customizing newsletters, and more. I would welcome the opportunity to help one of my readers!

- Blogger Buster (`www.bloggerbuster.com`): This site contains Blogger tutorials, templates, and up-to-date Blogger news. You may also hire Blogger Buster to set up and customize your Blogger site.

- RemarkaBlogger (`http://remarkablogger.com`): Recent articles include marketing tips, how to deal with competition, and how to write better content for your blog. The main focus of this site is its blog coaching and consulting services. You can schedule personalized sessions and discuss topics such as increasing blog traffic, how to get more customers using your blog, working with video and audio content, and ebook planning.

Blog Design Services

Many people start out using a template because they are just learning how to build a blog, or because they can't afford to hire a professional graphic designer. As you continue to grow your business and increase traffic to your blog, you may decide you want a fresh, new, customized look—a blog makeover. Here are three graphic designers I highly recommend:

- Laycock Designs (`http://laycockdesigns.com`): Michelle Laycock is a professional graphic designer. She can create blog banners, backgrounds, animated GIFs (graphics), and advertisements. She can also create business cards, gift certificates, and other business forms you may desire (for print). Furthermore, she has designed coordinating themes for Twitter, Facebook, Ning, Weebly, Grou.ps, EventBrite, YouTube, and other social networking sites. Your blog and all your sites can share a common theme.

- VK Design Company (`www.vkdesigncompany.com`): Veronica McCollum is another excellent designer. She specializes in blog banners, backgrounds, buttons and badges, sidebar graphics, and more. She can also provide animated GIFs, social networking designs, and print designs (including business cards, T-shirts, banners, and key chains).

- Webs By Amy (`www.websbyamy.com`): Amy Celona is the go-to gal if you are looking for a designer who can create a professional WordPress presence for you or your business.

Michelle, her assistant Jackie Steffen, and Veronica also provide custom illustration and caricature design (a cute and fun cartoon image of yourself), and offer a collection of premade designs for sale. Please note: these ladies are very talented and very busy, so they do have waiting lists.

Summary

In this chapter, we reviewed a few common problems that mostly involve HTML or CSS, as well as problems relating to image size and position. I know as you continue blogging, your blogging needs will grow and you may need additional help and have questions not covered in this book, so I also provided an extensive list of sites that can help as you try to do more with your blog.

If you prefer to hire a professional to assist with your blogging needs, I have included a list of sites where you may pay for blog-related and professional design services, and of course I would be happy to help you (visit `www.BlogsByHeather.com`).

I hope you have found this book helpful and I thank you for taking this journey with me. In concluding this book, I am honored to have had this opportunity to work with you and assist you in creating a new blog! Congratulations! You did it! I wish you much luck and success in your future blog endeavors.

Index

◼ T

You Need the Companion eBook

Your purchase of this book entitles you to buy the companion PDF-version eBook for only $10. Take the weightless companion with you anywhere.

We believe this Apress title will prove so indispensable that you'll want to carry it with you everywhere, which is why we are offering the companion eBook (in PDF format) for $10 to customers who purchase this book now. Convenient and fully searchable, the PDF version of any content-rich, page-heavy Apress book makes a valuable addition to your programming library. You can easily find and copy code—or perform examples by quickly toggling between instructions and the application. Even simultaneously tackling a donut, diet soda, and complex code becomes simplified with hands-free eBooks!

Once you purchase your book, getting the $10 companion eBook is simple:

❶ Visit **www.apress.com/promo/tendollars/**.

❷ Complete a basic registration form to receive a randomly generated question about this title.

❸ Answer the question correctly in 60 seconds, and you will receive a promotional code to redeem for the $10.00 eBook.

THE EXPERT'S VOICE™

233 Spring Street, New York, NY 10013

Offer valid through 8/11.